1|17

Hut

31.

D0130240

WITHDRAWN

Books should be returned or renewed by the last date above. Renew by phone **03000 41 31 31** or online *www.kent.gov.uk/libs*

s Registration & Archives

CUSTOMER SERVICE EXCELLENCE

CSE

Kent
County
Council
kent.gov.uk

C334008140

MOTHER OF A SUICIDE:

THE BATTLE FOR THE TRUTH ABOUT A MENTAL HEALTH COVER-UP

Joanna Lane

Published by Accent Press Ltd 2016

ISBN 9781786152473

Copyright © Joanna Lane 2016

The right of Joanna Lane to be identified as the author of this work has been asserted by the author in accordance with the Copyright, Designs and Patents Act 1988.

All rights reserved. No part of this book may be reproduced, stored in a retrieval system, or transmitted in any form or by any means, electronic, electrostatic, magnetic tape, mechanical, photocopying, recording or otherwise, without the written permission of the publishers: Accent Press Ltd, Ty Cynon House, Navigation Park, Abercynon, CF45 4SN

To our son Christopher, and to all sufferers of
hypopituitarism, whether diagnosed or undiagnosed

CONTENTS

FOREWORD

This is part of a letter I sent to a consultant endocrinologist a year or so after our son Chris died. It gives an idea of what he was like:

> Christopher was kind, friendly, amused. He was capable, clear-sighted, he understood people. I used to rely on him for advice when I felt worked up, and when I needed computer help he'd always give it. My mother-in-law called him "a lovely boy" and he was, he'd willingly do odd jobs for her. He always worked hard and was good at his job. I used to love visiting him at his home in Skipton. He'd be waiting at the station for me, a tall, slim figure spreading his arms wide to hug me. I remember his soft, snorting laugh. What a good host he was, improvising a bed for me in his living-room, with the reading lamp placed at exactly the right angle. When I stayed there he used to play pop songs by artists such as Dido on the piano by ear – he was good at hearing and reproducing chords and he had large, well-shaped hands. We found a big Lego-type model of a machine in his house after he died, and I could imagine so clearly his hands making it, with strength and precision.
>
> I miss him so much. But I expect I'll get over that eventually. What I can't ever, ever get over, is the

understanding I now have of his suffering and isolation, and my realisation of what great strength he showed, when I was so wrongly believing him weak. I can't ever erase the image of him putting on that nasty helium mask and taping it in place, and turning on the canister and getting on with dying, with his door considerately left unlocked so that the police could get in to find him. And the thought of his heart beating more and more slowly and uncertainly, and then stopping, as he sat in his boxer shorts alone in the dark.'

1 - BREAKING THE NEWS

On 26 August 2008 my doorbell rang. It was late afternoon, sunny and warm. I was feeling good because I'd tackled the garden and I'd enticed my feisty 84-year-old mother-in-law, Celia, out on a trip ('How about coming to the dump with me?'). She'd come, and we'd enjoyed it, and we'd had tea at her house afterwards. I smiled at the two policewomen. They didn't smile back.

'Are you Mrs Lane? Do you have a son called Christopher Lane?'

I stopped feeling good. I started asking questions, too fast. 'Has he had an accident? Is he in hospital? Was it his bike? He won't ever wear a helmet…'

A pause, and then I asked (it felt from nowhere), 'Is he alive?'

No answer, just a long, slow look. They asked if they could come in. 'Can we sit down somewhere and we'll tell you what he's done?'

'What he's done' made me feel better – it made him sound as if he was still alive. We went into the lounge while they told me. Chris, our 31-year-old son, who lived 200 miles away in Skipton, had put on a mask and inhaled helium from a canister some time during the night, and left time-delayed emails for the police to come and find him. He'd also sent emails to Mark and Em, two friends from university, one to his boss at Skipton Building Society, and one to his counsellor. I hadn't even known he was being counselled. No email for us.

1

I thought wild thoughts that eat into me now when I remember. 'How silly of him, how melodramatic! He's turned me into the mother of a suicide!'

One of the women asked if she could make me a cup of tea, so I showed her where the things were. I remember how neat and round her police hat looked, resting on the work surface. They told me, 'He's in Airedale Hospital' and immediately I visualised him in a hospital bed, alive.

'In hospital?' I said.

One of them cleared her throat. 'There's a morgue attached,' she said.

They were very tactful, and wanted to know if I had someone who could come and sit with me. My neighbour, Jill, I said. 'We'll do whatever you want, if you want us to stay, we'll stay.'

I fetched Jill. I told her briefly what had happened. She sat in the living room while I went to my computer. I just needed something to blot everything out, and the game Minesweeper seemed the answer. One policewoman stood in the conservatory, discreetly making calls on her mobile. I'd hardly located three mines when the phone rang. It was my mother-in-law, asking about an arrangement we'd made that my husband would call in on her when he came home. He was almost due. Oh heavens! I had to tell him. I had to tell my mother-in-law. I had to drive to the station to pick him up in a few minutes. I said 'I've had very bad news. I'll come round.'

The policewomen seemed to think I wouldn't be safe to drive. One of them drove behind me for the five minutes it took to reach my mother-in-law's house. But I drove more carefully than usual, focusing absolutely because I didn't want to think. I delivered the blow, and she sobbed aloud, but I couldn't stay with her, so I asked the policewoman to look after her while I went on to the station.

That was the hardest thing, to see John in his suit coming down the hill towards me, catching sight of me, pleased to see me, thinking it was just another ordinary day. I ran to him. I couldn't help clinging to him, stroking him desperately, as I told him our son was dead. He stopped still and listened to it all. My face was buried in his suit so I couldn't see his expression. He said in a very level voice, 'You never know what's round the corner.'

We picked up my mother-in-law and the three of us went to our house, where I can hardly remember what we said. I was desperate to go to Skipton right away. I couldn't help feeling that if I got there fast enough I would be able to see something they'd missed, spot some mistake, somehow get him back. But the police said the morgue wouldn't be open until the next morning. John asked a lot of practical questions, wrote down reference numbers and telephone numbers and names. I thought about our daughters. Jenny was in France on holiday with her husband, Nick, but Ruth, our youngest (I would soon have to start saying 'younger'), was only an hour away, in London. I couldn't tell her on the phone, I'd have to go in person. I think I even set off without checking she was in (I had a key to her flat) because I didn't want her to suffer for an hour in suspense.

I hardly want to remember telling her, and how we cried together most of the night (not proper crying in my case, just a painful filling of the sinuses and never-ending nose-blowing, and a terrible headache), and how when I did go to bed I couldn't sleep, because all the thoughts and memories came crowding in. It was the first of many nights like this.

2 - THOUGHTS IN THE NIGHT

My first thought was 'When did I speak to him last?' I felt I'd lived through aeons, but I worked out that it had been only the previous evening – the night before he died, in fact. He must have rung me with all the nasty paraphernalia of suicide in his house, waiting (perhaps right in front of him) to be used.

It had seemed a normal conversation. He'd talked about the allotment he shared with Mark and Em, about my brother's offer to find him a cheap car, how he'd been in the Dales the previous day, which was Bank Holiday Monday, walking on his own (why didn't that ring alarm bells?). I told him how we'd taken my mother-in-law, Celia, to the seaside on her mobility scooter, which she couldn't control very well, and how she'd created mayhem, scattering chairs in an open-air café. He laughed, I remembered. But then there was a little pause at the end, as if he didn't want to end the conversation. Finally I said, 'I suppose you want to watch that Al Pacino DVD, darling' (he'd mentioned it earlier), and we said goodbye. Why didn't I let that pause extend? What would he have said if I hadn't shut him up? But I put the receiver down, and sometime during that night, before 7 a.m. the next day, he did it.

I reached for my mobile and looked at his texts. There was one from Monday saying, 'What are you up to today?' and I'd answered that we were walking by the sea in Kent. So this was when he was on his solitary walk in the Dales, feeling desperate.

I'd asked him what he was up to too, and he texted 'Just getting on train back to Skipton after a walk near Keighley'. That was around noon. I looked at all the other ones for the past month.

July 30: Okay thanks Mum. I've left your key in the fridge in a bag with the carrots

August 2: Hi Mum. Can you text me Duniyul's street name before you go if you get this message. The address folder is in the study

(Later that day): Thanks Mum. Enjoy the play tonight!

August 3: Hi Mum, back in Skipton now. How was last night? Can you post me my mobile phone charger? I think I left it plugged in under your desk in the study

And then, only eight days ago on August 20: Greetings from Betws Y Coed! Today is the first day of our kayaking course. It's actually river kayaking, not sea kayaking. It's been very wet here so the rivers are all in full flow!

I could not believe there would be no more texts like this, that this ordinary, inconsequential living stream had stopped, that I couldn't any longer select 'Chris Lane' on my phone and tap out a message to him. These everyday messages had suddenly become relics.

Among my first thoughts when I got the news (along with 'how melodramatic and silly!') was the idea that he hadn't loved us enough if he could do this to us. But now, in the dark, I wondered if I had loved him enough. I'd always known that I hadn't been a good mother when he was a baby. To confess now: although John was Chris's father, he and I didn't start to live together until Chris was nine months old, and during those early months – and afterwards too – I was stressed and insensitive. When he was a toddler I used to smack him. I remember that when he was three he drew a picture of me and him – I was a giant, towering figure and he was a little, tiny one in the corner, crying. My heart smote me then and I grew gentler, and life gradually became calmer as I made friends with other mothers in the area. But I'd always carried inside me the wish that I could live those years again, better. I sometimes thought of how hypnotists can implant false memories, and I wished Chris and I could go together and construct an alternative past, where everything was as it should have been.

Had my failings all those years ago made Chris kill himself? Naturally, I looked round for an excuse for my character defects in my own upbringing, and I wondered if I could lay the blame for my failures at the door of my elderly, rather strict parents who didn't communicate with their own widely spaced children (my sister was six years older than me, my brother four years younger), or teach them interpersonal skills. My sister – though she would dispute this – bullied me sometimes, but I hadn't been too hard done by really. It was more, I thought, like the way toxins in the sea can get concentrated by one creature eating another, until the last one in the chain ingests a lethal dose and dies. Perhaps my poor Chris was the end one, paying the price for the failure of generations.

But the next few days were going to bring me circling nearer and nearer to the true reason for his death.

3 - THE JOURNEY TO YORKSHIRE

The next day the weather changed abruptly, absolutely, from summer to winter. I have never known the outside world to mirror human emotions so well. Ruth and John and I drove up to Skipton through driving rain, desperate to get there, while simultaneously dreading getting there. I half wanted to spare our other daughter, Jenny, (let her not know, let her enjoy her holiday with Nick and be happy a little longer!) but I knew she would not forgive us if we kept the news from her. I called her in France and said 'Is Nick with you? Can you get him? We've got bad news…'

They said they'd come back to England right away.

We reached Airedale Hospital. A nice, young policeman came to the desk to greet us and escorted us to a room where Chris lay covered by a shiny red cloth. How strange it was that I felt a little lift of the heart when I saw him, the pleasure of recognition, to see his dear face, his well-shaped, dark eyebrows looking much as usual above his large, closed eyes. I had been imagining something monstrous. But then reality took over. I felt his face, which was cool, and then his chest through the red cloth. His body was as hard as iron, frozen. I realised that the hospital must thaw out the faces of the dead, out of kindness to the relatives, but the mechanics of it repelled me. He had a little mark on his throat, which I later discovered happened when his boss, Avice, found him and ripped off the mask hoping to save him. But she was much too late, of course.

I am not a demonstrative person, but I gave a kind of

howl, deliberately, to see if it made me feel better, but it didn't. I stroked his eyebrows, because they at least didn't feel dead. Seeing him lying there reminded me so much of when he was seven years old, in intensive care after a terrible head injury falling from a tree. The same slightly open mouth with the top teeth showing, the same unresponsiveness. But there had been a happy ending that time.

Then it was time to go to his house.

It was in a terraced row ending in a high, blank wall where the canal ran. It stood out from all the other houses because the natural sandstone bricks were painted a thick cream. He hadn't been sure about this when he bought it, it wasn't a good effect, but in every other way he liked it. The front door opened straight on to the living room, from which you could either go upstairs or through another door into the kitchen. There was a little yard at the back where he had made a miniature polythene greenhouse to grow tomato plants, and beyond that an alley that ran between the backs of two terraces, which was usually festooned with washing lines from one side to the other.

The house had a dank feel. There was an armchair close to the front door. This, we learned, was where he had sat, his laptop running, with its dreadful emails biding their time, a book called *Final Exit* nearby and a mask over his face with a tube leading to a helium canister. He had left the front door unlocked considerately, so that the police (to whom he'd sent the first email, timed for 7 a.m.) could get in to find him. But it hadn't happened as he planned, because the police didn't see his email until after Avice had got hers at around 10 a.m. and rushed round with a colleague, to find him blue and stiff in his boxer shorts.

Her email, which she forwarded to us later, said:

'If you're reading this then it means I was successful this time.

It was always a pleasure working for you, Avice. You are an excellent manager and a truly lovely person to have known.

I didn't make it to the docs on Friday in the end. Medication might have masked the symptoms but it wouldn't have been the real me, and it wouldn't have addressed the cause. The counselling was therapeutic, but each time the warm afterglow feeling only lasted for half a day. Waking up the next morning I was always back where I was.

All the books and techniques seem to point to the need for change. But the ironic thing is neither do I want to, nor have I the capacity to change who I am. Perhaps it's as much genetic as based on life experiences. Whenever I try to visualise a 'future me' all I see is an empty space.'

We didn't linger near the armchair. We went up to his bedroom and started to pack his things. A copy of Dorothy Rowe's book, *The Successful Self*, lay half read, by his bed. I flicked through it and saw he had been reading about how parents can wreck their children's self-esteem.

His bookcase was full of DVDs. I wanted to take them home with us and watch them all, so that I could understand every experience he'd had, everything he'd thought, but John and Ruth talked me out of it. I looked in the cupboard at his clothes, all his familiar T-shirts hanging there. They too seemed cold, unaired, needing a wash. Were we going to throw these out? Would we keep them for ever? I decided then and there that I was going to wear them and wear them and wear them until they wore out completely, and then I would say goodbye gradually, throwing them away one by one.

4 - HIS WORKPLACE

We had arranged to visit Skipton Building Society to meet Chris's colleagues, and Avice. So, after stowing his clothes and papers in our car to take home, we drove there. I had never met Avice before, but could see immediately why Chris had liked her so much. Some people have an aura of unmistakable warmth and sympathy. She welcomed us in, showed us his desk, gave us an album which his colleagues had put together, full of photos and anecdotes about him. We could see he'd been loved. We could also see that he'd had fun at work. We stood, browsing other people's memories of our son – nearly everybody commented on his helpfulness and eccentric sense of humour.

He had a colleague called Graham who had an individual style of speech, which Chris had decided to record, with translations. Here is an example:

Ordering a Drink

Graham Speak
Can I moisten your ship with a beverage?

Translation
Would you like a drink?

The drink of champions
Tea with two sugars

If you could press the button that resulted in production of a chocomilk, I would be eternally grateful
Chocomilk please

One colleague, Mark, had written, 'I have a distinct memory of one particular morning when Chris came in looking very tired. After a small inquisition he told everyone that the previous night he had driven 200 miles down to London to see a friend for just a couple of hours before driving back. I think this is a good example of the type of person Chris was, and the lengths he would go to for the people he cared about.'

Another, Rachel, recalled how the two of them would chat about Smurfs: 'We spent at least a week discussing the female Smurf, where she came from and what she wore' – and how Chris made a penguin out of Blu Tac to be a friend for their mascot, a small plastic duck.

Yet behind this jokey persona had been despair.

Avice had found out more than I had. She'd given him a job review, at the end of which she'd asked the routine question, 'Have you any concerns or difficulties you'd like to mention?' and something about his expression had made her say, 'Is everything all right?'

He'd confessed to her that he was depressed. She'd done everything she could – arranged for him to see a counsellor through the company, lent him books, talked to him. She seemed almost to be apologising to me for not saving him, but I said 'You did more than me. When he came to visit us last month I left him and went off to have lunch with a friend!'

Avice arranged for us to talk to the counsellor, who was open and generous in her efforts to comfort us. She told us Chris had been worried about his sexual identity, hoping we would see this as something that wasn't our fault. He had said he didn't feel 'like a proper man', and felt that the gap between how he presented himself to others and how he felt inside had become enormous. She said he'd spoken of John and me with great affection. I could see how she would have given Chris a 'warm afterglow' because she did it to us, too. For a moment we felt uplifted and cheerful – but as Chris had found, the descent to reality was harsh.

Avice told us that Skipton Building Society was anxious to give us the use of a flat they used for business clients, but we had arranged to spend the night with my sister Caroline. We said we'd stay in the company flat when we returned for the funeral.

Arranging the funeral was what we did next. As we waited in the undertaker's parlour, John referred to a walk he'd done with Chris recently around Skipton, and his voice broke, for the first time in living memory. Ruth said 'Don't you cry, Daddy, too, I don't know what we'll do!'

The priest at the church was kind, like everyone else. We fixed the service for a week away. When we reached my sister's we were exhausted, glad to eat the meal she'd cooked and to go straight to bed afterwards. I couldn't sleep, and read more of the album by the bedside lamp.

5 - ANOTHER NIGHT

There were entries by Graham, whose speaking style Chris had documented so carefully. One was:

'The Monkey Wrench

When Chris cycled home from work, he would enter the back yard of his house and after depositing his bike would go inside through the back door. One day, the handle to the back door broke off. As Chris lived in a mid-terraced house this resulted in a fair walk to get around to the front door. For several weeks, to avoid having to walk *that* far, Chris carried a rather large monkey wrench to work and back each day. When he got home he could enter through the back door by using the wrench on the remaining stubby bit of the handle. Some may have bought a new handle for the door as soon as they could, Chris used the old wartime saying "make do and mend".'

The other described how 'the always resourceful Chris' had borrowed an enormous suction-cup handle from work, designed for moving heavy metal floor panels, and cycled home with it, to use it to move a small resistant strip of laminate flooring.

This side of Chris went with the way he had obviously put off repairing his central heating, and been content to live in a cold, mouldy house. It went with the way he had moved his piano from the house he used to rent, to his new one. He had trundled it on a little trolley by himself down a steep hill and along at least half a mile of streets, and broken a bone in his foot in the process. Why couldn't he have hired a removal van?

I suspected him of liking his 'zany' image and acting up to it. But I hadn't wanted him to be zany, I wanted him to be a person who mended his back door and his central heating and hired removal vans and – to get to the heart of the matter – went out and found himself a girlfriend, instead of hankering uselessly after Kate who had left him five years ago.

Tossing in bed I thought about that time, when Kate left. They had been living for three months in the house that they'd bought together in Leighton Buzzard, and I had thought everything was fine. But he rang up one day to say, very nonchalantly and as if it was unimportant, that she'd gone. I rushed over to see him but he didn't seem able to tell me much. They'd gone on holiday with her sister and boyfriend, and he'd felt the sister didn't like him much and was putting Kate off him. And then, after they got back, Kate had said, 'This isn't working, is it?' and she'd gone back to her parents. They had been an item for four years, ever since they'd met at the university conservation group.

She hadn't given any reason.

John and I had made the two-hour journey to his house for several weekends after that, going on walks with him, giving him support. He'd found himself two lodgers to help with the mortgage, one of whom he suspected of criminality. He used to tell us funny stories about them, and then one left. He carried on doing freelance IT work locally, and we thought he seemed to be coping OK.

Then, a year later, while John and I were on holiday in

Portugal, he disappeared. I'd been anxious as he hadn't answered my phone calls from Portugal but then, when I'd rung our house expecting to get Ruth, Chris had answered, and I had just thought, Oh good, he's OK, and rushed off to dinner at the hotel, without thinking it strange that he should be there, though on reflection it was.

We returned to England a week later to find his mobile answered with the message 'this mobile is switched off, please call again later'. There had been no response to any of his emails, and the answerphone for his landline was unable to take any more messages because the inbox was full. I felt ill with worry. We drove to his house and found his car gone. To our surprise, a policeman intercepted us as we approached his front door, and insisted on doing a swift search of every room before we went into the house. I didn't realise until afterwards that he thought Chris's body might be hanging from a ceiling somewhere, and that something must have led up to the police presence there.

Later, partly from Chris's computer, which John took home, partly from the police, and partly from Chris himself when, thank God, he returned, we learned a complicated story. Perhaps I should start with his computer. We quickly found that he had slid helplessly into debt, not able to find enough freelance work (perhaps too depressed to try) and not getting enough rent from his lodgers. That was the most easily understandable of the revelations. There was another. In 'My Pictures' there were two images of himself, one in his normal clothes and one, in an identical pose, wearing women's clothes, a wig, and makeup.

Apparently there are places that will do this for you. We learned from Chris later that he'd belonged to an internet cross-dressing forum under the name of Kayla, and that he'd had a semi-official role there as gatekeeper. He'd confided to the group that he intended to commit suicide. Having learnt that a type of metallic spray used for the symbols on the bonnets of cars was lethal, he had ordered some on the internet. One of his virtual friends – to whom I'm lastingly grateful because he gave us a few more years with Chris – was alarmed and contacted the police, who were somehow able to identify him and visit him at his house. Chris was so shocked by the intrusion that he instantly took flight, breaking into the family home through a back window and lying low. This was when I had spoken to him, ringing from Portugal. From there, if I've got this right, he went to the cross-dressing salon, then on, in drag, to Kate's parents' house, where she was holding a barbecue for the group of conservationist friends that they were both part of. His friends were discomfited and embarrassed and he didn't stay long. He then drove to Edinburgh, though I can't imagine why, armed with his metallic spray, intending to kill himself.

I wish I hadn't been so imbued with political correctness about sexual variation. I felt the internal blenching most parents would feel, but I believed that everyone was different, that I had to be reticent and respect Chris's choices and accept him as he was. I didn't realise that here, if I'd only followed it up, was a powerful clue that might just possibly have led me to the truth in time.

He was away for about a week after we returned from Portugal, during which we went through hell. Then he crept back into our house in the middle of the night, waking us up. I felt instant fury. 'Christopher! How could you put us through this?' He told me he'd tried to kill himself 'but it hadn't worked'. I could not understand anyone wanting to commit suicide, and couldn't believe that here, in my own family, where we were all 'normal', was someone seriously entertaining such a thought. So I decided, completely ignoring what I knew of his character, that it was all about being in debt, he was trying to scare us, hoping we would be so glad to have him back that we'd pay up without demur.

And of course we did pay up, and we arranged for him to see a psychiatrist, who said he didn't need medication, just counselling, so he had that. I wanted so much to know what he said to the psychiatrist and the counsellor – was he telling them what a bad mother I'd been? But he wouldn't talk much. He lived with us for some months, after the crisis, and I urged him to get a job, because I thought it would make him feel better. He said once, 'I want to get to the bottom of it first,' (i.e. why he felt depressed), but I thought, quite wrongly, that introspection and inaction would get him nowhere. So he got a job with Bromley Council, visiting people after waste trucks had reversed into their garden walls, getting details and, where possible, soothing them. He was apparently brilliant at this and he did seem to get more cheerful.

After a while he decided to leave us and move up to Yorkshire to be near his friends Mark and Em. I really wanted him to stay, and tried to tempt him with promises that we'd turn the extension into an annexe for him, with his own front door, but he was set on going. I thought his plan, which was to move there first and then find a job, was deeply unwise, but I was wrong again, because he instantly got a low-paid IT job with Skipton Building Society and then impressed them so much with his skills that he was taken on permanently, eventually being co-opted in to Avice's team.

I'd thought he was all right. His phone calls always sounded cheerful. He seemed sociable and busy, going to Jazz 'n Jive dance classes, playing football, digging his allotment, running marathons. I buried the cross-dressing episode at the back of my mind, getting irritated when Celia mentioned it to me once. Yes, everything had seemed fine. But he did tell me at some stage – when? that year? – 'I'm feeling a bit low.'

I kept tossing and turning in bed as I remembered. Why did I just say, 'Ah darling, I'm sorry', instead of asking him to tell me about it properly? Why didn't I realise that he almost certainly meant, 'I'm feeling suicidal, Mum'? Why was I so blind?

He'd visited us so much this year, more than any other year since he'd moved to Yorkshire. My birthday, Mother's Day, Jenny's wedding, the holiday in Scotland when we all went to stay with John's brother. I realised that all those times he'd been mutely pleading for help, hoping I'd notice and do something.

6 - GOING THROUGH HIS THINGS

We spent the next day taking Chris's possessions to the charity shop and his furniture to the dump, and, in John's case, repairing his central heating. We kept his bicycle to give to one of our nephews. It was a small house, so it didn't take us long to dismantle it. Looking round at it now, a bare shell, I felt desolate. He had been so pleased when he'd bought it, we'd helped him move in (except for the piano!), he'd laid a laminate floor in the kitchen (helped by the suction cup handle), he'd achieved everything with his own earnings, and I thought he would be happy there. What would happen to it now? We'd sell it, someone else would move in, his little greenhouse at the back would be dismantled. It would be as if he'd never been.

We made the long, wet drive back to London, loaded up with boxes that needed sorting through. At home I started on a box of letters between him and Kate. Both sides of the correspondence seemed to be there and I tried to jigsaw them together. I'd felt frustrated that the police had taken away his laptop (which we were not to be given for many weeks), and I wanted so much to understand what had been going on in his mind. Maybe it was voyeuristic of me, holding their letters in my hands, prying into their relationship, but it felt more like wandering round a bombsite, where personal possessions lay scattered, tattered, and privacy had been destroyed for ever.

The letter I lingered on, very neatly written in his small handwriting, said:

Hi Kate

You might think that this is a strange time for me to be writing you a letter. And at 11.36 p.m. on a Monday night I'd have to agree with you.

But I'm starting to think that the occasional spell of madness is good for me. And also there are a few things I'd like to say which are, quite frankly, far too rude to mention in conversation.

And since there really is no other way to bring it up (if you'll excuse the expression) I'm just going to come straight out with it. I would like very much to write to you about my penis but before I do I would also like to tell you about my trip to Pembrokeshire in South Wales at the weekend. If you don't want to read about Wales, skip to page 4 for the juicy bits.

How had he known it would be page 4, I wondered? Then I realised he'd left a space and added the 4 afterwards. I skipped Wales and arrived at:

Right. Enough of this trivial chit-chat and down to the case in hand. We have been going out for near on 9 months now, and one thing I can't seem to quite get the hang of is sex. You've been very sweet and understanding about it all, but I can't help feeling that your patience, as well as the tendons in your right wrist, must be wearing a little thin.

For some reason my little man seems to need a

24

lot of encouragement to do his job ... If there is anything you would like to try that we haven't already done ... If all you really want is for me to get a decent hard-on then we can keep trying ...'

The letter ended, 'I love you with all my heart. Chris x'

Poor, poor Chris, I thought. I couldn't bear to think of him trying, and failing. It was a catastrophe that must have eaten him up from inside. And I'd never dreamed of it. Had they ever overcome those difficulties? If not, no wonder Kate had left. Amazing that she had stayed four years.

I told Ruth, who said, 'Maybe it got better later.' I pondered, then decided I needed to know, and rang Kate, who had already been told about Chris's death.

She didn't seem angry that I'd read their letters and answered honestly that things had never got better in all their time together. 'I wanted him to see his GP but he wouldn't, and what can you do? And I thought it might be my fault, that I wasn't doing the right things. But I didn't leave him because of that. It was his depression. When we were in a crowd with the group it wasn't so bad, but when it was just him and me in our house I was always trying to lift him, and it got so that I couldn't bear it.'

I put the phone down and went shouting crudely round the house, 'I've asked Kate. He never *ever* got it up! He was impotent!' I felt half mad with a piercing kind of pain. How must he have felt this year, when Jenny married Nick, when his best school friend Duniyul (whose street address he had texted me for recently) had announced that he and his wife were expecting their second child, and when Duniyul's younger brother had just got married too? An explosion of fecundity going on all round him, and there he was, his girlfriend gone, no hope – or so he must have felt – of ever finding another one. He must have felt his life was pointless, that he had nothing to look forward to.

I thought about the anecdote in the album about his crazy trip down to London. I'd remembered, when I read it last night, that it was Duniyul he'd visited, and what had triggered it was the news that they were expecting their first child. I'd thought it was stupid, extreme behaviour at the time (he must have got so tired, driving 400 miles in a night and going in to work next day, he could have had an accident), but now I saw it in a different light. Duniyul had achieved what he, Chris, could never do. Powerful feeling had spurred him.

I seemed to be haunted by sea imagery at that time. Now I saw Chris as a seashell clamped tightly shut, impossible to open in life, but in death the halves hang loosely, open to the passing currents.

I rang my sister and told her what Kate had said. She said, 'I bet it was that bang on the head that did it. We ought to look it up.'

I agreed, but somehow couldn't summon the energy. I felt physically weak, I can understand what 'gutted' means, because I felt as if my stomach and intestines had all been scooped out. Terrible thoughts kept assailing me. When Chris had trundled his piano through the streets of Skipton and broken his foot, I'd found someone to stand in for my classes – I taught English as a second language for Croydon Council – and hurried up to Yorkshire to look after him, and we'd had a row in which he said I was like a cheese-grater, rasping him with everything I said. Then we'd made up and gone to a Chinese restaurant round the corner together, and he'd said he wasn't 'normal'. I'd stared at him in dismay, wondering what this meant. Was he saying he was homosexual? I said,

'Sweetheart, I love you whatever you are.' I wish so badly that I had instead said, 'What do you mean, Chris, not normal?'

Memories like this kept lurching at me, I couldn't cope with it. I spent time doing silly little things. I labelled all the things we'd brought back from his house – the Sellotape, the maps, cold remedies, some DVDs (I did bring some of those back), a bottle of TCP, a tin of cocoa – with his name, so that we would always know when we used them. I was obsessed with the idea of using everything up, so that in a way we were reabsorbing him. I thought of *Watership Down*, where I'd learnt that pregnant rabbits can reabsorb their foetuses in hard times. I'd brought back a set of his playing cards, and when I couldn't bear to think any more I played patience with them, pretending to myself that he was answering me through the cards. A display of red cards meant he was trying to cheer me up. If the game came out, he was telling me things would get better.

Jenny, Ruth, and John made preparations for the funeral and kept asking me to find photos or to answer questions. I distinctly remember thinking, 'Why have they got to hurry him into the earth? Why can't they give him the benefit of the doubt?' I still felt doubt that he was dead. I still couldn't believe it.

John and I belong to a walking group and would typically walk around ten miles on a Saturday. We went as usual five days after his death, but I found I could hardly walk half that distance.

Then, sometime during that first week after his death and before the funeral, an email came from my sister. It said, 'You would have found this, but maybe not till after the funeral, which would be too late to do tests for multiple anterior pituitary hormone deficiencies, which according to this 2007 paper are almost inevitable after traumatic brain injuries.'

It was a life-changing moment.

7 - THE RESEARCH

I sat staring at my computer screen for a long time before I could make myself read on. Her email continued, 'To me it explains everything about poor Chris's problems except how he soldiered on so bravely for so long and stayed so kind and patient with everyone.'

I scrutinised the research she'd sent, heart beating wildly, hardly able to think straight enough to extract the facts from the dense medical language.

The hypothalamus and pituitary are essential for childhood and adolescent development and are vulnerable to injury and dysfunction following brain trauma ... Well recognised in adults, data regarding hypothalamic-pituitary function in brain-injured children and adolescents are scant. It is necessary for physicians as well as patients and family members to know that onset of hypothalamic-pituitary deficits can occur even after several years following brain injury ... The key presenting symptoms are growth failure, delayed or arrested puberty, secondary amenorrhea, or reduced libido. Delay in the diagnosis was extreme in many cases...

What on earth did all that mean? I had to read it several times before I understood that it was saying that head injury often damaged both the pituitary and its 'control' (the part of the brain known as the hypo-thalamus). This damage could interfere with growth and puberty, make a girl's periods stop, and rob people of their sex drive. And all this could start to happen years after the injury. Everything seemed to fit with Chris's story.

I took in another sentence: 'It was notable that in six patients, multiple deficiencies were documented after relatively mild head injury without loss of consciousness.'

Chris's head injury when he was seven hadn't been mild, it had been very severe. He'd fallen from a tree and fractured his skull 'like an eggshell' according to the consultant. We'd thought he was going to die. After a week-long coma he had come round and slowly climbed back to normality, though his face remained half paralysed for months. I even remembered a nurse telling me as we left hospital, 'His pituitary may be damaged' – abruptly, as if she were flashing a personal warning. But my school biology lessons hadn't given me the full picture. I thought the pituitary just controlled growth, and though I didn't forget what she'd said and waited anxiously to see if he would grow, my worries subsided when he did (though I now know that growth and growth hormone deficiency aren't incompatible). I hadn't known at all about the sexual side.

Our first reaction was to approach the pathologist, but this led nowhere. All he did was to go and look at Chris's body and report that there were 'no clinical signs of hypopituitarism'. In other words, his penis looked a normal size and he had body hair. He did have body hair, but his facial hair had always been rather scanty, and his chest hair had an odd, lopsided look. I felt the pathologist could have done more, but I was told later that pathologists do not get paid much 'per death' and can be perfunctory.

I expect we could have insisted on a proper autopsy, in

the process of which his pituitary gland might have been physically examined. I didn't think of this. The funeral arrangements were in full swing, with letters and cards flooding in every day, and I felt it had turned into an unstoppable machine. And if we did find pituitary damage, what would it achieve? We wouldn't have sued. It wouldn't bring him back. I decided to let it go, though there have been times since then when I've wished we hadn't.

The general effect of my sister's electrifying information was to lift, slightly, my feeling that I was wholly responsible for Chris's death. Now I saw it as a double whammy. Misery from the impotence coming at him from one side, and the insecurity created by my early mothering failures coming at him from the other. He hadn't had a chance. My sister's words about his courage, and how he had soldiered on, being patient and kind with everyone resonated with me. Poor Christopher, poor Christopher! I wanted to comfort him, to tell him that I understood now, to say sorry for every time I had ever been impatient or thought him weak, that I could see now that he hadn't been weak but very, very strong. But no message from me would ever reach him now.

When he'd had his brain injury nearly twenty-five years before, what had sustained me then was a simple mantra: 'Let everything that can be good, be good.' What it meant to me was that though you could do nothing about the big bad thing that was going on, you could do little things. If the room you were in was untidy, you could tidy it, and that was then one thing that you had made better than it was. If your socks were dirty from being worn six days running while you were sitting in intensive care, you could wash them, and that was another good thing. Or if you were tempted to snap at someone because you were tired and miserable, keeping it in was better than not keeping it in. It is a way of feeling you have some power left.

Now my sister's information had given me something to do. If Chris had been affected by hypopituitarism and not been diagnosed, it was likely that he wasn't the only one. Maybe there were other people like him and I could save them by spreading the information.

I can't pretend that I felt any great desire to help anyone at that stage, but it fitted the mantra, so I decided, even in those early days before the funeral, that I would channel some of my wild, useless emotion into this.

8 - THE FUNERAL

The rain fell and fell. The priest at the service for Chris said it was the angels weeping. He was a nice man.

What I mostly remember from that day is how many people came. The church was bursting. I remember my mother-in-law wailing loudly at some point. And I remember Duniyul's eulogy, which took me back to the days when Chris was four years old. The full version is in the Appendix.

Afterwards, at the reception, I remember hearing Dido singing, 'I will go down with this ship, there will be no white flag above my door, I'm in love, and always will be,' over and over again, until it was like a torture, while the sequence of photos projected on the wall repeated endlessly – Chris as a baby crying in a rucksack; Chris as a little boy playing on the beach; Chris as a young man sitting on the ground, his arms loosely propped on his knees with unconscious grace. I just wanted to get away and hide in the dark somewhere.

And in the end we did get away, making our way to the flat that Skipton Building Society had offered for us to use. It was high, and from the window I could see how Skipton was laid out, and the Yorkshire Dales beyond. On ground level I had often been puzzled about how the river and canal and railway and roads were interwoven, but now the riddle was clear – rather as Christopher's death and our subsequent discoveries had given us a bird's-eye view of his own sad geography. I thought about him and his sister Jenny, both little, round-headed babies born at the same time of day, weighing much the same, both blond-haired and smiley, and I thought how happy Jenny was, newly married, adored by Nick, brilliant at her job, whereas Christopher … There's a poem by William Blake which goes, 'Some are born to sweet delight, Some are born to endless night.'

Thinking about Christopher's endless night made me want to be alone and huddle into myself, but John wanted to make love, and this was probably the first time I felt the difference in the way men and women face tragedy. To me, it was as if John was triumphantly flaunting something he could do and Christopher couldn't, and it felt like a profound breach of taste. To him – I didn't feel like asking him – maybe he wanted comfort for himself and thought it would comfort me too. Anyway, I applied the principle of doing what would make things better rather than worse, and I didn't reject him.

Afterwards we talked. John said, 'I just want to get on with life and forget this as soon as I can.' And I said, 'I feel the exact opposite. I want to go over it and over it and understand it as much as I can.' And somehow, we agreed to accept our different strategies and support each other. Much later I read Lee Woodruff's autobiographical *In an Instant* where she says, after describing a miscarriage and hysterectomy, 'Men and women grieve differently. I needed to chew it over and roll it around, and Bob wanted to bury it like a bone.' This just about sums it up.

9 - GRIEF

What I felt as August gave way to September and the weather remained wet and autumnal, as though summer had ended on that far distant sunny day when I was happy and got on with the gardening, will be familiar to anyone who has suffered a sudden, close bereavement. I couldn't sleep, or when I did I would wake up, heart lurching, staring into the darkness, with the impossible thought, 'Christopher's dead!' propelling me from the bed with terrible force. I did Sudoku puzzles with mechanical concentration until I couldn't think any more and then I switched off the light and twisted and turned.

I was frustrated by my inability to cry. I felt that if I could only let out a great flood of tears it would ease my heart, but I couldn't. Somehow over the years my tear-glands, from being exceptionally copious in my teens, had withered, and now the sharpest grief only produced the merest drop. I conceived the bizarre idea of collecting what tears I could shed for him in a little plastic tube with a cap, letting them mount up into a quantity I could see. So I woke in the night and cried into the tube, seeing the level rise barely perceptibly.

Then I collected coins that had been dropped in the road and put them in Christopher's money box, a miniature telephone box I had given him long ago, which we found stuffed with 2p pieces in his house. I got strangely fixated on this. I remember seeing several coins in a workmen's pit fenced off by posts on the pavement – several 2p pieces, a 5p even! – and creeping down early next morning before anyone was up, so that I could climb over the barrier and get them without embarrassment. Actually a passing man did see me, and I had to give a nonchalant shrug and smile like Kristen Wiig caught astride a security gate in *Bridesmaids*. Then I went home to post these grimy, defaced coins through the telephone box slot like all the others, whispering, 'For you, my darling.'

Tragedy is a magnet that draws out other people's secrets. Juliet, a friend from our walking group, a slight, blonde girl with a sunny, childlike smile, told me how her only daughter was murdered by her boyfriend. 'When it happened I told the whole world about it, I couldn't stop talking, but then that wore off and I hardly mention it now. But sometimes when people talk about their children I feel like saying, "I have been a mum."'

To have your only child die, and die in that way, is a benchmark of horror. I used to think about people in Beirut who went shopping and came back to find their home destroyed and their whole family killed. Before Christopher died I would read these things in the papers and be hardly touched. It was too dreadful to imagine, so I didn't try. But now I had a way in.

And I thought of Victorian families, where there were often a dozen children and you'd lose one or two as a matter of course. Maybe those families had a more real understanding of life than we have, we who are cosseted and protected by modern medicine so that premature death strikes us as an outrage.

Another friend, whose son died of leukaemia when he was only twelve, told me how she'd read that the faulty gene could be triggered by trauma, and how she thought her son's had been, which made her feel as if his death had been her fault. She was telling me this to assuage my feelings of guilt. When he was a little boy she had come home from shopping, put her car in the garage, letting him sit on her lap to 'drive' as he liked to do. When she lifted him out of the car he ran back into the house and tripped over the step knocking his teeth out. 'The times I've relived those moments, over and over again, wishing and wishing I hadn't bothered to put my car away.'

Thinking about other people gave me perspective, but I still felt as if I could hardly function. I felt like I was struggling hopelessly to steer a small ship over a vast, heaving sea. It seemed a matter of survival to brace up and do something practical, which meant campaigning, though I thought of it simply as writing emails, and didn't give it that name at that stage.

10 - DR BABU'S TUTORIAL

But where to start? I was in that state of shock where you can take in very little, remember less, and rational thought is almost impossible. All I had was this inability to rest without feeling dreadful, and as Juliet had, a compulsion to tell my story again and again, to anyone who would listen. I was obsessed with a sense of urgency, that I might save someone like Chris from suicide if I worked quickly enough (and eight years on, I know I was right to feel this and am sorry that the feeling has faded). I spent all day at my computer, googling and emailing, exposing myself late into the evening to that stimulating blue screen light that I've read is an enemy to sleep, and which in my case certainly seemed to be.

I wrote myself diagrams of a four-pronged approach with headings – MEDICAL, MEDIA, CHARITIES, GOVERNMENT ORGS – and added intricate sub-branches to each, but in fact I did nothing systematically, I simply did whatever anyone suggested, immediately, uncritically, and though I made tables now and then, listing what I'd done and what responses I'd had, they were incomplete and I often failed to follow things up.

I spent hours scouring the internet for articles about post-traumatic hypopituitarism (PTHP), but when I found them it was hard to read them with anything like intelligent comprehension. By a kind of osmosis, though, facts did slowly filter into my brain.

I cannot replicate this experience for the reader so the most sensible thing is to give a bald summary of what, in the end, I absorbed about the pituitary. I was greatly helped by the Pituitary Foundation's leaflets and also by a kind consultant psychiatrist who lives at the bottom of our road and who summoned me into his dining room to give me an impromptu tutorial.

I will follow my neighbour's example in giving you a picture of the pituitary gland first. I was struck by how tiny it is, for something so important. It is not much bigger than a pea.

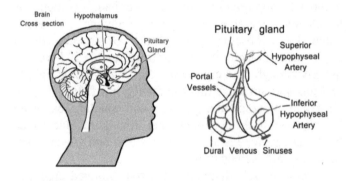

The picture on the left shows its position, hanging by a fragile stalk from the underside of the brain behind the nose. The right-hand picture shows the stalk and its blood vessels in more detail. The gland itself rests in a bony hollow below, called the sella. This means that when the brain swishes about in the skull during impact, the stalk cannot swing freely and escape damage, but is stretched because it is anchored at both ends. This matters because the veins that supply the gland travel down it, and if the gland is starved of blood, it can die. If it dies, it stops making the hormones that it should.

There are five important hormones made by the front part of the gland that can be affected. My own trick for remembering them is to count them off on my fingers. My thumb stands for growth hormone. It not only makes children grow, but is responsible in adulthood for muscles, strength, and vitality. Athletes get into trouble for abusing it to build up body strength. Cattle are fed it to bulk up their lean meat. Elderly American ladies take it to keep their skin smooth and elastic. If your body doesn't make enough, you grow fat and flabby and fatigued, and you can't think straight. Another serious consequence is depression.

The next pituitary hormone is adrenocorticotropic hormone, or ACTH for short, and as its name implies it stimulates the adrenal glands above your kidneys to produce adrenaline and cortisol (the fight or flight response). Not enough of that, and you may lose weight, feel faint when you stand up after sitting, and, again, suffer fatigue and depression.

Then comes the thyroid stimulating hormone, which I count on my middle finger. It triggers the butterfly-shaped thyroid gland in your throat to do its job. Without it everything slows down, both in your mind and body, and you will put on weight you can't shift, be tearful, not be able to remember things or concentrate. Your body temperature may go out of control, you may feel either too hot or too cold, your hair will get lifeless, your skin dry, and you may have high cholesterol and liver problems.

Next come the gonadotrophs, that I believe failed for Chris. They are luteinising hormone and follicle stimulating hormone, which are generally referred to as a pair – LH/FSH. The gonadotrophs are what tell your sex organs to make oestrogen or testosterone, and if you don't have these you are in serious trouble. It's not just that you lose your sex drive and fertility, but again, just as with

41

deficiencies in the other hormones, you can be constantly tired and depressed.

Finally, the little finger. This is for prolactin, the hormone that controls the production of breast milk. Paradoxically, if the pituitary is damaged you may have too much of this, and whether you are a man or a woman you may find your breasts ooze milk. Too much prolactin is associated with depression.

Coming now to the more protected, back part of the pituitary, which is less likely to be affected because it is fed by shorter, less fragile blood vessels, there is one more hormone to mention. This is the hormone that controls how much urine you produce. Its name is anti-diuretic hormone, or ADH, and if you're short of it you can be doomed to produce vast quantities of urine all the time, and will need to drink constantly to make up. Again, you may feel ill and depressed.

Finally, one has to remember that a damaged pituitary may not cause every hormone to fail. It's more usual for only one or two to be affected. This is what makes hypopituitarism so difficult to diagnose, because the picture varies from person to person. Another confounding factor is that your hypothalamus, a part of the brain that is upstream from the pituitary and controls it, may also be damaged, causing your autonomic nervous system to malfunction too, affecting sleep and appetite.

If you have hypopituitarism the outlook is grim. You may be too fatigued and fuzzy-brained to hold down a job. You may become grossly fat and lose all your friends. Your relationship may fail because you can't perform in bed or because you can't have children, or simply because your partner can't understand why you're so miserable all the time. The worst-case scenario is that your depression may get so bad that you kill yourself. A substantial

Danish study by Teasdale and Engberg in 2001 covering around 150,000 hospital admissions showed that someone with a brain injury is three or four times more likely to commit suicide than other people.

There are two obvious questions: how many people have hypopituitarism, and can they be treated? The answer to the second question is yes, they can. They can have the missing hormones replaced on an ongoing basis and generally return to normal life, have sex, conceive children, and work. Although some people are miraculously transformed by treatment, others may still feel below par, perhaps because artificial hormone replacement cannot perfectly mimic the subtle action of the body, which produces hormones in little bursts according to the time of day and how much stress you are under. As one diagnosed friend put it, years later, 'I don't feel a hundred per cent, but I've got my life back.'

The question of how many people have hypopituitarism is harder to answer, and my ideas about this have changed gradually over the years since Chris's death. The truth lies somewhere between many and shockingly many. When I began reading the research, which was mainly about people with serious injuries like Chris's, I believed that about seven thousand people were laid low by it each year. This seemed a huge number to me, and I couldn't understand why government officials and patient safety organisations didn't respond more urgently. Then, later, I read more carefully and saw there is plenty of evidence that mild brain injury, or concussion, causes it too. There are over a million concussions a year in the UK, and some research claims that a sixth of them cause PTHP. The real figure then, it seems, is likely to be considerably higher than seven thousand.

I found two important academic papers stating that

between 30 and 50 people suffer PTHP in every hundred thousand each year. Multiply that by 600 for the UK population, and then multiply by, say, the past forty years that it's been ignored … My hair stood on end.

But when I started writing letters I was not too focused on the statistics. Even if just one other person in the whole world had suffered what Chris did, I'd have tried to save that person, because that was the only way anything good could come out of his death. I didn't even care too much either, whether PTHP was what Chris actually had. Supposing it had been something else, what did it matter? He'd been robbed of his sexual confidence, he'd lost his partner, he'd been given no medical help, no sympathy, and here was a group of people who were going through those exact same things. How could I not want to help them?

This is why the people I was about to encounter, who would try to persuade me that Chris didn't have PTHP or that the problem was small, seemed so off-beam. Why on earth would they think such considerations would matter to me? How could anyone possibly imagine they would make me stop?

My emails to organisations and individuals followed a pattern. I would describe Chris's death in the first part, and give general information about PTHP in the second, and at the bottom I would list the many academic papers that I had found, that showed the high risk. Telling the same story so many times ought to have been a means to make it real to me, but in fact I reached the stage when I would reel it off mechanically as if it concerned somebody else, and the pain would lurk, untouched, to spring out at me at night time.

As I cried my sparse tears in those dark hours, drowning in my emotions, I sometimes felt distaste at the way I focused on myself all the time, as if it was all about me. I remembered the comedy *Nighty Night*, where Julia Davis, faced with her husband's terminal illness, cries, 'I mean, why, why *me*?' and her long-suffering husband says, 'Let's keep this in perspective Jill. It's me that's got the cancer.' And I would imagine Chris saying, 'It's me that's dead, Mum.' But thinking of him, trying to imagine what he went through, was just unbearable, and it always brought me up against the bleak truth that he wasn't there any more, he was beyond all reach of comforting, so now it *was* all about me, the one who was left.

11 - RULE 43 AND THE INQUEST

It was, of course, about John and Jenny and Ruth, and Celia, too, but I wasn't much help to them. Meanwhile, the impulse to tell the whole world and not stop talking helped in practical ways, because I told everyone I met, and when people weren't telling me about the sad things that had happened to them, they were thinking inventively and coming up with good ideas, all of which I wrote down and set myself to do.

Early on, one of these ideas was Rule 43. This came through my old university friend Frances who had risen high in the legal profession and had a colleague, Linda, who was knowledgeable about inquests. Rule 43 is something the coroner can invoke if someone has died in such a way as to highlight a risk to the general population. It means the coroner can write to a person or organisation, in this case the NHS, where he believes that action should be taken to prevent future deaths. The recipient is obliged to reply within 56 days. Linda advised me to get hold of Chris's medical records as a preliminary. I thought this would be straightforward, but when I wrote to his GP he replied that he could not send them 'because it would contravene the Data Protection Act.' Linda said this was rubbish and drafted a strong letter to them ('Your response appears to misunderstand the intention of the Access to Medical Records Act 1990...'), which resulted in my sister, who lived near Skipton, driving over to pick them up within the week.

I opened the big, brown envelope and drew out the

crookedly photocopied sheets with that same feeling of looking through the ruins of a blown-up house and finding private things. Poor Christopher! There were parts of his notes that I could hardly bear to read.

There was a letter dated 16 November 1999 from his GP of that time, referring him to a depression clinic. The GP had had a 'long discussion' with Chris and learnt that he had:

> 'a feeling of low mood which can happen up to several times a week, but sometimes doesn't trouble him for a couple of months. Looking further into the past, he had an episode in his last year of university for two months when he was unable to work due to low mood and inertia. At that stage he had some counselling ... he tells me that he didn't pass his final exams and although he re-sat them, he didn't pass his re-takes and had some difficulty getting a job. When he was out of work for a number of weeks recently he felt more low in mood, but over the last few weeks he has started working for Rover and feels a little bit better in himself. He says that whilst he was feeling better he would like to have it sorted out as to why he keeps getting these low moods.'

So that was why he didn't get his degree! I'd thought he'd been lazy, just not working hard enough. I'd been disappointed in him, and shown it. Another stab to the heart, seeing how I'd failed him, but I drove down the thought. How sensible of him to tackle the problem while he was feeling well, rather than wait until he was overwhelmed by it and would have no strength to do anything. He must somehow have felt, his body must have known, that it was a physical problem.

So, on his side he'd done everything right. But oh, why hadn't the clinic known about the link between a past head injury and depression and, come to that, suicidality? Why hadn't they been given the training that would have told them he needed endocrine testing?

Then there was the entry when Chris had been tested (negatively) for chlamydia. I remembered him telling me, some years after Kate had left him, that she had got in touch having apparently found she had it, and had asked him to be tested. In view of what she'd recently told me I could only imagine she thought it might be transmitted by heavy petting. Maybe it could. At any rate, the entry read, 'Ex partner from 5 yrs ago has screened +ve for chlamydia, would like testing. Not currently sexually active.' When I showed the notes to my psychiatrist neighbour, he paused on this last phrase and said, 'Not currently sexually active. That's another thing they should have picked up.'

But overall, I could not see why the GP's practice had been so reluctant to release the notes to me. It was true that his doctor had definitely known about his childhood head injury (the section on his headaches actually commented that I, the 'mum', had been worried about a possible tumour following on from his head injury – 'nil to suggest this'), but I could hardly blame him for not investigating Chris's hormone levels when nobody in the NHS apart from my neighbour seemed to know they should have.

While we were waiting for the inquest I wrote to his GP in Skipton about the research I'd read. I wanted them to do an SUI report (Serious Untoward Incident) which would warn other GPs. They refused.

I was in a very delicate frame of mind. As long as everyone responded to my information with human sympathy and a readiness to do what they could to stop the same thing happening to somebody else, I was fine. But as soon as anyone did not respond in this way, like the GP practice, and later, NICE, I was extraordinarily upset.

I wrote to the practice manager, 'I'm sure if you and I had met as friends and I had told you about our son, you would have been shocked and saddened at the needless death of a young man, and you'd have been eager to do anything you could to stop it happening again. But something extraordinary seems to happen to people once they work as part of an organisation …'

She did not reply.

Nor did Dr Adrian Winbow, the psychiatrist we'd sent Chris to privately after he'd disappeared for two weeks and come back saying he'd attempted suicide. I wrote to him twice, but there was absolutely no response. I believe, six years on, that he was more to blame for missing the chance to diagnose and treat than the GP, because the psychiatrists' 'bible', the *Diagnostic and Statistical Manual of Mental Disorders*, has a section about medical conditions that can produce psychiatric symptoms, and head injury is listed there. At the very least he could have told us about the associated high risk of suicide. But I wasn't on a witch hunt. I was focused on rescue, not vengeance.

Sadly, the coroner did not respond in the right way either. He picked on the chlamydia episode as a reason to doubt that Chris was impotent, even though I produced Chris's own letter about the failures of his 'little man'. The inquest happened on a cold, snowy day, in Skipton of course, and my sister came with me, sharing the bleak trudge to the Registration Office. We both spoke up about hypopituitarism, and afterwards the policewoman who had been there commiserated with us. 'They do all this research,' she said, 'and all they're interested in is furthering their careers.' Actually I felt grateful to the researchers, because where would we have been without them, but I was comforted that she believed us and seemed on our side.

That day marked the end of my attempts to persuade those who were professionally involved in Chris's story to do something. From then on I felt I was on my own – one individual trying to tell the sixty million people in this country something that for their self-protection they need to know. I used to think if I just told twenty people a day for the rest of my life, that would be 150,000, that would be something (I was optimistically counting on living to my eighties). In fact, during the tail end of 2008, telling twenty people a day was pretty well what I did, despite getting odd looks from strangers on trains. Gradually, however, I drew in my horns and tried the more conventional routes of email shots, the media, and conferences.

12 - THE FISHPOND

Long ago, when video games had only just been invented, there was one called *Minotaur*. I believe it still exists in a far more sophisticated form, but when I played it the graphics were primitive – a black screen on which you could progress jerkily along a corridor etched in thin white lines that tapered towards a vanishing point. Pressing function keys enabled you to turn left or right through mysterious openings in search of ingots. As you made your way, a deep creaking sound like a heavy footprint might warn you that the Minotaur, unseen, was five moves from you, but then, with luck, there would be silence once more. Then perhaps you would make a mistake and the creaks would start up once more, rising in pitch and menace – becoming beeps in fact – and your heart would pound as you tried to escape, until suddenly, there was the monster filling the screen! He was drawn in thin white lines too, a simple, smiling creature, and his eyes, white as stars in a night sky, would wink at you in triumph, first one eye, then the other. That was the end of the game.

At the start of my campaign, the complexity of the NHS and the multiplicity of medical organisations and charities did make me feel as if I was entering a labyrinth, but I had no thought of a minotaur. I believed that when I met with obstruction or failure, it was because of institutional inertia or because in some way I had approached an organisation clumsily. It was perhaps two years before those deep, almost sub-audible creaks became too insistent to ignore.

Christmas came, our first without Christopher. We were lucky because Nick, by marrying Jenny that year, brought our family members up to five again, which meant we were spared the desolate sense that we were diminished. But it was a subdued day and I was glad when it was over.

As New Year approached, I tried to take stock. Had these past three months of chaotic, driven emailing achieved anything?

Well, there had been some progress. I'd learnt a lot about hypopituitarism, for a start. I'd built up a collection of papers that filled a whole filing cabinet drawer, throwing out all my teaching papers to make room for them. I'd persuaded a couple of important medical websites to include the crucial information. I'd made slight inroads into the medical press – a couple of letters in magazines for GPs. I'd had encouraging replies from some of the hospitals I'd written to. I'd learnt that Dr Tara Kearney at Salford Royal Hospital in Manchester was 'addressing the issue' of PTHP. Thanks to one of my brothers-in-law and a nephew I had a website, Headinjuryhypo, that set out the salient facts, but all this was like throwing bread on the water. I did not know where the ducks were, or if they were eating any of it. I was reaching out into the void, desperate to find somebody like Chris (I always visualised a young man, though I knew it wasn't only men who suffered) who would learn about PTHP and get his life back.

As well as learning about hypopituitarism, I'd made other discoveries. My learning had happened in a random, experiential, incremental way, rather as a lab rat learns that pushing certain levers will bring food, and others not, and what I learnt was this: that approaching any government organisation set up to protect the health of the patient or the population at large, would produce no rat-food. The Health and Safety Executive, The Patient Safety Organisation, The Secretary of State for Health ... in other words, anyone *paid* to address the kind of risk I was pointing out, would find all kinds of reasons to avoid taking responsibility. Their replies were too tedious, and somehow disgusting, to summarise here. I learnt that charities were a mixed bag, some good, some bad, and that medical professionals, who work hands-on to help sick people, and who have no obligation to respond to emails sent by strangers and yet sometimes replied at 11 o'clock at night, could be brilliant.

Their replies were about a twentieth the length of those from government organisations and charities, and their sympathy was human and real. I particularly treasure an exchange with a consultant paediatrician, in which he said nice things about my mailshot and, when I told him how useless government organisations had been ('It is people like you who [...] are almost too busy to breathe let alone engage in anything extra, who have been wonderful'), he replied 'and thank *you* again, Joanna! I'm actually breathing quite easily just now and enjoying a piece of cake with a mug of tea whilst answering e-mails, so please don't fret for me!'

It was human exchanges like these that kept me going. Sometimes I felt I shouldn't enjoy the occasional praise that came my way – how could I enjoy anything that came out of Chris's death? – but the truth was I needed comfort, and took any that came along.

I'd met a friendly statistician who told me about a website that lists how many people have been diagnosed with a particular ailment in any one year. I looked up hypopituitarism and found that – from all causes, not just head injury – there were fewer than two thousand diagnosed cases in 2008. According to what I believed at the time, there should have been at least three times that – and in the light of what I know now, it should have been fifteen times as many. I was pleased to know about the website; I realised that now I had an objective measure. If I looked up the diagnosis figures every year, and saw them rise, I would know I was getting somewhere.

I look back at my 60-year-old self now, as I sat waiting for the end of the year, trying to make sense of my life. I was probably sitting at my computer in our study, wearing one of Chris's T-shirts. There was a khaki one I especially liked with cream letters saying DIESEL IND 1978 on the front, one which I had often hugged him in, feeling his warm living chest through the thin material. I wonder what I looked like in December 2008. I still straightened my hair and tried to look younger than I was. I don't think I had visibly started yet to hurtle into old age as I have now, though the process had already begun inside.

What I can see now, as my past self couldn't, was that though everything I'd done had been a muddle, and I had been like someone randomly stabbing fish in a pond with a spear, missing far more than I hit, during those three months the *dramatis personae* of my story had been assembling, one by one. They were the larger, darker fish who swam more deeply, the big players, and as time went on I would aim my spear with more precision.

13 - THREE BIG FISH

Apart from Dr Kearney, the consultant endocrinologist researching PTHP, who did not make her appearance in my life until the following year, the three big fish were Headway, the Pituitary Foundation, and NICE.

Headway is the biggest charity for head injury survivors and everyone said that I should contact them. When I did, they responded with great speed and sent Luke Griggs, their communications manager, down to see me. He had a terrible time fighting his way through the south London traffic, I had a series of frustrated phone calls from him apologising for being late and giving his current position, and when he eventually arrived, looking hot, I took an instant liking to him, which has remained ever since despite Headway's sometimes questionable behaviour.

Luke said that Headway had links to women's magazines and that if I wanted he could get a journalist to write about Chris. He warned me that these magazines might sensationalise the story, and showed me examples that were indeed rather lurid. I decided privately at that point that I would write my own article to keep control. When I changed my mind two years later, swayed by the consideration that it wasn't just *Guardian* readers who needed to know about PTHP, Luke was the string-puller behind an article in the popular magazine *that's life!* headed 'A BROKEN MAN, SEX SHAME FROM THE GRAVE'.

That first morning he had no other suggestions for

publicising PTHP, and after having a cup of coffee he made his way back into the awful traffic, and that was Headway's rather low-key entrance into the drama.

The Pituitary Foundation was another obvious organisation to approach, since it supported people with all kinds of hormonal illness. When I wrote to Kit Ashley, their CEO, she wrote a kind and sympathetic letter back, enclosing a copy of their 'Needs Analysis Report', which I found useful as it demonstrated a link between hypopituitarism and depression, which did not always get a mention online, and an invitation to call their telephone counsellor to cope with my grief. She asked permission to show my letter to her medical committee, which I gave. She ended, 'You are in our thoughts.'

Her next letter said that the medical committee had provided 'thoughtful responses'. They felt it was 'conceivable that Chris had secondary hypogonadism to allow puberty to occur.' (If you have some difficulty with this sentence, so did I. I did not know then that 'secondary' in this context meant 'caused not by the testes or ovaries themselves, but their failure to receive instruction from the pituitary gland. 'Primary' hypogonadism is caused by the sex glands themselves.) I think she meant to write '*delayed* secondary hypo-gonadism.' She went on, 'This could link to depression and erectile dysfunction. If puberty occurred normally, then there would be no outward reason to perform tests in adolescence to diagnose secondary hypogonadism.'

She sounded as if she was trying to defend the medical profession against a negligence charge, while not answering my point, which was that *because* PTHP was hard to spot, doctors needed to be warned. She said the incidence of PTHP in children was 'not clearly defined' but research was being done and awareness raised. She signed off again with, 'You are in our thoughts'.

I was reminded of a video our younger daughter Ruth made at school when she was about twelve, learning about the plague and the Great Fire of London. She and her school friend Alison can be seen, suitably dressed in long skirts and 17th century shawls, rocking their babies and talking about the fire. Alison says with utmost tranquillity, 'We hear the fire be very fierce. People do say that it has reached the next street...' and she and Ruth take another sip of tea.

The inertia of government bodies had dismayed me, but the apparent indifference of a charity that above all ought to have felt an obligation to act, was baffling. Why wasn't Kit Ashley more shocked at what I had told her? Why didn't she feel any pressure to do anything? The fire was crackling in the next street, but nobody seemed inclined to budge.

Finally, there was NICE, the National Institute for Clinical Excellence (or as they now call themselves, the National Institute for Health and Care Excellence). As well as their more high-profile role rationing expensive drugs, they produce guidelines for the treatment of medical conditions, which are what hospitals follow. I found that they had another role. When I wrote to my then MP, Richard Ottaway (now Sir), or the Secretary of State for Health, or the National Patient Safety Agency, and so on, a number of very long letters would be solemnly generated and passed from one organisation to another. The replies that came back to me generally expressed profound sympathy, explained that PTHP didn't fall within their remit, and that NICE were the people to approach. NICE were, in other words, the organisation the buck got passed to. As I had early on been disturbed to find that NICE's head injury guideline did not contain a word about PTHP, I was keen to approach them, and did. Their communications department told me that they would pass my letter to the group who produced the head injury guidelines.

I was thoughtless enough at that stage to imagine that NICE had only to see my letter to put things right at once, but when some weeks later I casually mentioned this to Frances' friend Linda (of Rule 43) who knew all about NICE, she did that thing with her eyes that means, 'Are you *sure*?' I checked back and was told that there were 'no plans to conduct an unscheduled review.' I'd wanted them to revise the guideline immediately to warn of the risk, even though the next update wasn't due for several years. Reading this email was like walking smack into an unseen glass door. How could they refuse, when somebody had died, and when all I was asking was the inclusion of a few words to save other people?

At that time I hadn't the faintest understanding of NICE's character – this huge reptilian organisation, slow-moving, cold, enmeshed in procedures and protocols, quite devoid of a sense of human feeling. I was stupid to expect human feeling. How could it feel? A large organisation is a phenomenon, not a person. This setback upset me far more than the response, or lack of it, from Chris's GP surgery and Dr Winbow.

Luckily for me, I was cheered by the help I continued to get from individuals in other matters. For example, Jo Derby at BUPA was a truly sympathetic (virtual) friend when I tried to get something on to their website. She passed on my information to BUPA's clinical team and I imagine was quietly persistent when they were obstructive. I couldn't believe that they demanded my membership number before they would do anything, but luckily I did happen to be a member. When they eventually did post something under 'erectile dysfunction' she wrote to tell me, and later wrote, off her own bat, to suggest ways I could attract visitors to the website we'd set up.

Another person I had real help from was Stephanie McNamara, who worked for the General Medical Council. She understood my frustration and had suggested approaching the media early on, with advice to ignore editors' obsession with exclusivity. She also warned me to arm myself against the ways Chris's story might be sensationalised, saying she'd hate me to get hurt by insensitive treatment. But I didn't care about that. She was right; it was a way to get things moving, and I had in fact been considering it ever since Luke's visit. When she wrote in December suggesting the *Guardian*, it was all the prodding I needed.

14 - THE GUARDIAN

So I set to. I had qualms about exposing Chris's story to such a large audience, especially his sexual failure – I couldn't imagine anything he would have hated more – but he was dead, and if I didn't do anything, I was sure other people would die too. Out of deference to Kate, who didn't want her name used, I wrote under the pseudonym Caroline Churchill, a combination of my sister's first name and my mother's maiden name. I called Chris 'Andrew'.

I opened with a poem I'd written in the weeks after his death, about how he'd cut down a tree for us only a month before he died, how good he was, and how good the tree was too, and how 'He was the woodman and the wood, he was the sawyer and the sawn. He cut himself down.' It had been my way of expressing something I couldn't get my head round, that he was both victim and murderer. How could he have killed someone so dear to me, and hurt me so deeply, and yet be the innocent sufferer too? Sometimes I thought my head and heart would burst with it.

I wrote about my bizarre tear-harvesting ritual, and made it the framework for the story. I found the process of giving my experience a shape oddly consoling. However ugly and jagged the shards of one's life may be, one can still arrange them in a pretty pattern. Perhaps this is the purpose of art.

I wrote about the timeline his laptop showed – how he'd ordered the suicide manual weeks before he died, then the equipment he needed, in bits, then written his last email to Kate apologising for the depression that had wrecked their relationship, then the final emails to Mark and Em, and Avice, and his counsellor. For me, I wrote, tracing this sequence was:

> 'like watching him slowly falling away from me, as if he were behind glass and me powerless to help him. I do not believe that he completely wanted to die. Why would he have had the counselling? I wanted to smash through the glass to this past Andrew, to take him in my arms and comfort him, to tell him how much I loved and respected him, how brave I knew he had been, say all the things that might have helped if I had said them at the time.'

I sent the article off to Homa Khaleeli who edited the First Person section of the *Guardian* and waited. A few days later she rang me saying she wanted to use it. She asked if I wanted to refer readers to further sources of information and we fixed on Headway's helpline and website. She said she would pay me £500. I instantly decided that I would give that to Headway.

To say I was euphoric would be too simple, but I had an air-punching 'yesssss!' sort of feeling. At last I was getting the warning out there, making a difference.

15 - HEADWAY

The article didn't appear until February 2009 and when it did I was on tenterhooks all day, waiting for something momentous to happen. My friends and family kept a watch on how it was doing in the 'most read' *Guardian* list, and it crept up to number two, but I knew that was because the headline – My Son's Secret Destroyed Him – was good, thanks I imagine to the editor, Homa.

Of course nothing momentous did happen, except that Peter McCabe, the CEO of Headway, told me the article 'had moved him to tears'. The one useful thing to come out of the experience was that it alerted me that Headway had put nothing on their website about PTHP in the four months since I had first contacted them – I was directing *Guardian* readers to a dead end. I rang Luke and said, 'I'm sending all these people your way, but you haven't put anything there for them!'

I decided I needed to speak to Peter face to face. On the advice of my scientist brother-in-law who understands the world of medical lobbying and charities, I went with the scrapbook of pictures and mementoes of Chris that his work colleagues had given me, and made no aggressive demands (I am mortally shy, and the very idea of my making aggressive demands would have made anyone laugh.) Peter gave me an hour of his time, which I kept thanking him for, but he at no point committed Headway to any action on my behalf. He suggested approaching my MP, which I had already done without result. He theorised about flagging up head injury on patients' notes so that

PTHP symptoms might sound alarm bells, but he did not say how this could be done. He seemed to think that amending the hospital discharge advice to warn patients and families wouldn't do any good, particularly if the effects showed years later, 'because parents would just put it away in a drawer and forget.' Could he really have believed this? I said I wouldn't have forgotten. His reply was to the effect, 'Ah, but you're middle class,' as if middle-class people didn't count. He did not seem to look at the pictures of Chris properly, even, I felt, avoided them. When I gave him a cheque for £500, my payment for the *Guardian* article, he didn't look pleased, but waved it away almost as if it disgusted him. He told me to sign a 'tax paid' form and go through their donations department. Bizarrely, he ended the interview by telling me how much Headway were doing to encourage people to wear cycle helmets. It was not until after a discovery I made more than a year later that I could guess what was going through his mind. I believe he was very uncomfortable that day.

I went home low after this exceedingly unsatisfactory interview, but was cheered up soon afterwards by an email from Isabel Sargent at the BBC, saying that they wanted me to speak on *Woman's Hour*. Hurray!

16 - A MEETING WITH AN ENDOCRINOLOGIST

I had to live through more than a month before the broadcast, which was scheduled for March 26th, with my nerves jangling. During that time I had an interesting interview with an endocrinologist, triggered, oddly enough, by my mother-in-law Celia.

In the months after Chris's death everything had gone wrong for her. A woman broke into her house at night and appeared suddenly in her bedroom demanding money. Celia said, 'You wicked woman!' and brandished her walking stick at her. They wrestled and then Celia, eighty-plus and infirm, made it across the room to the window and bawled, 'Help!' into the street with all the force of her choir-developed lungs, which was enough to put the wicked woman to flight. This gave Celia a dramatic story to tell for weeks afterwards and we were very proud of her, but it must have taken its toll. A little while later she had an accident in her car, shunted by a truck on a busy main road, and only a few weeks after that she had a stroke.

The stroke didn't seem at first to have affected her, but soon she began to complain of depression, which seemed unlike her, and to obsess about possible ways in which John might have breached minor requirements of the Catholic faith. We tried to be patient, and thought that losing a grandson who was dear to her (he was very fond of her and used to help in her garden when he came south), being robbed, having an accident and then a stroke

– all within the space of less than a year – would be enough to make anyone depressed. Also her diabetes had worsened and she now needed injections rather than pills. However, quite soon during my late-evening, blue light computer sessions I found that depression happened after a third of strokes and could be caused by biological mechanisms affecting neural circuits involved with mood regulation. I thought, 'Why didn't somebody tell us?' It would have made all the difference between my suppressed irritation and real sympathy.

I wrote a letter to *Therapy Today* telling Chris's story and Celia's, complaining about how patients and families weren't warned about physical causes for depression. Then, googling further, I found that strokes could cause hypopituitarism. This made me sit up. Suppose it was hypopituitarism that was causing her depression? Suppose she could get hormone treatment and feel better? How ironic if the death of one fit young man could improve the life of his old Wabby (as he called her).

And then I remembered Dr Stephanie Baldeweg, who had come up in my searches as an endocrinologist who knew about post-traumatic hypopituitarism and who was based at The London Clinic. Perhaps I could take Celia there, and pick Dr Baldeweg's brains at the same time? I made an appointment and dragged poor Celia from Purley to Marylebone High Street. I took her by car, a nightmare journey taking about two hours through terrible traffic, and she bravely hobbled into the clinic.

Dr Baldeweg's view was that her diabetes wasn't being well managed and that we should look at 'the nose on your face' before searching elsewhere, and she fixed for us to see the diabetes nurse. I expect she was right. Beforehand I'd asked if we could spend part of the consultation discussing Chris. When we had finished with

Celia, Dr Baldeweg looked at me and said, 'Well?'

I told her the story, and she stared at me and said, 'If he had his accident at the age of seven, and then went through adolescence normally, as you say, then his pituitary was obviously working after the injury, so it couldn't have been damaged. Also, the only pituitary deficiency that can cause depression – or depression-like symptoms – is growth hormone deficiency and you're telling me he grew normally.'

I felt extraordinarily shocked, as if the ground had been cut from under my feet, and could only stammer, 'But the research exists, and even if Chris wasn't affected, a lot of people are.' She nodded. She agreed in principle to sign a letter to NICE asking them to update their guidelines, so that was one good thing. We left her surgery, went to see the diabetes nurse, and made our way back to the car.

My lowest point was when I found a parking ticket there demanding £80. I'd thought Celia's handicapped badge protected us, but when I looked at the small print I found it didn't.

All the way home I thought about what Dr Baldeweg had said. Although I hadn't been able to challenge her at the time, I knew there was research showing that you could go through a 'normal' adolescence after an injury and still have hypopituitarism.

It took me nearly a week to gather my ammunition before I wrote to her in March. The full letter is on my headinjuryhypo website with all its footnotes, but the gist was that I needed to get my facts right for the press (I superstitiously didn't tell her about *Woman's Hour*), and it would be very kind if she would look at the references I'd found, and tell me if they were reliable. I then quoted a paper saying, 'Diminished pituitary hormone secretion

[…] may occur *at any time* after traumatic brain injury.' I pointed her to three other papers that said the same thing.

So didn't that mean that Chris's pituitary could have worked fine through his adolescence and then packed up after that? And similarly, even though he grew normally, couldn't he have suffered growth hormone deficiency, with the depression that went with it, after he'd reached full height? Could I then legitimately write, 'It is possible that our son suffered delayed pituitary dysfunction after his brain injury' and that 'head injury survivors who are depressed should press for a referral to an endocrinologist'?

To her credit, Dr Baldeweg wrote back promptly, in effect retracting what she had told me and agreeing that PTHP could develop late and that Chris's depression could have been a symptom of hypopituitarism. I was relieved, but was left puzzled that, in some areas at least, I seemed to be better informed on PTHP than the supposed experts.

17 - WOMAN'S HOUR

My interview for *Woman's Hour* was recorded on 25 March 2009, six months to the day after Chris's birthday and exactly seven months after his death. I'd arranged, for Kate's sake, to stick with the pseudonym Caroline Churchill.

As I arrived at Oxford Circus and made my way northwards through the crowds to Portland Place, my hair whipped upwards by the spring wind, I felt like something small – a mouse, say – snatched up to the clouds in an eagle's talons while the landscape grew vast below me. However could I have ended up here? Speaking to more than five people at once was an ordeal to me, yet I was about to speak to thousands. But I blocked these dizzying thoughts and held on to the fact that this was my chance, I mustn't blow it. This was my present for Chris, a present too late, which he couldn't receive, but still, I had to give it. Pain and grief are powerful rocket-fuel.

In the lobby, I changed out of my trainers into smarter shoes that hurt, but I didn't have time to flatten my hair down before I was greeted by Isabel Sargent who escorted me through. She had a benign and comfortable look, which stopped me worrying about my hair – she wasn't that smart herself and reminded me of my university tutors forty years before, who always looked as if they valued thoughts more than clothes.

Old Broadcasting House is a round building, with window-lit corridors encircling it on each floor, and lots of little offices of varying degrees of scruffiness opening on the inward side. It would be easy to get lost here, I thought, and in fact I soon did, after Isabel parked me in an office with a polystyrene cup of coffee and I went hunting for the loo. When I eventually found my way back, I sat sipping coffee and obsessively going over the points I had to get in. One: the police coming with the bad news. Two: the letters in Chris's house that told us about his impotence. Three: my phone call to his ex-girlfriend who confirmed it and said she couldn't get him to go to the doctor. Four: my sister being so sure his childhood head injury must have caused it. Five: her discovery of the research about hypopituitarism. Six: How he could have had treatment for it if we'd only known. Seven: how important it was to warn people.

Before I'd had time to repeat it all into gobbledygook, Isabel appeared and took me through to the recording studio – an eerily private-seeming, small, round, sound-deadened room. A circular counter with microphones at regular intervals ran round it. I would have to speak into one of those! But all that mattered in the long run was to speak clearly enough for people to understand, and not miss anything out. I had to focus on that.

Isabel introduced me to Jane Garvey who was doing the interview. Jane reassured me that any mistakes would be edited before the programme was aired – 'if anyone boobs it'll be me' – but despite this I found her intimidatingly crisp and sharp, and began to worry about my hair again – probably with reason, because her first words, said with great heartiness, were, 'Well, Caroline, *you* don't look like someone who would deliberately put themselves in the spotlight … so tell me, what's brought you here today?'

I felt this was a little unkind (in fact another opening was substituted before the broadcast), but was too hell-bent on getting my seven points out to take much notice. Jane Garvey didn't have to say much, I just went on and on, until it was time for Dr Kearney to speak. I had chosen her myself after learning about her PTHP research. She took part in the interview via telephone, and in a crystal-clear voice she corroborated everything. Yes, hypopituitarism was often missed after brain injury, yes, 'the link was often missed' if people's symptoms appeared late. She agreed that Chris's stress during A-levels and Finals could have been a sign of low cortisol or thyroid hormone. Diagnosis was relatively simple, she said, hormone treatment was effective and the person could have a 'normal fulfilling life with a normal life expectancy.' If only Chris could have had that.

When I mentioned the NICE guidance she said, 'We're working towards getting the revised version to include endocrine complications.' I pricked up my ears at that 'we'. So she was part of the NICE team?

Afterwards Isabel and Jane gathered round me and said I'd done well. 'If I could only know,' I said, 'that just *one* person had been diagnosed after what I've said, it would make it worth it.' But they were quick to say that this might never happen. Isabel told me that Dr Kearney had said she was willing to meet with me and that she would forward contact details.

I hung around a bit longer, senselessly, just wanting companionship after this huge putsch that had left my knees trembling, but it gradually dawned on me that I had to go, so I did, back to my friends Connie and Moira who were waiting for me. They'd sent me off to London three hours earlier giving me the usual wise advice about staying calm and imagining the people I was talking to were naked, and it had helped.

Afterwards, Isabel kept her promise and sent me Dr

Kearney's details. She also sent me some of the listeners' comments that had come in. These had been carefully topped and tailed to anonymise them, and she had written, 'I must stress that these are for you alone and must not be forwarded, quoted or published in any way.' I will just mention that one mother wrote that she stood in her kitchen in amazement, recognising her daughter's symptoms and feeling that at last there was a glimmer of light. This thrilled me. At last I was finding some real people with this illness, rather than abstractions from my reading. Maybe her daughter would get treatment and feel better – but I would never know.

A few days later Isabel forwarded another anonymised email which made a deep impression on me. After a head injury at the age of seven the sender had suffered from problems similar to Chris's which had only been picked up by doctors twenty-eight years after the accident. He or she thanked God every day for referral to Dr Kearney who was doing everything possible to help, and said how tough it had been, and 'lonley', not being understood.

I was desperate to answer this email and pleaded for the address. However, Isabel said it had been destroyed. The only thing she could remember was that she thought the sender was a girl. I was surprised. Somehow, because the sender had used the word 'guy' about Chris, and had identified with him, I had imagined someone male.

A friend who works for the BBC said it was nonsense that the email would have been destroyed because there was a rule that all correspondence had to be kept for some years, but I don't know if that's true. All I know was that my heart reached out to this person who had been 'lonley' and 'in a place he/she was finding it hard to get out of'. This was how Chris must have felt, and he chose the only way of getting out of it that he could.

18 - MEETING DR KEARNEY

So there I was a month later at Manchester Piccadilly, frowning at a street map. The pub where I'd arranged to meet Dr Kearney wasn't far away. I often have dreams that I am lost somewhere, urgently have to get to Yorkshire to visit my mother, or be observed teaching a lesson. I plunge on and on through the maze, fruitlessly – this reality was exactly like that.

When I arrived I was as on edge as an exam candidate, and I recognised a similar uptightness in Dr Kearney. She had long, blonde hair and one of those fair delicate skins which I associate with people who are super-conscientious and hardworking. Her greeting was abrupt.

It was noisy and hard to hear each other and I took out a notepad, explaining that I didn't trust my memory and I wanted to remember everything she said. One of the first things she told me was that her research was showing that PTHP was quite rare – they were only finding it in six or seven per cent of head injury patients. I opened my eyes and said, 'But surely, the research … there's a paper by Lucy Behan…?' I couldn't remember the names of any of the other researchers, I was as wordless as I'd been with Dr Baldeweg. Dr Kearney said the higher figures published were because of biased series, and that there was a tendency for the pituitary to 'shut down' temporarily during trauma, which made the figures come out falsely high because once the trauma was over the hormones went back to normal. She gave the example of anorexic girls becoming so thin their periods stopped, but once they put on weight they started again. She talked about new, unpublished research that showed the numbers were lower.

I felt somehow that our meeting was going in a direction I hadn't anticipated. I hadn't thought that Dr Kearney would spend her time trying to persuade me that the problem was small, I'd thought we would be discussing what we (or I) could do to solve it. Also, I was really surprised to hear her quoting such a low percentage. I wanted more evidence, more explanation.

She listed the tests that were needed to diagnose hypopituitarism, which was helpful. When I asked about my *Woman's Hour* listener, the patient of hers who I so wanted to contact, she gave me her secretary's email and suggested I write to her. She mentioned her head injury nurse who used to go round the wards putting up posters warning people – 'this was the spirit', I thought.

What I most remember about her is how, when our food came, she stared into the distance and said, 'But it *is* a serious condition, isn't it? It can cost a person their marriage.' Even at the time I thought it was strange she should say this to me, when I believed it had made Chris kill himself. Surely she didn't think I needed convincing? Later, thinking about it, I wondered if she was mentally addressing NICE.

After our meeting I wrote to her repeatedly, asking her to send me details about the new research she'd mentioned. She sent me some slides from a talk she'd given, but nothing there suggested the problem was minor. Her secretary gave me no joy finding the anonymised patient.

Later, when my email campaign prompted the chief executive of a Yorkshire hospital to ask for Dr Kearney's protocol at Salford Royal, I wrote more urgently. Still no reply, but I knew she must be very busy. Finally, when it seemed as if she must have forgotten, I wrote, 'Dear Dr Kearney, I know that you care about the patients who will not get diagnosed unless you send Salford's protocol...' and at last she replied to Dr Greep, copying me in. She attached the protocol adding the caveat that in her own experience, and that of her colleagues, the true incidence of pituitary damage after head injury was far less than had been quoted in earlier studies 'where there was an obvious selection bias' and that most people believed only around 7-10% were affected – 'clearly still clinically significant but not the 20% previously quoted.' She said the studies showing the new figures had not yet been published.

On that unsatisfactory note my dealings with Dr Kearney ceased for a little while.

19 - THE PEOPLE OUT THERE

I heard the thin gnat-voices cry,
Star to faint star, across the sky.

'The Jolly Company', 1908

Oh! often among men below,
Heart cries out to heart, I know,
And one is dust a many years,
Child, before the other hears.

'Fafaïa', 1913

These lines come from two poems by the war poet Rupert
Brooke. They note how light from extinct stars goes on
travelling through space for millennia, and lament –
though not explicitly – how Ka Cox only started fancying
him after he'd stopped fancying her. The gnat-voices
bring back the feeling I have described before, of reaching
and reaching for someone like Chris, sending faint cries
across space, yearning to find the people who needed to
hear me. In fact, I still feel like this, hoping I'm not dust
before I'm heard. Or perhaps I am more like someone
circling in a helicopter over dark seas, knowing there are
shipwrecked people there, but unable to see them, unable
to find them in time.

That woman in the kitchen who heard my *Woman's
Hour* broadcast, suddenly understanding what might
be wrong with her daughter, the young man (I think it
was a young man) talking about identifying with Chris
and being in a place which was hard to get out of – these

had been faint beeps answering my signals, but I wanted more. I wanted dialogue.

I was baffled by the silence. Surely, if the numbers quoted in the research were right, these people must be everywhere. Where were they hiding? I was like a scientist, theoretically convinced that something must be so, but dying for tangible proof.

I thought I had found my proof in May 2009. I'd written an article for *Mental Health Today*, and got an email from a youngish man whom I shall call Jake saying he'd been moved to tears (echoes of Peter McCabe's tears – but I preferred Jake's). Jake had had a brain injury and suffered from depression, and felt his sexual performance was no longer what it was. Rapturously I drove over a hundred miles to his home. Not a recipe for a successful friendship, you would think, and yet somehow it is still going strong seven years later. Jake has made two more suicide attempts in the time I have known him, but it has been proved, after exhaustive testing, that his pituitary was not damaged by his injury. Knowing him is a good antidote to my tendency to think that all depression after brain injury must be PTHP. His story is not relevant to this book, except that he exemplifies the kindness and decency that I have almost always found in the people that life has been particularly unkind to. His marriage broke up soon after his accident and he has struggled for many years with the problems that follow brain injury – chronic fatigue, lack of motivation, and the inability to plan. Yet with all this to contend with, he spent a lot of his limited energy on helping an alcoholic friend to find accommodation, and he has been a good friend to me. He also has a penchant for terrible puns and has made me laugh more than anyone else I know. I'm glad to say that he has remarried now and his depression has lifted. Long may he remain happy.

But I was still no nearer to finding the people in the dark sea. When I set up my website it seemed essential to include personal stories, and I scoured the internet for them. I found one on the Stop the Thyroid Madness website about a man called Phil who, I guessed from his vocabulary, was American.

It came with the following introduction: 'Phil's story is enough to make you weep – years of being sick, not looking sick, being harassed by family, friends, and co-workers, losing his job, multiple doctors and multiple wrong diagnoses [...] until he finally finds the right treatment and lives again. A must read...'

It is truly a 'must read'. For me it was a confirmation of everything I theoretically knew. I will give his story in full, because it was key to my understanding of what hypopituitarism means.

The trouble began when Phil was forty, and had just bought a new house and received a big promotion. Fatigue struck, but he hid it and pushed himself to act normally for four months, until he collapsed. He'd recently recovered from a bad car accident. His GP put him on sick leave, and soon afterwards a specialist diagnosed him with Ménière's Disease – 'an unknown problem in the inner ear' which was causing him balance problems.

A bout of pneumonia and left side numbness prompted steroid treatment, which gave him six months' respite ... until the fatigue came back, and once more he couldn't do his engineering job at Chrysler.

The next doctor specialised in Chronic Fatigue Syndrome (CFS) and told Phil he had major depression. Phil had to go along with this to keep his job and sick pay. A psychiatrist prescribed counselling and anti-depressants.

This 'crap', to quote Phil, went on for five years. He walked around in a drugged up fog, on a cocktail of anti-depressants. The psychiatrist told his work colleagues that he liked being depressed and didn't want to get better. 'After this my wife turned into some kind of monster, telling me I would be better off dead, there was nothing wrong with me, and just go to work. And I could see this was it for us.' She left, taking the kids.

They had to put up their new house for sale, and the divorce was a week from being finalised when he was put on Prozac, with side-effects so bad he wanted to die. The Prozac also gave him a bladder infection, but indirectly this was a blessing because at last, in a urologist, he found someone who looked at his condition with fresh eyes. The urologist thought his problem could be low testosterone, not depression at all. It took him 30 days in rehab to wean him off all the anti-depressants, and after testosterone treatment he returned to work.

His wife returned, but in Phil's own sad words, 'We are still together today, but it's not the same between us.'

He was still not right, health-wise, and had to take frequent sick leave. His colleagues, family, and friends could not grasp that he could look OK and yet not be OK. His sick pay was stopped.

A big fight against this discrimination brought him early retirement at 55 with a huge settlement, but his life was no better. He was sitting at home, jobless, and still ill.

Then, after some internet browsing, he changed his testosterone treatment from gel to human chorionic gonadotropin and discovered that his low testosterone was not caused by his testes themselves, but by the failure of his pituitary to stimulate them. In other words, his doctor now realised that his car accident all those years before must have damaged his pituitary. This was why he'd had borderline low cortisol, thyroid, IGF-1, DHEA, and testosterone for 23 years – and nobody had spotted it.

'Now I am damn mad about all those years and all those Doctors and Endos [endocrinologists] that missed this. My life would have been a lot better if they had done their job right.'

Even then his troubles continued. His doctor wouldn't treat his low cortisol or thyroid, saying they were adequate. It was only when a debilitating bronchial infection drove him to self-treat with thyroid and hydrocortisone preparations that his visible improvement convinced his doctor to prescribe.

Even then he was not completely better. Thanks to his own research he found two other adrenal hormones were low and at last he was put on medication that cured his sweating, fatigue, frequent urination, and intolerance of heat. He now goes to the gym and isn't wiped out for the rest of the day.

As I read Phil's story now, I see it had classic elements that were to become familiar to me as time went on: the ignorance of the medical profession despite all the clinical signs being there; the lack of sympathy; the Chronic Fatigue Syndrome label, with its implication that Phil was somehow being ill on purpose because he liked it or wanted attention; the damage to his relationship; the serendipitous meeting with a medic with an open mind; and most of all, Phil's own tireless research into his condition that made him see solutions, self-treat when he had to, and marshal arguments for dealing with medics.

I can see in Phil what I was to find later in other people in his situation. Not just the bloody-minded determination to find a solution, but the generosity to share the story to help others.

Bev Maiden, a former volunteer with the Pituitary

Foundation, was generous too, sharing her own story of a fall from a horse that affected her pituitary, disrupting her sexual development, her weight, her appearance, causing her untold misery. I posted her story, though pointing out that there was no actual research to link her pituitary tumour with the fall. She passed on to me another story that fitted the parameters of PTHP more closely.

Hayley, 17, had been a champion ice skater from childhood. About three years ago, Bev told me, Hayley had had a very bad fall on the ice. She'd suffered a severe concussion and had to stay home from school for almost six months. Her neurologist advised her to stay in a dark room and not exert herself. Soon after, her menstruation stopped and she gained a significant amount of weight.

Further investigation revealed that she had caused damage to her pituitary gland and she was put on steroids that made her gain even more weight. After the steroids, she was given other medication to help start her periods again and eventually they returned. From the time of her injury until just recently, Hayley had been depressed and angry. Her mother told Bev that it was very sad to see her daughter not enjoying her teen years like her friends, and especially not having any boyfriends.

When Hayley had first suffered the concussion, a friend of Bev's had taken her to two different neurologists in Toronto who did nothing about her symptoms. Eventually, a neurosurgeon in Montreal figured out that Hayley's problems were caused by damage to her pituitary from her fall on the ice. By the time I heard her story, Hayley was finishing her last year of high school in Switzerland and also had a boyfriend.

These stories were like tiny scraps, doing little to feed my hunger. It would be more than a year before my gnawing emptiness found solid food.

CATHERINE HUGHES' STORY

Hi, let me introduce myself. My name is Katie Hughes and I am one of those thin gnat-voices that Joanna longed to hear as she began her campaign. Even though she and I did not encounter each other for another three years, she does not see why the reader should have to wait that long, and she has asked me to write my story for her at this stage to explain, in a way that she cannot, what it's like to have hypopituitarism. So here goes.

The very worst thing was the not knowing.

There were things that I *did* know: that I wasn't well; that I was experiencing fluctuating, seemingly unconnected symptoms; that I was unable to persuade any doctor, bar my GP, to listen to me; that I wasn't believed by those who did at least hear me out.

But I had no idea why I was so unwell so much of the time, and that in itself was as frightening as the variety of symptoms I experienced: dizziness, fainting and palpitations; poor recovery from surgery; weight gain; exhaustion; profound depression and overwhelming anxiety; hair loss (and, ironically, hair growth where no woman wants to see it); skin discolouration; apathy; nausea; agitation; a lack of emotional control; social withdrawal and isolation – all of these things and more were less frightening than the simple fact that nobody could give me a reason for my suffering. No one understood.

Just prior to my diagnosis, I was living such a secluded life – trapped in an abusive relationship – that I rarely left my house. I had almost, but not quite, given up hope of ever comprehending what was wrong with me, or of being given the simple credence I so desperately needed.

Statistically speaking, it is likely that my pituitary malfunction is the result of a small, benign brain tumour – a microadenoma – but this has not been proven, as the one MRI scan of my brain was not targeted. Other possible origins for my condition are a simple congenital defect, a previous head trauma, haemorrhage during childbirth, or some other, idiopathic, cause. I will probably never know, but it seems likely that a congenital defect would have manifested sooner, whereas I was already symptomatic when I did indeed haemorrhage during the birth of my second child. The only head trauma I have ever suffered occurred at the age of three and, although I still bear the scar in the centre of my forehead, I don't believe the accident was severe enough to have caused brain damage.

I suppose it doesn't really matter, but I like to think of the cause as a tumour – an actual, physical entity that I can blame for the awful things that I have to endure.

From the vantage point of knowing and understanding what is wrong with me, I can look back and realise that I first showed signs of being unwell in my late teens and early twenties, my college and university years. I would come home from my classes every day and go straight to bed, despite having had a proper night's sleep the night before, sleeping for two hours between 4 and 6 p.m. before getting up, feeling somewhat discombobulated, and studying or socialising for the rest of my evening. I wasn't the most gregarious of students, instinctively avoiding the usual high levels of alcohol consumption, nor did I do particularly well in my degree studies notwithstanding the evident potential that had earned me a place on a prestigious course in the first place.

I countered my constant malaise and exhaustion with another instinctive measure – exercise. I rode my bike everywhere, swam almost daily, went roller skating and horse riding, and attended aerobics and trampoline classes. My weight fluctuated but never reached a point at which it became impossible to buy high street clothes. I reached a size 16-18, although in today's sizes I would probably have been more like a 14-16, and, much as I would have liked to have been slimmer, I had less trouble in accepting myself then than I do now.

Thus, I was twenty-six and pregnant with my second child before I began to suspect that something might be significantly wrong with me. Multiple thyroid function tests had previously returned apparently (just about) normal results but, when I became pregnant again, having had a completely normal first pregnancy, I found myself unbelievably, incredibly sick. Unable to properly articulate the severity of the nausea and exhaustion I was experiencing, I allowed my doctors to write my symptoms off as a difficult pregnancy, but I have never forgotten those harrowing nine months.

Life went on – another difficult pregnancy ended in a beautiful home birth – until my third child was a few months old and I began to feel agitated and nauseous. Initially, my weight plummeted, then my body expanded with horrifying speed, all my weight piling on to my belly to the extent that my GP ordered pregnancy test after pregnancy test. Desperate, I begged for every test that might explain what was happening and, for the first time, my thyroid function tests came back as abnormal and I thought that I finally had an answer. Relieved, I took my thyroxine tablets and waited for them to take effect.

They never did. I briefly regained control of my weight after taking up running, but I wasn't ever well again. My weight ballooned once more, before my fourth pregnancy caused such extreme agitation, sickness and exhaustion that I was placed under the care of a psychiatrist in the hope that he would be able to ameliorate my distress. Powerful anti-psychotic drugs – almost certainly contraindicated in pregnancy – did nothing to suppress the daily horror of my existence during that time, but the idea that I might be physically ill, in some way that was exacerbated by pregnancy, was dismissed. I found myself begging for a Caesarean section at 28 weeks pregnant, longing for the misery to end. It was refused. My last child was, miraculously, born healthy at 41 weeks thanks to the support of my family, midwife and a community psychiatric nurse. I now know that many hypopituitary mothers lose their babies long before that late stage.

My memory of my son's early years is dim and incomplete, thanks to the anti-depressants which were deemed necessary for my continued existence. With a supportive GP on my side I attended clinic after clinic across four different hospitals, each time being told that I was mentally not physically ill. One doctor told me that people in Belsen hadn't got fat and that if I wanted to lose weight and be less exhausted, I should stop eating. When reminded that I was fully breastfeeding a six-month-old baby and therefore unable to resort to starving myself, he shrugged and remarked that that was my problem and not his. Another doctor at a different hospital used my appointment there to sell the bariatric surgery that he undertook in his private clinic. Yet another insulted me and spoke over my head to my then-husband, suggesting I be 'suitably medicated' so that I would 'stop making such a fuss'.

I researched my symptoms avidly, spending hours on

the net, and initially suspected that I might have Cushing's disease, another form of pituitary dysfunction.

The next doctor I saw suspected the same thing, and noted that the endocrinologist who had seen me during my last pregnancy, when my levels of the active thyroid hormone T3 dropped to almost zero, had suspected the same thing and had begun testing me accordingly. He had retired, however, leaving me in the hands of the consultant who clearly believed that fat people belonged in concentration camps. Similarly, this latest understanding doctor went on maternity leave, and the registrar who saw me in her absence was all too quick to condemn me as greedy and lazy and very, very stupid. When I told him that I had once been a runner, he laughed.

Somehow – and to this day I don't really know quite how – I continued to fight. I weaned myself off the anti-depressants, knowing in my heart that they were simply numbing me to the wretchedness that had become the overriding characteristic of my life, and I complained about the shabby, shoddy manner in which I had been treated.

The breakthrough, when it came, seemed almost inconsequential and yet I very clearly remember walking down the hill from my GP's surgery to my house, clutching a small piece of paper with my latest thyroid function test results written on it. All three of my thyroid hormones were low – an anomaly since one (TSH) should rise if the other two (T3 and T4) are low. I remember wondering how that might be possible. I remember the search term I used to try and find out. I remember seeing the word 'hypopituitarism' in the results. And I remember reading and reading, tears pouring down my face unhindered, with one thought and one thought only running through my brain: *'I know what's wrong with me.'*

It all changed from there, although my battle, which ultimately involved two MPs, my GP and practice nurse, a psychiatrist and a huge amount of correspondence, did not end as quickly as I would have hoped. After yet another failed plea to yet another NHS consultant, I sought the opinion of a private expert, whose services were paid for by my father. He agreed with me that pituitary dysfunction had to be ruled out.

My care transferred to a different hospital, I then endured a variety of dynamic blood tests during which substances were introduced via IV cannula to challenge my brain to respond. It didn't, but the tests themselves made me unwell and distressed.

When told of my results, I sobbed incoherently for the best part of three-quarters of an hour in my latest consultant's office. 'It's all right,' he soothed. 'We can deal with this.' What he didn't understand was that I was crying from sheer relief, not from fear or distress. I was *glad* to know that I had hypopituitarism. I wasn't crazy after all, nor a liar, nor a hypochondriac. I had been right all along.

Confirmation of my results was then sought by means of an insulin tolerance test, during which my blood sugar was lowered to dangerously low levels to see if my pituitary would respond. It tried, but the test was compromised by the fact that my known resistance to insulin was not factored into the analysis of the result. Referred to yet another hospital, I was told that my results overall were inconclusive and I once again had to plead for the chance to undergo a third type of test. At first, this last chance at diagnosis was also denied me until, in frustration, desperation and despair, I lifted the leg of my trousers and showed the consultant my leg muscle tone.

'I was a runner,' I sobbed. 'I'm not lazy, or greedy, or stupid. I'm not delusional. If I'm depressed, it's because I'm ill; I'm not ill because I'm depressed. You are my last hope. Please don't ignore me.'

I didn't know, then, that this consultant was also a runner. My plea was heard. The next time that he saw me, my weight had dropped dramatically and I was clearly very unwell, to the point that he sought to admit me to hospital (only no bed could be found for me). I later went on to have that final dynamic test and to be formally diagnosed with Adult Growth Hormone Deficiency, an element of hypopituitarism.

It is likely that I am also ACTH-deficient – which means my adrenal glands are not stimulated to produce sufficient cortisol – but not yet to the point where I need exogenous steroid replacement. I'm fairly sure that time will come, but who knows? Obviously, my thyroid deficiency is now known to be secondary to my pituitary disease, rather than a primary illness, and all my weird and wonderful symptoms can now be united under a common cause – my malfunctioning pituitary gland; my broken brain.

I'm a runner again. It's hard, but it helps me to stay well, probably because it stimulates my brain to produce what ACTH it can. My quality of life is not wonderful but, with replacement T3 and T4, HRT, a supplement regimen that I designed for myself after extensive reading and, of course, the growth hormone that I inject each night, it is a great deal better than it used to be. Steady doses of replacement hormones can never properly replicate the responsive, reactive hormone-release of a healthy pituitary, but it's certainly better than going without. I cannot remember how it feels to be normal and

healthy, and there are yet days when I feel I cannot carry
on.

There are also days when I am amazingly proud that I
do.

20 - ANOTHER ENDOCRINOLOGIST

A couple of weeks after the *Woman's Hour* broadcast I got a letter which seems odder to me now than it did then. I had earlier, as part of a 'gender dysphoria' mailshot, written to a Dr Belchetz at Leeds General Infirmary but had no answer. Now a Dr Robert Murray wrote saying my letter had been passed on to him as Dr Belchetz had retired from the NHS two years before (Six years on I see that Dr Belchetz still works at Leeds General, so his retirement was short-lived.) Dr Murray wrote me a genial two pages, which began by claiming that growth hormone was the commonest hormone affected after brain injury, but on the whole, hormone deficiencies were rare. He claimed that research indicated that 10 per cent of survivors were affected, but said it had used biased populations and inadequate tests and thought the real figure was 'a lot lower [...] One study performed in Oxford has failed to find any evidence of hypopituitarism in survivors of TBI and I do wonder if this is nearer the truth.'

He went on to say that the research suggested far fewer children were affected than adults. The fact that growth hormone was the most likely deficiency, and most children grew after brain injury, suggested that childhood injury rarely caused it.

He agreed that the PTHP risk hadn't been aired enough, but blamed it on the 'roughly one in four' claim, which 'we truly do not see' and which he felt was counter-productive. 'Until we are more realistic about the true incidence [...] I do not think this finding will be believed or acted upon.'

He didn't think there was a link between gender dysphoria and hypopituitarism.

He hoped to set up a study to examine the incidence of PTHP in the survivors that went through the unit, his team just needed time and extra funding. Once they had the data and assuming they found more than five per cent PTHP cases, they would hope to start screening.

At the time, it didn't occur to me to wonder why he should have written at such length in reply to a letter not addressed to him, replying to a question that my letter hadn't asked. Now I do wonder about the mixed messages. Why talk of screening for something that according to him hardly existed? Why blame the ignorance about PTHP on what were, in his view, alarmist claims about how common it was? Nobody was aware of these alarmist claims, nobody seemed aware of *any* claims, alarmist or otherwise. But I was naive. With my head bursting with studies that quoted figures of 20-30 per cent, all I thought was, 'Ten per cent? Where on earth did he get that from?'

I sent him a revamp of my Stephanie Baldeweg letter, expressing gratitude, diffidence about my medical ignorance, fears that I might spread disinformation in the media, saying I would like to set before him what my reading had led me to believe, hoping that he might find time to 'shoot me down' or at least tell me which studies I could trust and which not.

I sent him the research showing that 25 per cent of brain injuries caused PTHP, and that children were at risk. I quoted an expert who said that unlike other problems in paediatrics, studies suggested that the younger a child was when severe brain injury occurred, the worse the prognosis might be in the long run, and added 'which challenges your own view.'

I questioned him about his own claim about the 10 per cent figure, and indicated that I would also be interested in reading the Oxford study he mentioned.

Then I waited for him to shoot me down – *could* there be something wrong with all those papers that said one in four? – or, at the very least, send me a reference to the Oxford paper he mentioned, but I never heard a peep out of him.

My follow-up letter was ignored. I was disappointed. I'd thought that here at last was someone who would talk to me, and now he wouldn't. I could only think that he couldn't challenge my arguments. But how could that be? How could an endocrinologist who had gone through years of medical training, who professed a special interest in hypopituitarism, not answer a novice like me who had spent a few months googling?

As a child I believed that everyone who wore glasses was kind. Later, it took a long time to dislodge my view that all clergymen must be very good people. And at 60 I still thought that doctors were by definition humane and moral. Between then and now I have encountered many doctors who are, and I love them for it, and in fact it is doctors who have helped most of all. But I no longer see life so simplistically.

21 - THE PITUITARY FOUNDATION

I didn't research the Pituitary Foundation properly before I first approached them a month after Chris died, and I didn't learn until later about their honourable history of lobbying on behalf of pituitary patients when the government wanted to stop free prescriptions of human growth hormone to adult patients in 2002. It was thanks to their hard work that an appeal against the decision was at least partly successful.

But when Kit Ashley, an ebullient, blonde American, became CEO in 2005 the climate changed. Maybe the charity's staff had been exhausted by that campaign and left wary of becoming involved in another. Kit was full of praise for my *Guardian* article, ready to 'share information' with Headway, happy to put my story in their newsletter, but came up short on doing anything that would make a real difference. The only concrete outcome of my letters was that some information appeared on their website. This posting in itself gave me pause for thought.

It said that there was no clear agreement among academics on how frequently pituitary damage happened after brain injury: 'It is observed, it is more common in severe traumatic brain injury.'

My unspoken reaction to that was, What? No consensus? What about the international *consensus* statement of 2005 that talks of 'significant risk' and recommends screening all moderate to severe TBI patients? Why the implication that people with milder brain injuries were relatively safe, when the 2005 statement said, 'the severity of the symptoms is not necessarily related to the severity of the injury'? One of the most sinister aspects of PTHP is that concussion – an occurrence so common you'd be hard put to find a circle of friends without someone who'd suffered one – can cause it too.

The website item ended with the words: 'As traumatic brain injury is common, but pituitary dysfunction following this is a rare but serious consequence, we would advise that you contact your GP if you have any concerns and experience some of the following symptoms' (which they did list correctly). 'For information and support for Traumatic Brian Injury visit.'

I liked Traumatic Brian Injury. It had a Monty Python ring.

At that stage I did not want to cause offence. I was thankful to see anything on the website. In a way I wasn't too troubled by the heavy emphasis that PTHP was rare – I thought a sufferer would recognise the symptoms and go to his/her GP anyway. But what I really wanted was for Kit not to preach to the converted, in however muffled a way, but to send the message wider to GPs and in particular to sign a letter to NICE asking them to amend their head injury guidelines. It was this second wish that transformed the initial sweetness and light of our exchanges into sourness and dark.

I asked her, inauspiciously on Friday 13 March 2009, if the Pituitary Foundation would join me in writing to NICE. Kit replied, in effect, that they wouldn't do that unless Headway signed too, but couched the statement in such indirect language that I did not pick up the message or contact Luke. Two weeks later, having not heard back from me, she wrote refusing, saying they were too small a charity to commit to that kind of project. She hoped I didn't find this too disappointing.

Disappointing! How was signing a letter an expensive time-consuming 'project'? It would take a minute! NICE clearly needed to change its guideline. Why wouldn't Kit sign?

I fretted for three weeks. I hadn't been expecting a refusal. As I had with Chris's GP and NICE, I'd thought naively that I only had to explain about PTHP and how common and dangerous it was, for everyone to rush to do my bidding. Now I had a resurgence of despair, feeling that they were treating Chris as if he was nothing, that I was failing him, and I would forever twist and turn in my bed at night with bitter words whirling through my head, my stomach churning and my heart pounding, and with those meagre tears, which were all I could squeeze out, doing little to relieve me.

We went away to the Isle of Wight for four days, and I found that particularly hard because I could neither shake off my angry thoughts against the Foundation, nor – being away from my computer – do anything constructive about them. When we came back in mid-April I decided that in spite of my telephone phobia, I must ring Kit, and after a fortnight of screwing up my courage I did, at the end of the month. I caught her at a tense moment when she was very busy dealing with a lawsuit and she said would ring back later – which she did. The conversation was not a success. It ended with her positively shouting me down with, 'You don't need to WASTE EITHER MY TIME OR YOURS in telling me that undiagnosed hypopituitarism is a serious issue!' and cutting our conversation abruptly short.

I wrote to her the same day repeating what I'd said, with evidence, but she didn't answer. Nor did I get an answer to any of my later emails, and when I wrote to Pat

McBride, their patient support manager, with whom I had been exchanging friendly, gossipy emails on many topics including her own medical history, and the possibility of writing her story for the press, she didn't reply either. There was complete silence. I felt very snubbed and hurt. Did I deserve to be sent to Coventry like this, only eight months after my son had died?

After some thought, I decided no, I didn't. It was surely an improper way for a charity to behave. I surfed the net for other dissatisfied customers, and found several. The most articulate was Jon Danzig, whose by-line I vaguely remembered seeing in the quality papers some years ago. I discovered that the threatened lawsuit which had put Kit under such stress was his.

His story, though it shocked me, made me feel better about myself. It wasn't me, it was them.

22 - JON

I learnt that Jon used to work with the broadcaster Roger
Cook as an investigative journalist, but later became ill
with acromegaly, which is caused when the pituitary
produces too much growth hormone. The appalling
symptoms include joint pains, fatigue, sweating,
headaches, eye problems, sexual dysfunction, abnormal
bone growth in the feet, hands, and face, and internal
damage. Sufferers are twice as likely to die early,
particularly from associated heart disease.

Pretty serious then – enough to prevent Jon supporting
himself as a journalist. When a neurosurgeon on the
Pituitary Foundation's committee wrote that 'for the
majority of patients, perhaps over 90%, acromegaly is
relatively symptom-free' Jon was not only personally
outraged, but concerned that statements like this might
affect benefits or private insurance. He went on the
Pituitary Foundation's forum asking people with
acromegaly if their illness was relatively symptom-free
(provoking an overwhelming vote that it wasn't). He also,
more controversially, asked for another vote on whether
the charity's medical committee should give out correct
information and got another 'yes'. Kit banned him from
the forum and told all the Foundation's volunteers
throughout the UK not to communicate with him, because
he gave 'misleading and inaccurate information'. So I
wasn't the first to be excommunicated.

When I came to know Jon, I realised that this was the
most wounding accusation anybody could make, because

he took inordinate care to be honest and accurate. He frequently pressed Kit for examples of his inaccurate information but never had an answer.

His next move was to make a request under the Data Protection Act to see all the data the charity had processed about him. Eventually, after appealing to the Information Commissioner, he was given over 400 disturbing documents, calling him a 'sad guy' and a 'prima donna'. The chairman, Terry Lloyd, had written before the forum debacle, 'I will follow my usual procedure of "sleeping on it" before ripping the guy's throat out, whoops, wrong attitude!'

Yes, wrong attitude indeed. Jon was one of the people the Foundation was set up to aid, and one of the rules for charities is that they do not harm their beneficiaries or, in other words, those whom their organisation was created to help. Jon was not well, but instead of helping him, they attacked him. What he was doing, however inconvenient for the Foundation's medical committee, was fighting the cause of all patients with acromegaly, and it was Kit's role to support him and, if necessary, to do battle with the Committee herself rather than actively opposing him.

By the time I met Jon, his solicitors were in communication with the Foundation's. I visited him at his home in north London. He impressed me: partly because of his striking looks – he's tall with intelligent, light green eyes that gleam at you from under jutting brows; partly because of his voice, which has a calm and relentless insistence, very polite, very hard to interrupt – a good interviewer's voice; and most of all because of a dogged quality about him. He is immune to banter, not overly distracted by other people's feelings (though not in an uncaring way), and his obsession with justice means that despite frequently being wiped out by headaches and fatigue, he never gives up. He has helped me profoundly over the years and I am proud to have him as a friend.

I have a horror of conflict. I used to cry on the school bus if a conductor spoke sharply to me. I never stood up for myself in any way. But Chris's death had made me see that there were times when I had to fight. Jon's story emboldened me to write to Kit on 5 June, after nearly two months of silence, in much stronger terms than I would ever have dreamed of using before. Much stronger than I would ever use face to face either – there were limits to my courage! I sent the email as an attachment to a shorter one to her that said, 'This is a letter I'm considering sending to you, copying in the Trustees.'

In the letter itself I repeated that the charity needed to act, and reminded her that the charity's core aim was to inform the public and the medical profession about pituitary illness. Raising awareness about PTHP was exactly the kind of thing the Foundation was set up to do, that was why it had charitable status, and why people gave it money.

I asked her to write to NICE, to allow Pat McBride to collaborate with me on articles, and to produce a leaflet to circulate to GPs.

This email did at last goad her into replying, with a crisp email saying she was busy, had done what she could, was short-staffed, had little money, and that 'It does not help to have to take the time to explain or defend what we chose to do.' She said their strategy for the next three years was based on the needs and concerns of the majority of their community. She gave a 'no' to approaching NICE, a 'perhaps' to Pat helping me, and an emphatic 'no' to the GP leaflets, which would be 'crippling to our budget.'

She ended with, 'I'm sorry you find this lacking […] I

am simply asking for your understanding of these limitations and further asking for you not to create more. I apologise but I must tell you this will be the last communication I will have on these matters.'

Have a nice day, I thought.

I did not copy in the Trustees as I'd threatened. The conflict with NICE (which I will describe later) and with her was taking it out of me and I was in a constant heart-pounding nervous state, unable to sleep, suffering from night horrors. August was when Chris had died, a golden month when you begin to feel that summer is slipping away, and everything reminded me vividly of how it had been a year ago. I didn't think my heart could break any more than it had, yet somehow it did. John and I went north to Skipton and did a memorial walk with his friends and that gave me some solace.

On 21 September I recovered enough to send a fairly conciliatory email to Kit, still reiterating the urgency of the issue, the need to tackle NICE, asking her to raise the subject again with her Trustees. She didn't answer. Four days later, which was Chris's birthday, when he would have been 33, I wrote again out of a full heart, copying in Peter McCabe's secretary.

Dear Kit

It is now a year since our son died, and during these twelve months at least 10,000 people have been discharged from hospital with a condition that will destroy their confidence and relationships, make their lives miserable and may lead to worse consequences. These people are not just numbers on a page. They could be our cousins and friends, in future even our own selves if we're unlucky … I have been campaigning for a year with limited success, and this is partly due to lack of support from the Pit F, and Headway. *Apart from some information-sharing between you, you have done nothing. I do not believe either of your organisations has been responsible for a single patient being diagnosed who would otherwise have been missed.*

I vowed again to approach the Trustees and the Charity Commissioners if the Foundation did not write to NICE.

Silence. So then Jon and I rolled into action. I approached the Trustees and, as one might expect, I got some venom from the throat-ripping Terry Lloyd about my 'threatening and extremely offensive remarks' and my 'ill-informed judgements concerning operational matters' which questioned 'the integrity of our Board of Directors and our Medical Committee.' He said Pat was, 'not comfortable working with a third party on the *Daily Mail* piece' and asked me to 'Please understand and respect her wishes.'

There was nothing left to do but approach the Charity Commissioners who were later to refuse to investigate the complaint without giving a reason, and without even asking him for evidence. All they did was to impose a 'requirement' (later watered down to a 'recommendation') that the Pituitary Foundation enter into mediation with Jon. The Commissioners' regulator criticized the Commission's handling of Jon's complaint, prompting them eventually to offer him a consolatory payment of £100 which he asked should be given to charity.

To pause here, looking back I feel more kindly towards Kit than I did then. It was true she had shouted at me and blanked me out as if I were a pest, and that was certainly inappropriate behaviour, but it was not a hanging offence, and she was under strain. My demands that she should raise the alarm about PTHP must have felt rather like being told, when you're having a dinner party and you've just divided the food carefully between the guests, that there are 200 other people queueing outside. It's not only the hassle of re-dividing the food, but the reaction of the existing guests you have to worry about. And it was not her fault that the medical committee put together a misleading information sheet that said there was no consensus when there was, and called PTHP rare.

However, against this must be set Jon's discovery from the Foundation's 2008 Report and Accounts (no longer displayed on the Pit F website, but available from Companies House), that the pharma giant Pfizer gave the charity an £18,000 grant towards an 'outreach project' which Kit was obliged to refund that year, unused. I don't know what the project entailed, but if it meant reaching out to the thousands of undiagnosed patients suffering pituitary disorder, then eighteen grand would certainly have come in handy for sending a leaflet to GPs.

Kit resigned a year after the Charity Commissioners responded, and returned to America to write steamy novels (a second career which had been on the back burner while she was CEO). Terry Lloyd left at the same time, after a curious interlude during which he was terminated and reappointed as a director of the foundation no less than four times. No explanation for this was given by the PF spokeswoman to Ben Cook, who reported the episode on 29 March 2011 in the online magazine *Third Sector*.

Since Kit left, Pat McBride has resumed relations with me, being as helpful as always. Menai, Kit's successor, has been friendly and cooperative in many ways, though she stops short of saying anything that the charity's medical committee would disapprove of.

It was really to support Jon that I complained to the Charity Commissioners. There were times when I regretted it as a time-consuming project (to use Kit's word) that diverted my energies from my primary aim of publicising PTHP, but on balance I'm glad I spent the time on it because of what I learned.

Part of what these recent years have given me is an insight into the workings of our democracy. I have sometimes felt as if I were being led by the hand by some Dickensian ghost and shown what lies behind the imposing façades of our charities, our health service, and our watchdogs. Those gracious porticoes, those architraves, those carved pillars ... and behind them, very little. Sometimes the façades have no more substance than flats on a film set; they are all show.

I had already felt disillusioned with the Pituitary Foundation's and Headway's apparent wish to do the barest minimum they could get away with, in the face of what any impartial person would agree was a massive, urgent problem. But I can hardly describe my feelings when I discovered that the Charities Commission was an entirely inadequate brake on misbehaviour. Charities, it seemed, could get away with anything – and if you can count it as murder to withhold information about a condition that it is known could end in suicide, that is what they got away with. There have been many complaints about the Commission, and googling shows that the National Audit Office has expressed concerns. According to them, 'The Charity Commission is not regulating charities effectively. It fails to take tough action in some serious cases and makes poor use of its powers.'

My own case was dismissed as a personal dispute and so was Jon's. He persisted for longer than I did, and achieved some good coverage in the online press as well as that derisory offer of £100 I mentioned earlier. I do not know if the Pituitary Foundation ever publicly retracted the statements they made about him.

23 - NICE

During the same year, 2009, that I was writing to the Pituitary Foundation I was doing battle with NICE, in a fitful way, with long pauses between the various stages. The pauses were partly theirs, and partly mine. I found it extraordinarily hard to write to them, and even harder to read the turgid and pompous responses that came back. In the later stages of our correspondence even the sight of an email from them in my inbox produced quakings of the heart and sick dread – dread of the waves of rage and disgust that would crash over me when I read it.

It was a hard year for me. I was still failing to believe absolutely that Chris was dead. In the night, I still woke up to the horror of it with a thudding heart. I still had flashbacks of things he said, times when I could and should have asked questions, things I should have done differently. In fact, these persist to this day. In April or May we learnt that my older daughter Jenny and her husband Nick were expecting their first baby in November – dear Jenny, promptly setting to, to repopulate our depleted family – and this helped, but only in the dimmest, most theoretical way.

NICE is run by many august, often titled professionals with letters after their names, and my earlier approaches to the organisation were marked by respect, hesitancy, and timidity. I have already described how I was naive enough to believe writing a single letter to them would be enough for them to correct their guideline. When I learnt that NICE had no intention of doing any such thing I asked my lawyer friend Frances what to do, and she told me to look in their statement of aims and objectives and the regulations governing them. It was good advice, because there I found that if one of the guidelines contained an error that 'may result in harm to patients' NICE could do an exceptional update – in other words, amend the guideline immediately without waiting for the appointed time. I wrote to them in April 2009 saying so.

The weeks passed and no reply came. I didn't know how to chase politely – this is how in awe I was – but another lawyer friend gave me the right phrases and I finally got a reply two months later, from a Dr Fergus Macbeth. It said:

> 'Through the President of the Royal College of Physicians, I sought the opinion of a senior endocrinologist in the UK. Interestingly he has just completed a study similar to the ones from Italy and Dublin [...] His study which has not yet been published but will be submitted in a few months shows a very much lower incidence than previously seen. Although I am not denying the seriousness of this condition and the scope for a disastrous outcome if not recognised, this information [...] leads us [to] conclude that an immediate update is not justified [...] However, when the guideline is updated we will ensure that this issue is addressed.'

I was astonished. My first thought was, 'So if there aren't so many affected it doesn't matter? It isn't worth adding a few words to save their lives?' My second thought was, 'Well, how many *are* affected? What does this new research say?' and my third was puzzlement as to how one study could possibly overturn the findings of the score or so that I had read. Surely NICE was supposed to base decisions on the consensus of published research, rather than rely on one unpublished study? What was to stop that study being unrepresentative?

I thought I could solve the mystery by ringing Dr Macbeth up, but he was unobtainable. When I put my question in writing I was told, 'Unfortunately we are not at liberty to release the name of the author of the as yet unpublished research [...] nor are we able to comment on the precise incidence of the condition in the report.'

What could I do? Jon Danzig's advice was to make a Freedom of Information request to see all the correspondence my communications with NICE had generated and I did this. What came back was a fascinating series of emails, the sensitivity of which could be judged by the number of black rectangles where names and whole sentences had been blanked out. I would say there were more black rectangles than on the average MP's expenses form at the height of the scandal.

The most interesting email was from the endocrinologist whose name NICE had kept from me. It said, 'With regard to head injury and hypopituitarism we have actually done our own study which has just been completed.' Then five lines were blacked out. 'We have only just finished this study and so we have not published it but we will definitely do so.' Then two blacked out lines obviously constituting half a sentence because the train popped out of the tunnel with the words, 'but we feel our patient group is the same as others and that our findings are endocrinologically secure. Thus, hypopituitarism can definitely occur but is uncommon. Most people do not recognise it at all. Certainly pan hypopituitarism has been described. Therefore it is uncommon, potentially serious and under recognised. I hope this is helpful. Best wishes,' and then a blacked out Christian name, four letters long.

I homed in on, 'but we feel our patient group is the same as others' in particular. Clearly the first half of the sentence had said something along the lines of, 'There have been studies that imply a high incidence' to account for the 'but'. So they knew about the 'others' but were choosing a study that said something different? Why would they do that?

However, that little chink of light apart, the FOI didn't help much. What was much more helpful was a late answer from Professor Chris Thompson in Dublin, a world expert on hypopituitarism.

I had written to him as soon as Dr Macbeth's letter reached me, even though I knew him only by reputation, begging him to tell me how common PTHP really was, and now, at last, here was his reply. It was forthright. 'The vast majority of the published papers suggest figures of 20% to 30% for PTHP after traumatic brain injury.' He stated that NICE was 'incorrect' to suggest a lower figure. This just confirmed what I already believed, but somehow his letter came as a shock. I rushed to find John, shouting, 'NICE have been telling porkies!'

I could hardly believe that an organisation like NICE, with its international reputation and such power, would stoop to such behaviour. Half-truths with the fingers crossed behind the back, as it were, were one thing. Direct misinformation was another. At this point my respect for them completely vanished.

I wrote back to Dr Macbeth with some glee, quoting Professor Thompson's letter. NICE's reaction was telling. They did not try to justify themselves, or apologise, or in fact refer to the topic at all. They simply, with a breathtaking and acrobatic change of direction, like a kitesurfer swivelling in mid-air, announced that the guideline only covered the acute stage of head injury and therefore PTHP, a 'long-term complication' according to them, wasn't covered by the scope. This despite telling me the issue would be addressed when update time came round.

I was stunned.

I had so many responses to this: that PTHP wasn't just long-term, the research said it could kill you during the acute stage; that the scope clearly intended medics to spot complications that might show up later; that to fail to warn the patient was flouting the principle of patient autonomy, his/her right to 'be aware of the risk and possible treatments of one's condition.'

Our Headinjuryhypo website gives all NICE's emails so anyone interested can see all the twists and turns, the way NICE would quote the beginning of a sentence that appeared to support their stance, while remaining silent about the ending, which supported mine, or the way they would claim that a reference to PTHP in the discharge letter would alarm rather than inform patients.

It was useless. I went through the complaints procedure, appealed to the Parliamentary and Health Services Ombudsman (PHSO), all with no result. I was obsessed by the image of desperate people trapped in a burning building, a cinema perhaps. NICE and the Ombudsman were like imposing, uniformed officials with gold braid on their coats who told you with the utmost politeness and regret that their regulations did not permit them to open the exit doors – when in fact their regulations required them to open those murderous doors as fast and as wide as possible.

The correspondence ended with Sir Andrew Dillon writing to me suggesting a separate guideline – the equivalent of a gold-braided guard saying, 'But there *is* a little door at the back, Madam, which we might open at some future date.' I preserve his letter mainly because he admits in it that one effect of pituitary damage – life-threatening adrenal crisis – can happen in 12% of cases during the acute stage, while still maintaining that PTHP does not belong in a guideline devoted to the acute stage … an anomaly you wouldn't expect to find anywhere outside Alice in Wonderland.

I do not know why I accepted his empty offer. Of course the separate guideline did not materialise. The proposal died an early death a few months later at one of the procedural hurdles. I think I was just tired and didn't know what else to do.

I was left baffled by NICE's resistance. It would not take much time; it would not cost much to insert a few paragraphs into the guideline. What was the problem? It was only as time passed and I experienced more and more orchestrated opposition that I began to suspect an explanation that was almost too dark to believe.

The NICE correspondence took its toll on me. It made me so angry that I couldn't give my mind a rest from it, and I was continually rehearsing pithy phrases to demolish their arguments, even as I tossed and turned in the middle of the night. What I never managed to articulate in my emails was the thought that their guidelines were supposed to look after the patient, so that their attitude should have been to find any excuse to get the information *in*, rather than any excuse to keep it *out*.

I remember going to Chris's house in Skipton a while after his death and looking over the wall from the little alley that ran between the two rows of houses. It was the kind of alley you often find in the north of England, between two rows of terraced houses – narrow, cobbled, criss-crossed with flapping washing lines – and if you walk along you can see into people's back yards. I could see Chris's. To my pain I saw that the little plastic-covered shelter he had made for his tomato plants had been blown or ripped away, leaving a rectangular raised bed of soil, which dogs were clearly using as a toilet. Nothing could have been more desolate than to see his careful, caring work come to nothing, and turned into a foul quagmire. NICE made me feel the same.

HENK GRIFFIN'S STORY

It would be another two years before Henk first made contact with me, but I have brought his story forward to complement Catherine's. Here it is.

I am fifty-three years old and live in Amsterdam. However, I was brought up in the Casco Bay area of Maine in the United States.

I enjoyed my childhood, and I did well at sports. I was one of the best defence soccer players in the state; I could seize the ball from the other team and kick it a very long distance in the opposite direction. In later years I became a strong long-distance swimmer and cyclist. I worked in Los Angeles, San Diego and Prague, where I was always active and social.

However, when I moved to the Netherlands, the good times ended. I came there as a highly paid advertising executive, but problems with my work permit extended for four years, making me lose my place on the career ladder and forcing me to do poorly paid work with long hours, under constant pressure, not eating or sleeping enough. Eventually my health suffered. It took many years before I was finally diagnosed with hypopituitarism. Now, unfortunately, I can no longer work and have to live off disability benefits.

Although my stressful life obviously contributed

to my illness, I am still not sure what caused the actual damage to my pituitary. Over the years I have hit my head countless times. I was in bad car accident as a kid, split my head open on the end of the pool multiple times, was beaten about the head twice, and was tackled badly by a group during an ice hockey game and lost consciousness. My doctor thinks head injury is the cause, but I also wonder about a raging infection I had in my jaw bone between 1996 and 1999 which just would not go away. I had to have five operations during that period, and in 1997 I had terrible flu-like attacks which came every month for five months. I wonder if I had undiagnosed encephalitis or meningitis then, which caused some damage.

My real problems started in 2003, just after I had some heavy blows to my head which burst my eardrum. Perhaps my earlier head injuries had a cumulative effect. Gradually I started to get more and more thirsty. It got so bad that I would go to the tap and drink five glasses of water as quickly as I could, like an addict. Then 15-30 minutes later I would have to do the same again. I was so constantly thirsty at that point it was obvious something was very wrong, and although I had other symptoms, the doctors focused on that one. I was repeatedly tested for sugar diabetes, and it took three or four years before they discovered that I had neurogenic diabetes insipidus (caused by my pituitary). Then, unfortunately, they didn't do any further investigations and my health carried on going downhill for another five years.

I finally ended up with the right doctor because I had to have tests for something else at a different hospital, because my normal hospital could not do them quickly enough. Someone there was talking to me, heard my story and felt bad for me and told me there was a really good doctor there who could maybe help. She called upstairs and then sent me up to make an appointment and I left the do-nothing dysfunctional hospital I was at previously. So luck played a part in my diagnosis coming when it did. Even so, it took nearly nine years to give me a more complete diagnosis.

The doctor at the new hospital was open-minded and relished the challenge of finding out what was wrong. I was diagnosed in less than six months from first seeing him. I was given the insulin stress test three times, because I am unusually resistant to insulin and had to be given three times the normal dose (enough to kill an ordinary person) before my blood sugar went down to the level it needed to be for the test.

Even now that I have been diagnosed with hypopituitarism after testing positive for diabetes insipidus, secondary hypoadrenalism, and prolactin deficiency, I still have a horrible fight with people that always want to believe it is all in my head, especially with people that work for the government.

As to how I live with hypopituitarism, well, hormone treatment is not a magic fix. The cortisol and vasopressin replacement medicine I take is life-saving, but I am still not well. I suffer from varying degrees of chronic pain, extreme fatigue, muscle weakness, and cognitive dysfunction. I frequently have internal infections and viral illnesses and must contend with parts of my body being stiff and numb. Breathing and swallowing can be difficult. I used to tolerate stress better than other people but cortisol deficiency makes everything much more stressful as your body loses its mechanisms to process stress and sometimes you can develop more serious life threatening Addisonian / Hypo-adrenalism Crisis but right now I can't take even the smallest amount. When I hear a sudden noise it can make me jump out of my chair; before, nobody could make me jump. I seem to have a food intolerance to carbohydrates and lactose. I also suffer from sleep deprivation. I broke my leg and ankle a couple of years ago because of osteoporosis, perhaps caused by my medication. I also have serious, ongoing visual disorders.

Now that I am on disability benefits I have to fight every step of the way to try to get enough money to live on. I am subjected to endless government initiated demands and bureaucracy as a result, which force me to work very long hours executing tasks when I am too ill to work at all. When I am at my most ill, I am typically sent on a psychiatric detour owing to the false assumptions made by some of my medical and government contacts that my problems are all in my mind. I have to avoid making appointments with people or making plans in advance as I am too ill to leave the house more than 50 per cent of the time.

Since I never know until after I wake how well or how ill I am, I cannot have much of a social life or do things with friends like I once did and my financial situation also limits me socially. Every year, I become more and more isolated from family, friends, former colleagues, and acquaintances. From the outside I look well, so everybody expects me to be as active and as communicative as someone that is healthy and it can be very draining trying to meet the expectations of other people. I have to take multiple medications, some several times per day and at precise times. After years of this, I am so tired of taking medication I wish I could have a medication vacation.

Incidentally, there are links between hypopituitarism and other conditions. A significant proportion of hypopituitarism patients have ME, fibromyalgia, neuropathy, and/or hypoglycaemia, though the reason for this is unknown. I have all four.

24 - MORE EMAILS TO CONSULTANTS

After my battle with NICE, which had cost me so much emotionally, John thought I should forget about them and carry on writing to consultants. He was right. They were human beings and they took action.

Emailing consultants isn't easy. They understandably want to protect themselves from the potential avalanche of time-consuming – possibly time-wasting – queries from anxious patients, and they have their strategies for making sure they're not too easy to reach. There are exceptions, of course, and some hospitals, such as Charing Cross, list all their staff with email contacts.

I enjoyed searching out their addresses on the internet. It was curiously absorbing, like chipping away at a tough rock-face, where every now and then a crystal would dislodge itself and fall miraculously into my hand. It never occurred to me that I could have bought a database and saved months of this patient chiselling. I found it an escape from the anguish that was waiting to pounce if I ever allowed myself to think. It was like Minesweeper, but more productive.

There is a website called drfoster.com that lists all the consultants and their specialties in any given hospital. If you then discover the email suffix of the hospital, as it might be srft.nhs.uk for Salford Hospital in Manchester, you can then experimentally feed the name of your consultant – for example Dr Alfred Bloggs – into Google as alfred.bloggs@srft.nhs.uk and if you are lucky, bingo! It will appear, possibly as the author of some learned paper. Sometimes if you are desperate, researching the name of a colleague of the consultant you are after will unlock that magic formula of the suffix. Sometimes googling the consultant's surname with the initial tacked on to the end (Addenbrooke's does this) will yield gold. I became expert. I sent off email after email, gradually honing it from a mammoth screed to a briefer, more readable one, with the key research highlighted in unmissable yellow. Occasionally there would be the odd yelp of pain ('I would be grateful if you would inform me where you obtained my email address'), but on the whole I was impressed and heart-warmed by the kindness and energy of the responses.

For example, Dr David Shakespeare, a neuro-rehabilitation consultant at the Royal Preston Hospital in Lancashire, circulated a letter in August that year to all the local GPs describing the symptoms of hypopituitarism and warning them to be vigilant. Dr Stephen Kirker, a re-habilitation consultant at Adden-brookes, asked Professor Thompson (the expert whose letter I hoped would vanquish NICE) to write an article about PTHP for a professional journal for rehab consultants and neuro-logists. He suggested writing a letter for publication in the *British Journal of Neurosurgery*, which I successfully did, and he gave me a list of people to contact, and that is how one of the good angels of this story made his appearance. Professor Mike Barnes of the UK Acquired Brain Injury Forum (UKABIF) has been a kind and instant source of medical information over the years, and has invited me to speak at conferences and workshops, and even colla-borated with Carol Jackson on an article about PTHP for a legal website.

Apart from the satisfaction of reaching these important people who met patients face to face, I enjoyed the linguistic challenge of mimicking consultant-speak. Like an immigrant in a foreign land I felt instinctively that I would prosper if I mastered the language, and I hoped it might make them take me more seriously. I do not know if I fooled anyone, but I gradually acquired their stately polysyllabic rhythms and adopted their little habits such as using data as a plural. Whenever I came across an unfamiliar medical term such as *sequelae*, meaning 'consequences of an injury', I would look it up and, if I could, use it (though with extreme caution). Transmuting what had happened to Chris into words derived from Latin and Greek distanced it mercifully from me, but just now and then, looking perhaps at a medical diagram, I would think, 'This was Chris's brain' – as much a part of him as his face and hands, even though hidden – and I would think of that tiny little dangling blob that had been so badly hurt.

Even when rebuffing me, consultants wrote to me as human beings, taking in what I said and answering my questions courteously (even if unsatisfactorily). They have not been trained to swamp their correspondent with verbiage, NICE-style, and I hope they never are. I wrote to Professor John Wass, a consultant endocrinologist practising in Oxford, in 2009 because his position as Chair of the Pituitary Foundation's medical committee made me hope he might sign a letter to NICE about the guideline. He replied that he knew of the literature about PTHP, but his own study testing fifty people found growth hormone deficiency in only two of them, and no deficiency in the sex hormones, so he felt he could not sign. In reply I made the point, as tactfully as I could, that the bigger the sample the more accurate the result, and if his own fifty patients were added to the thousand-plus from other studies, it would dilute the 27 per cent figure down to around 25 per cent – surely still high enough to write to NICE about.

He'd suggested that the tests in other studies were carried out incorrectly, so I asked if he would look at an individual study (I gave an example) and explain in detail where the methodology was wrong. He did not do this, but the following year he sent me a link to an article by Kokshoorn (beloved by both the Pituitary Foundation and Andrew Dillon), which said that PTHP research had exaggerated the figures through inaccurate testing.

I felt out of my depth and wrote to Professor Thompson for help. Two months later I reported what he told me to Professor Wass, which was that although the figures for growth hormone deficiency had been exaggerated in some research, just as Kokshoorn said, Professor Thompson's own studies used the gold standard tests and still found that 12-16 per cent of the patients were low in cortisol and growth hormone. And he confirmed that the figures for sex hormone deficiency still held good – a question of mine that Professor Wass hadn't answered.

I received no reply. By this time, I was pretty sure, thanks to Professor Thompson's broad hint and to the fact that Professor Wass's first name had four letters, that he was the author of the unpublished research that NICE would not divulge. I decided he was too hard a nut to crack and left him in peace for a while.

Dr Kirker, the Addenbrookes consultant neurologist who had helped me before, was a mine of good advice. Besides putting me in touch with Professor Barnes of UKABIF, he also suggested I should write to Professor Derick Wade, editor of the medical journal *Clinical Rehabilitation*, and this led to an interesting correspondence in late 2009, which could be summarised as follows:

Me: PTHP happens to between a quarter and a third of head injury survivors.

DW: Rubbish! You'd have much more success if you quoted realistic numbers, instead of making such ridiculous claims.

Me: Here are 22 papers that support me.

DW: [In a different tone of voice] Oh, I had no idea! Well, I'm an old man but it's never too late to learn. Can we meet sometime, maybe in London?

There was something endearing about his readiness to change his mind and I was very keen to meet him. Around Christmas I wrote reminding him of his suggestion, but he didn't reply, and a further prod yielded nothing. Some time later we corresponded about getting an article about PTHP into his journal, and he consented in a guarded manner (quite different from his earlier impulsive email) to considering a submission if it was from a qualified author.

Enter Mr Antonio Belli, a consultant neurosurgeon who at that time was at the Wessex Neurocentre in Southampton. He told me he was screening his head injury patients and finding that one in four had hypopituitarism. I was ecstatic to get such forthright support, and thought of him immediately as a possible author.

He kindly agreed to co-author a paper with someone on his team. I had to nag, of course, but I had become less hesitant about this. I pointed out that women took less time to have a baby than his article was taking, and he agreed that it was taking 'longer than the gestation of a human child' – but in the end the child was born and submitted to Professor Wade. However, to my mortification, he turned it down! Luckily Mr Belli found a home for it in another medical journal.

But why had Professor Wade changed his tune so dramatically? I had further correspondence with him the following year – leisurely, gracious, and ultimately pointless – about risk and screening, in which he told me that even a five per cent figure for hypopituitarism after head injury was likely to be a gross over-estimate. I was amazed that he could say this only a few months after he'd apparently been convinced by my list of papers demonstrating more than four times that. He presented the argument that if, say, testing patients gave five per cent of them hypoglycaemia and seizures, they would be doing more harm than good and screening wouldn't be worth it.

I was aware of these risks and I agreed with the principle of his argument, but only if the figures were right, and I was deeply sceptical of his. I pressed him as gently as I could, asking him what he based them on (I had checked on the internet and discovered the seizure figure was much nearer one per cent) and he answered that, 'The side effect rates etc. are guesses/estimates and you can run at any figures you like. The point is that they have to be factored in...' He said his statement about the percentage with PTHP was based on research at their own unit in Oxford, adding, 'but I fully agree with you that it is not acceptable evidence until and unless it is published and I'll push the two researchers.'

Ah, I thought, and took the opportunity to ask if the research was Professor Wass's study that had found only two people out of a group of fifty had growth hormone deficiency, and to ask – assuming that this study would pass peer review and be published – in what way it would nullify the results of other research.

He answered honestly. Yes, it was Professor Wass's study. As for the research, 'it will not be definitive but add to the totality of evidence.'

I thought, but did not write, that there would have to be an awful lot of 50-patient studies before, say, Professor Schneider's 1,100-patient review was overturned. In the event Professor Wass's study was never published. Perhaps the peer review process, whereby other academics have to vet a paper first, got in the way.

Not all correspondences took as much time, with as little result, as the one with Professor Wade.

A heartening breakthrough came when Mr Peter Whitfield, a consultant neurosurgeon in Plymouth, managed to change Derriford Hospital's discharge advice after head injury to include a warning. It was just a line or two, I have marked his additions to the NICE template in bold below:

> If you start to feel that things are not quite right (e.g. mild headache, feeling sick, problems concentrating, poor memory, irritability, tiredness, problems sleeping, lack of appetite, **sexual and fertility difficulties, weight problems**) then please see your GP, so that he/she can make sure you are recovering properly; **occasionally further investigations (e.g. pituitary blood tests) may be required.**

Just sixteen extra words, yet I'm prepared to bet that they will have made a profound difference to several people's lives by now. They won't know, but they will owe that difference to Chris's death. If only all hospitals would follow Derriford's example.

As 2009 came to a close I took stock. I looked at the statistics website and found that the number of diagnosed hypopituitarism cases had risen by nearly 100 since

Chris's death, from 1,848 to 1,941. Did I have anything to do with that? But no, because I could see the numbers had fluctuated in the past (for example in 2004-2005 there had been 1,956 cases). And in any case there should have been thousands more. So no, not much result there.

All those emails to the Pituitary Foundation, Headway, and NICE had achieved little, but I do think that my obsessive chiselling at the rock face for consultants' email addresses had been valuable – more valuable even than the *Guardian* article and the *Woman's Hour* broadcast. This was not just because of what I've described in this chapter. It was because writing those emails had brought me into contact with a group of medical professionals who wanted PTHP diagnosed as much as I did. They were my allies. They told me things I needed to know.

In particular, it was through them that I heard about Mr Belli's seminar on head injury that was due to be held at the Wessex Centre in April 2010, and was able to get his permission to attend. This was an event that loomed large on my horizon, as it would be my first chance to meet professionals face to face and hear what they were saying about head injury. As it turned out, in fact, the seminar would prove to be even more momentous than I'd imagined, changing my ideas about how the world worked for ever.

25 - WINTER 2009

In November 2009 Jenny had her first baby, Katherine, by Caesarean section, so the year 2010 was lit up for me by the joy of being a grandparent. During that year Jenny and Nick were still living near Finchley Road in a second floor flat that looked out at the back on to a weeping willow tree gracefully drooping its fronds over the lawn of a quiet communal garden. I was always round there visiting, walking down the road from the tube station, up the broad old-fashioned steps to the front door, then climbing up the stairs and stopping on the threshold to breathe in the delicious scent of baby and baby milk and baby powder and baby poo. I was completely enchanted by Katherine, in the way that grannies always are. I would have done anything for her. Also I felt that Jenny, cooped up with a baby in a second floor flat with no lift, still recovering from her Caesarean, needed me a lot, and I was torn between my wish to campaign and my determination to be a good mother to my surviving children. I had vowed right at the start that I would never sacrifice my family to a cause.

Jenny was taking a year's maternity leave and was due to go back to work at the end of the year. She planned to put Katherine in a nursery, a decision that worried me. Some years ago I'd read Sue Gerhardt's book *Why Love Matters*, a summary of the scientific research on child-rearing, and had been disquieted by the chapters about babies and the effect of stress on their brain development. The research established that if a baby was separated from his/her mother you could measure its distress by the high levels of cortisol in its blood, and in the nursery context the alarming thing was that even when the initial phase was over – those first few weeks spent crying – and had been replaced by apparent tranquillity, the high cortisol levels still continued, showing that though the child had become outwardly resigned, he or she was still suffering. Exactly the same effect has been observed in dogs that are left alone when their owners go to work. And worse still, the effect on the brain is lasting, in that not enough cortisol receptors are grown, and so for the rest of the child's life it will be harder for him or her to calm down and feel happy again after being upset. My other daughter, Ruth, who had studied psychology for her degree, confirmed this.

The image of the child who looks content but is inwardly suffering acutely meant more to me than most people. I still vividly remembered my sister-in-law's suicide more than twenty years ago, which had happened three weeks after she had given birth and was, ironically in view of my life since 2008, clearly hormonally related. Her older son was three at the time and may have seen his mother jump off the kitchen table in a frenzy on to a knife. When my sister and I rushed there from various corners of the country to do what we could, we found this little boy playing placidly with his cars, and I thought – shame, shame on me – 'he's too young to understand'. But of course he wasn't, and the terrible effects of what he went through have probably marked him for ever. He stopped putting in any effort at school in early adolescence, refused to take any exams and now, in his adulthood, has so far never done any work, paid or otherwise.

All this back story meant I was determined to protect

Katherine's darling cortisol levels, even if it meant throwing myself into the breach as a full-time childminder, and I pleaded to be allowed to do this. Meanwhile I worked away at my PTHP emails with a sense of urgency, not knowing what free time I would have in 2011 when Jenny's maternity leave ended.

Another competitor for my time during 2010 was my poor mother-in-law Celia, whose health was deteriorating. As soon as we put one arrangement in place for looking after her, when things seemed to be going smoothly, the wheel would ratchet round one more notch and we would find we were failing her again and she needed more care. We always seemed to be one step behind, and I was often round at her house fire-fighting, since we only lived five minutes away. Even when she was extremely ill she never became ill-tempered. She bore everything bravely. Even so, I felt exhausted and stressed, and loved escaping from the atmosphere of human disintegration, to glorious babyland.

26 - DR KEARNEY AGAIN

I kept thinking ahead to Mr Belli's seminar in March. At the end of January, he surprised me by asking me who it was I'd mentioned as researching PTHP. This was of course Dr Kearney. I gave him her details, but I had been worried by how she'd tried to persuade me that PTHP was rare. In fact, wondering if I was being indiscreet, I confided this to Mr Belli.

He didn't however seem troubled, and booked her anyway. For the next few weeks I worried intermittently about what to do if she still claimed the incidence was six per cent. Would I have the guts to stand up and challenge her? I consoled myself remembering how on Woman's Hour she had supported what I said, and how the 'topped-and-tailed' patient whom I had so wanted to contact had thanked God for the day he met her. I felt instinctively that she was a good doctor.

I was fretting too about a planned holiday in Sicily which ended only two days before the seminar. Suppose something happened to delay our return?

My misgivings about Dr Kearney weren't helped by what happened next. A medically alert friend, Sue, told me that there were going to be four new centres opening soon, set up to help new research make it over the academic barrier into real-life treatment of patients. Sue and I both thought that PTHP was a tailor-made case for them. After receiving a dense information pack, I wrote a long, careful letter showing how addressing the PTHP problem would meet their aims. The area I applied to was Manchester, as I knew that at least they had heard of the issue there.

I wrote in August 2009, but it wasn't until the following March, shortly before the seminar, that an answer came. The email was long and contradictory, and I puzzled over it a long time. Readers who want to decipher it for themselves can see it on headinjuryhypo.org.uk. What I extracted from the verbiage was that they'd asked the advice of Dr Kearney, who said everyone was talking about PTHP, and they were drawing up guidelines for screening patients. But this was expensive and the 'observed frequency of hypopituitarism in this patient group is probably a lot less than originally predicted [...] although still significant.' There was disagreement about the tests and treatment and finally, the killer statement: 'this particular area of research has not been identified as a priority [...] at this stage.'

If a problem is rare, it's generally not economical to screen for it, especially if there are a lot of people to screen and the tests aren't cheap. I knew that and I also, of course, knew from my reading that the problem wasn't rare. Why was Dr Kearney telling them that it was? She had declared in the past that, 'Hypopituitarism is found in between one and two thirds of patients, even those with less serious injuries.' Why had she changed her opinion?

Despondently I filed the papers away as yet another failed project and went back to my consultants.

27 - HEADWAY 2

Once more, it was consultants who told me the things I needed to know, and shortly before our Sicily holiday, I had an email from a consultant surgeon pointing out that Headway had nothing in its online leaflets about pituitary dysfunction. 'As they are an important national charity working with NHS Trusts it would be useful for you to contact them.'

A bolt of shock went through me. Could it be that after all that attention from Luke, and after an hour's interview with Peter McCabe, they *still* had not put anything on their website?

I wrote a careful email to Luke three days later, asking him how he was, hoping everything was going well for him, then reminding him that the Research section on Headway's website still contained nothing about PTHP. He'd originally told me that no research had come out recently enough to warrant inclusion, so now I gave him links to two papers that had come out since then, and suggested that he included them.

Then I came to the nitty gritty. I pointed out that Headway still hadn't updated its leaflets to include the information, in spite of having produced a host of new booklets and factsheets during the year, and even winning an award. I wrote, 'I first alerted Headway to the research in October 2008. Headway's leaflets are a valuable, much-used resource for NHS Trusts. It is a tragedy that the information is not there. The consequence is that patients may have failed to get treatment that would have helped them greatly.'

I waited eight days but no reply came. When I chased Luke he immediately sent a long, obviously carefully prepared reply. He said they had posted a relevant article in their research section (This was a lukewarm study acknowledging hormone abnormalities after brain injury but casting doubt on whether treating them did any good.) He said he would post the research I'd sent.

On the leaflet side, he argued that the pituitary information was just one issue among many, and each booklet took a long time to produce. PTHP remained 'a possible inclusion in our library.'

He then talked of the need to be measured, and not to offer false hope to people 'who may think [they] can be easily treated with hormone replacement therapy' when their symptoms could stem from something else. He spoke of disagreement among experts. He said they thought a seminar organised by the Department of Health bringing the experts together would be helpful, and Peter McCabe had asked through his MP for this to happen.

It took me a while to control the distress (in fact, rage) I felt. I was particularly incensed by the idea of PTHP being only a 'possible inclusion' and revolted by Headway's pretence of concern for PTHP patients – protecting them from 'false hope' – while doing them the greatest injury possible. It reminded me of NICE. While I thought about what to say I continued to write to Luke in a normal tone of voice about getting Chris's story into the popular magazine *That's Life*, which to give him his due he did organise for me. It was about a week later, a fortnight before I was due to go to Mr Belli's seminar, that I replied directly.

I should have learnt from my experience with NICE that when an organisation is trying to justify the unjustifiable you get nowhere by arguing. However many of their reasons you demolish, they will always find others. In fact, argument is as useless as attacking the false timbers of an 'Elizabethan' pub. The roof will always remain in place, supported by reinforced steel joists that you cannot see.

However, against my better judgment, I hacked valiantly at Luke's fake Tudor beams, thanking him and Peter for the time and trouble they'd spent so far, but saying I owed it to our son to fight for other people in his position.

Yes, I agreed, Headway had other issues. Did any of them affect such vast numbers of people, were any of these other disorders treatable?

As for 'measured' – was he suggesting that any mention of endocrine complication was unmeasured? A risk didn't have to be quantified to the nearest decimal point before you mentioned it – you didn't wait to discover the precise size and whereabouts of a blaze before you shouted FIRE!

As for giving false hope, 'Inaction results in no hope at all! What is wrong with saying "If you suffer from any of the following symptoms there is currently estimated to be a one in five chance that you have treatable pituitary damage and you should get your GP to refer you to an endocrinologist"? This does not give false hope. It's the kind of statement that medics give all the time.'

On the subject of the government seminar, I said that the huge numbers of PTHP patients and the expense of treating them made it natural for the government to 'focus in a blinkered way on those vanishingly few research papers that suggest the problem is minor or disputed, and try to keep the issue out of the public eye.' I reminded him that Headway's agenda was different – it was to lobby on behalf of head injured patients and champion their right to compete for the NHS's scarce resources. In this past year of inactivity on their part, 'around 10,000 people … will be grappling with sexual problems and depression that could be treated if they only knew. I wonder how many related suicides there have been?' I took care to copy everybody I knew at Headway into this email. I wanted the whole organisation to know what was happening.

Still on a high of eloquence, I reluctantly had to drop the argument there and leave for Sicily.

28 - VOLCANIC ASH

For at least four years after Chris died I hated holidays. I could never sleep properly and when thoughts of him tormented me, I couldn't do what I did at home, convert sadness into action and get up, make a cup of tea, and write a few awareness-raising emails. Instead I had to lie in the darkness, defenceless. I knew that the sunshine and exercise – it was a walking holiday – would be good for me, and I wanted to meet our friends whom we only saw occasionally, but all the same I would rather have been at home.

As it turned out I was right to feel negative, and not just for that reason. The Thursday before the Monday of the all-important seminar was the day that Eyjafjallajökull chose to spew out its ash cloud, grounding all flights from Sicily to the UK. Desperate not to take chances, I abandoned my luggage, John, and our two friends, and made my way alone across Europe by car, coach, ferry, three trains, a taxi, two more trains, a ferry, and a lift in someone's car. It took me three full days to get home and my memories are of an over-taxed transport system, long, unmoving queues of displaced persons, anxious refugees, a continent in turmoil.

My journey isn't relevant to this story, but as crises often do, it loosened me up. Strangers helped each other, formed groups. I met interesting people, including – even – a primary school teacher whose brother had developed the milk-oozing breasts that pituitary damage can bring and went through a distressing battle to get diagnosis and treatment. In a crowded, rocking train corridor I temporarily became part of a gang of UK-bound travellers, one of whom used his smartphone to get us tickets for the only ferry that still had places left, and generously paid for them, trusting that he would be reimbursed (as of course he was). I remember relaxing at last as I sat in an open-air restaurant on the French side of the channel, ticket in hand, ferry place assured, noting the apocalyptic reddish tinge where the ash, up until then invisible, blurred the horizon and dimmed the luminosity of the sea.

What really sticks in my memory, though, came a few hours earlier, when we'd arrived in Paris. Strung out and beyond tired, since it was now the small hours of Sunday morning after two solid days of travel, I checked the time and place of Monday's seminar. I made a discovery.

Dr Tara Kearney was booked to speak, as I'd expected, and there was a little paragraph about her topic. It said:

'The first case of TBI-induced hypopituitarism was reported in 1914, followed by several case series over the ensuing decades. However, more recent systematic enquiries suggest that TBI-induced hypopituitarism is much more prevalent than previously thought, and this has been supported by several prospective well conducted studies.'

I sat staring at the blueish screen in the quiet hotel lobby. Much more prevalent than previously thought! I read the words again and again, hardly believing my eyes.

So, nothing about biased series then, or anecdotal evidence for a low incidence? Dr Kearney was going to say exactly what any other reader of the research would say, what I would have said myself. I wasn't going to have to challenge her after all. I could relax.

But what did this mean? It meant that this story – what

I was tempted to call a Tara-diddle – about the tiny incidence was not something she was spreading to everyone. But why would she say it to me? To put me off? To make me think 'this is just a minor problem, I won't bother?' Perhaps I should have felt flattered. But why would anyone want me to go away? What was going on?

This moment was when the Minotaur-creaks became too loud to ignore.

29 - THE SEMINAR

I should say here that I have no wish to attack Dr Kearney's character. Everything I've ever heard about her from her patients – and as time went on I heard in this back-door way from many of them – confirms what an excellent, thorough doctor she is, and attests to her sensitive kindness. It is her job to make people better, not to campaign. I believe that those who read on will feel sceptical that it was her own idea to mislead me, and will understand where the blame truly lies.

On that day in April 2010, however, my thoughts and feelings were all over the place. After a late homecoming from my epic journey the previous night, followed by four hours' sleep, I found it surreal to walk through the Wessex Neurological Centre, that quiet building with its glass partitions, pick up a name badge, and settle myself in one of the lecture room seats like a normal civilised person. I was afraid I might nod off before quarter past four, when the seminar finished. Dr Kearney's talk was scheduled for two o'clock, quite late. Would I be able to take in what she said?

I was interested to see Mr Belli in the flesh. He was a likeable, quicksilvery kind of man with a boyish, smiling air. I shook his hand, thinking, 'What those fingers can do!'

When he introduced the seminar I was surprised – life seemed to be full of surprises – to learn that the volcanic ash had prevented Dr Kearney from coming. She had sent him her slides and he would give the talk for her.

Mr Belli talked to me during the lunch break. When I raised the topic of warning patients, he was quick to say that until it was clear what diagnostic tests should follow, it would just cause mayhem and confusion. I said, 'Let there be mayhem. The tests will never get sorted out until there's a fuss.' He said that, at present, he would find about a quarter of his patients had pituitary dysfunction, but when he sent them on to the endocrinologist at Poole he would be told they hadn't. I wasn't at all convinced by his arguments. I wish I had said, 'Never mind any of that, it's the patient's absolute right not to be kept in the dark.'

When two o'clock came I had no difficulty in concentrating, despite my fears. But there was nothing in Tara's set of slides as delivered by Mr Belli to suggest anything but what I had learnt myself from my reading. She listed the same studies and reviews, all suggesting around a third of head injuries caused pituitary damage. The only surprise was that there was no surprise.

In the discussion after the talk I was warmed by everyone's openness and goodwill and felt that perhaps, somehow, I was mistaken in my suspicions. Perhaps there was some explanation for Dr Kearney's two versions that I hadn't thought of?

On the bus back to the station I told Chris's story to the man next to me and he reciprocated. His wife had had a head injury when a horse kicked her which caused early onset Alzheimer's, he said. His voice broke, describing it. She was dead now.

What a terrible thing head injury is, with its deadly, insidious consequences spreading so far into the future. Hypopituitarism, I saw, was only one possible consequence among many others.

I wasn't saddened for long. When I finally got home

and into John's arms, I felt an extraordinary elation, as if I'd had an unexpected, exhilarating bounce on life's trampoline and come to no harm.

I slept for a long time.

30 - DR KEARNEY ONCE MORE

As soon as I was back in my old routine I googled Dr Kearney, looking for something that might explain the discrepancy between what she had told me, and what she was saying to others. By this time I was reasonably confident that the general research consensus was that around twenty to thirty per cent of moderate to severe brain injuries resulted in hypopituitarism. I based my conviction not just on Professor Thompson's statement to me, but on that list of papers I had painstakingly compiled and sent to Professor Wade. A trawl through these yielded the following figures: 11%, 16%, 16%, 20%, 21%, 22.7%, 25%, 27.5%, 28.4% 23-69%, 35-40% 36%, 30-80%, 40%, 42%, 50.9%. There is a startling gulf between eleven per cent and eighty per cent, certainly, but the figures from the totality of the research were serious enough to prompt two international consensus statements, each written by a consortium of leading endocrinologists. One was dated 2005 and the other 2009 and they both considered the risk significant enough to call for screening.

I charted a timeline from what I found there and from Dr Kearney's emails. When I looked through the references to Dr Kearney, I found a summary of a talk she'd given at conference in Salford in November 2008 – three months after Chris had killed himself. She had said that brain injury was common in young men and described its effects. 'Hypopituitarism', she said, 'is found in between one and two thirds of patients, even those with less serious injuries.' She described two patients who showed dramatic improvements after hormone replacement therapy. She urgently advocated awareness-raising and screening.

So far, so good, she was on the side of the angels. 'Between one and two thirds of patients ... even less serious injuries.' She was putting the case powerfully.

Then came my *Woman's Hour* interview in March 2009 when she'd supported me so well, though she hadn't talked about exact percentages. But she *had* said, 'it isn't really until about 2000 that there was a literature search performed that suggested that this problem was much more common than we'd previously known about.' Much more common – yes, that was OK too.

What next? The lunch in the Manchester pub a few weeks later when she'd told me there was new research giving a lower incidence and that she was finding PTHP in fewer than ten per cent of her patients. And then the long email silence when I asked her for details of the new research.

Then there was her email to the CEO at Hull, the one I'd had to nag so persistently to get her to write, sent in July 2009 after he asked for Salford's protocol. This said that far fewer people suffered PTHP than had been thought and most investigators/clinicians believed the incidence was only seven to ten per cent, 'clearly still clinically significant but not the 20%+ previously quoted. The studies are still in progress and the data are as yet therefore unpublished.'

I guessed she was talking about Professor Wass's study of the 50 patients in Banbury, unpublished to this day. Her statement that most investigators believed the incidence was 'not the 20%+ previously quoted' was clearly at variance both with the research mentioned above, and with her own presentation as delivered by Mr Belli at the Wessex Centre for Neurology. I could not understand how she could be delivering two apparently incompatible messages so close together in time.

So far, the sequence was high-high-low-low. Then another low, the email from the Manchester Academic Health Science Centre, sent the following March, quoting Dr Kearney as saying the observed frequency was probably 'a lot less than originally predicted.'

I had a fresh piece of evidence too, now. I had just received an email from Dr Kearney, sent two days after I'd seen Mr Belli deliver her Southampton talk citing 30 per cent, saying, 'Most of the researchers that are currently investigating PTHP have the sense that the actual incidence of PTHP is in the order of 7-10 per cent in those with moderate to severe disease.'

So, finally, the pattern was high-low-low-low-high-low. A sandwich, then, with a dubious filling and an extra layer on top. I can see now why she could have been finding small numbers herself, and yet have continued to point out to the medical world the peer-reviewed research on the topic in the hope of effecting change, but what I couldn't understand was why she should tell her colleagues that the problem was common, and me that it was rare. I reflected that the long-delayed email to Hull must have presented a problem, addressed as it was to both audiences simultaneously.

I needed to have it out with her, but didn't know how. When I talked much later to a journalist friend, he said, 'No problem. You just say that you're writing an article, you need to check your facts, and ask her what the facts are.' I wish I'd done this. As it was, all I could think of was to write her a kind of impact statement about Chris, under the pretext that it might be useful to her work, and segue into a paragraph about the incidence and how I didn't believe it was low.

'Dear Tara, I began, Here's my "essay"…'

The first part of my statement to her forms the foreword to this book. It described Chris's character and how I missed him, and then went on as follows:

> 'Here is an extract from a suicide email he wrote, not to us but to two friends who lived in his road.
>
> *"It's really hard to find the right words for this.*
>
> *The only way it would make sense is if there was some way to link into another person's mind and really feel what it's like inside.*
>
> *So, instead of trying to explain it, I'm just going to say a last few things.*
>
> *1.   I am doing this with a clear head and it's something I've been thinking about for a long time.*
>
> *2.   I tried before in 2003 but I really hadn't researched it properly and I was unsuccessful*
>
> *3.   This is nobody else's 'fault' and nothing anyone did or didn't do is to blame*
>
> *4.   The responsibility, guilt, weakness and shame rests entirely with me. I am who I am and I can't change that."*

He goes on to thank them for helping him through some very dark times, and ends, 'You have a long happy life ahead of you, and the ripples I leave behind will soon fade.'

I went on:

'But the truth is that if he'd been diagnosed he wouldn't have felt guilt, weakness, or shame – he'd have *known* it wasn't his fault. He'd have had our understanding and support, and we would have fought to the end of the world to get treatment for him.

He had the genes for happiness, he had strength, good looks, intelligence, and a sweet, kind nature. If he hadn't had that terrible injury he would have been like my husband – successful, popular (and he had such good friends anyway, even as things were), and by now, I'm sure, he would have been a loving husband and father himself. He absolutely didn't deserve the misery that blighted him, nor that second, exacerbating misery of thinking everything was his fault.'

Of course, I was doing my best to make Dr Kearney feel bad, but it was all true and I made myself cry writing it. I went on to say how many sufferers there were, and how so many were young men – the group we needed because their work would pay our pensions.

'I don't think we can avoid the conclusion that there are thousands of undiagnosed people suffering terribly and in despair, and if we keep them in ignorance it condemns them to isolation and denies them the understanding and support of their families. Diagnosis alone might have saved Christopher, whatever disarray there is in current thinking on treatment. If we don't reach out to these others, some of them will follow in

Christopher's footsteps this year, I'm convinced. I wonder how many already have, over these past 18 months?'

Then, finally, the tricky part, the whole reason for my letter. I said I'd like to put to bed, finally, the myth that PTHP was less common than previously thought, with its implicit conclusion that delay didn't matter. The studies suggesting this were small and unrepresentative. I'd been assured by two eminent endocrinologists that current thinking was 20-30 per cent, and I'd seen that in her slides for the Southampton seminar she had implied something similar.

I ended with a plea about the discharge letter and a suggestion that we had another lunch together to discuss what I'd said.

She sent a warm, prompt answer thanking me, but not referring to the crucial paragraph about putting the myth to bed. Then I thanked her for thanking me, adding that she might have skim-read and missed the end of my email, which I quoted again in full, with that laden sentence, 'I see that in your talk you implied something similar...' What did she feel?

I knew that there were many demands on her time, but I was disappointed not to receive a reply.

31 - HEADWAY 3

The other thing I did, apart from writing to Dr Kearney, was to take up my fight with Luke at Headway again. Two days after the seminar in Southampton he sent a vigorous defence against my charge that the charity had done nothing for a year.

Far from it, he said. They'd spoken to medical experts, they'd drafted detailed information for their website (but not posted it, I thought sourly), and lobbied for national guidelines to be produced.

They had added a raft of studies, positive and negative, to their research section.

He said they had asked several medical experts who'd all had different views on how common PTHP was, and this showed there was no medical consensus. Peter McCabe had written to NICE and spoken with his MP, who had written to the Department of Health asking for a seminar on PTHP where a consensus could be reached.

But the bottom line was that while I'd been away, they had at last posted the information sheet they'd been quietly preparing in the background. Thank God it had happened at last! I called up the Headway website and looked at it. It began, 'Brain injury may occasionally cause damage to the hypothalamus and pituitary gland...' and next to the text were displayed, in prominent positions, references to articles by my old friends the PTHP-minimisers Kokshoorn and van der Eerden. As an example of seeming to do something while not really doing it, it was almost comical.

However, on balance I felt happy. The word 'occasionally' (later dropped) didn't worry me unduly. I reflected, as I had when the Pituitary Foundation had posted their own information sheet, that people are always inclined to think they are rare and special. It works in tempting them to buy lottery tickets, and it works with negative things as well. It wouldn't stop people checking whether they had PTHP. Also, as Luke had said, they had displayed positive research, albeit tucked away below the two negative papers. One of these papers intrigued me, for reasons I will explain later.

Meanwhile I thanked Luke and apologised for not realising how hard he'd worked. Then I talked about consensus. I told him about NICE, and how swiftly they had dropped their claim that PTHP was rare when I quoted Professor Thompson's 20-30 per cent at them. 'If there had been any mileage in that argument [I believe] they would have persisted.'

As for the conflicting views of the neurologists, yes, I'd found the same thing – practising neurologists were often too busy to be *au fait* with every new piece of research. 'In my view it is better to rely on published research than on anecdotal opinions from a small number of practitioners,' (ouch! I hoped). I reminded him of the two international consensus statements in 2005 and 2009, both calling for systematic screening of pituitary function. 'Clearly the numerous experts who prepared these two consensus statements do not regard PTHP as "occasional" or "rare"!'

But I had reached Luke's limit. He wrote, 'we believe that the information posted on our website and the language used is appropriate at this time.' He went on to discuss NICE's proposed 'separate guideline'. This guideline never in fact materialised, confirming my suspicion that it was a ploy to distract me. However, to be fair, Headway may have believed it was a real prospect then.

There matters rested, as far as the Headway website information was concerned.

As mentioned, I was interested in one item in Headway's newly plumped-up research section. It was an information sheet or poster about PTHP for display at a brain conference, co-authored by Headway's information officer, Richard Morris. The date of the poster was given as April 2010. It was a brilliant summary of the research – in fact, its wording was stronger than my letters to Luke. I was amazed. Its conclusion was that permanent hypopituitarism after head injury 'is not uncommon and may remain undiagnosed in many survivors of TBI'. Yet as far as the authors knew, it was not being screened for anywhere. The poster mentioned the 2005 consensus statement that I had quoted to Luke already, though (strangely for a document dated 2010), it didn't mention the second consensus statement of 2009.

The poster concluded that there was no point in the academic world producing endless studies and proposals for screening, if nothing was done to help the patient. Of course financial constraints meant that screening should be targeted at the most 'at-risk' population, but it was hard to decide who *was* most at risk, 'as the severity of TBI does not indicate the potential for hypopituitarism' (i.e. concussion might pose as great a risk as serious head injury). The possibility that PTHP could show for the first time 'many months, even years, after the initial trauma' meant that screening needed to happen more widely for everyone, however mild or severe their injury was.

Bravo! I wanted to shout. Hear, hear!

But if that was Headway's stance – and expressed in such a recent document too – why were they dragging their feet so with me? I looked more closely at the references at the end of the poster and was puzzled to see that there was no paper listed there more recent than 2007. Wasn't that rather odd, for a 2010 paper? I googled further and eventually found, from the Researchgate website, a networking site for scientists and researchers, what I suspected. The poster hadn't been written in 2010 at all, but in 2007, for a conference held by the British Society for Neuroendocrinology (The poster as it is displayed on the Headway website now bears this date.)

So Headway had done its own research a year before Chris died – and kept quiet about it for three years! I was as shocked at this as I had been when I discovered Dr Kearney had been telling me one thing and her colleagues another. The implications were enormous. For one thing, I now realised that Headway's CEO, the tearful Peter McCabe, had known all about PTHP the previous March when I'd had my hour with him, and hadn't breathed a word. I'd thought I was telling him something new. I remembered how he wouldn't look properly at my scrapbook about Chris, and how offhand he'd seemed when I gave him a cheque for £500. In his shoes, I'd have felt a bit queasy too. I even realised why he had talked about cycle helmets before we parted – he'd been saying, at least to himself, 'Look, I know we're not doing much to help people like your son, but at least I'm acting to stop more Christophers happening.'

All kinds of thoughts rushed through my head. For example, there was Luke's visit to my home when I first approached Headway. Was it normal for their communications officer to pay a personal visit to every family that had been affected by head injury? I didn't think so – the logistics would be prohibitive. So why had I been singled out? Had I been seen as a potential threat, someone to be distracted by the suggestion of getting articles into popular women's magazines from approaching more influential outlets? Not kindness at all then, though it had felt like that...

The past was changing in front of my eyes. It was like discovering your husband had been unfaithful. But finally, after all this revising, I was left with the fact that Headway had been sitting on this poster for three years without publishing it on their website, and what was I going to do about it?

My spirit shrank from confronting Luke and Peter. Ridiculously, something like embarrassment, or maybe cowardice, inhibited me – as if to accuse them would amount to a breach of good manners, or be in poor taste. If you have been exchanging lengthy emails for more than a year with someone, you do feel something like friendship towards them. Yet I had to do something. Headway received substantial donations on the understanding that they were fighting for the rights and welfare of people with brain injuries. What possible reason could they have for holding it back?

I deliberated for a while and then decided to do two things. One was to approach Headway's trustees. And the other was to contact the main author of the poster, Paul Goodwin.

In fact I did not write to all the trustees, only the Chair, as I remember – a Jersey MP who had become involved with the charity after his nine-year-old son had a severe brain injury cycling. His son's name is Christopher, like ours. I confided my discovery about the Morris/Goodwin research. Apart from an acknowledgement I never heard back from him, but this does not necessarily mean he did not act.

I wrote asking the author, Paul Goodwin, if I could see his research, and perhaps speak on the phone. Would he be willing to write an article for the Westminster Health Forum seminar transcript? He had no research apart from the poster, and said his research had moved to a different field. He suggested I contact Headway, and didn't give me his phone number. On the proposed article, however, he was very helpful. After a friendly, two-month correspondence he produced a well-written, informative overview which was duly printed. I suggested taking him out to dinner as a thank you, and he seemed to like the idea, but when I complicated the invitation by suggesting Richard Morris and Luke came too – I had a vague dream of plying them with alcohol and loosening their tongues – nothing came of it.

I eventually screwed up the courage to phone Headway's Richard Morris, the co-author, to confront him with the true production date of the poster. My state of mind can be gauged by the fact that I'd bought myself a telephone bug to record our conversation. It was a small, silver device with a slim box and I gave myself some practice-sessions beforehand on John. When I felt bold enough I made the crucial call, but I was not very bold. My heart thudded and my voice came out squeaky. I would not cut it as an investigative journalist.

To my relief I needn't have bothered. Richard was open and friendly with me – he must have felt pleased that his long-suppressed hard work was seeing the light at last. He readily agreed that his poster had been written in 2007 and the 2010 date was an error. He agreed to add 'delayed onset' to the hypopituitarism information sheet, and to insert sexual difficulties as a possible symptom in the concussion sheet. Then, with evident satisfaction in his voice (I thought, 'this man is on my side') he pointed me to the wonderful plethora of papers he had recently added to the Research section, new since I had last visited the website in April. It was all wonderful. I felt like the Prince in *Sleeping Beauty* who rides up to the castle expecting to find his way barred by thorns, and instead the hedge, all fragrant with flowers, opens up to let him through. I put away my bugging device.

Headway's change of heart felt like a breakthrough, and is what I chiefly remember 2010 for. It led, a whole year later, to the definite knowledge that what I was doing had helped someone.

32 - THOUGHTS ON GROWTH HORMONE

But, pleased though I was, I was still left wrestling with my suspicions. Whichever way you looked at it, NICE did not wanted to investigate; Headway had suppressed vital information; The Manchester Academic Health Science Centre had refused to include PTHP in their programme, for no clear reason; and there was Dr Baldeweg whom I'd visited with my mother-in-law, and Dr Murray who wrote me a letter saying the incidence was ten per cent, to think about too. Had I been vain, too ready to imagine that I knew more than these well qualified, long experienced professionals?

I could not understand this apparent keenness to deflect me. Surely adding a few words to a medical guideline cost next to nothing?

But I was obtuse. Everything always comes down to money in the end. Mulling everything over, I remembered the Pituitary Foundation's battle to stop the government banning NHS growth hormone prescriptions, and it occurred to me to look up what the actual costs were.

I had an interesting Google journey. I learned that growth hormone treatment only started in the 1950s. At that time, it was prohibitively expensive, because it could not be made artificially and had to be extracted from the pituitary glands of corpses. In fact, children receiving human growth hormone were sometimes, tragically, infected with diseases like Creutzfeldt-Jakob Disease from a dead person. In 1985 cadaver-derived growth hormone was withdrawn in America, thanks to a technical breakthrough in manufacturing a synthetic equivalent, called recombinant human growth hormone, or rhGH. From then onwards rhGH became steadily cheaper and more widely available.

However, growth hormone treatment still cost several thousands of pounds a year. My first Google searches came up with £12,000 a year, but Pat McBride of the Pituitary Foundation later gave me the more accurate figure of between two and three thousand a year. Treating a person with total pituitary failure (i.e. giving them all the other hormones as well) will cost six to seven thousand a year. Not too alarming, one might think – it can cost many times that to treat a cancer patient. However, it has to be remembered that this is not just for a few years; it's life-long. If I was right, that the number of undiagnosed patients must now have reached the hundreds of thousands, then one could see a motive there for maintaining ignorance. Yet how could they? All these people who could be made better, being deliberately kept in the dark and denied treatment ... I could understand that money might be short, but everyone has an equal right to the NHS's resources. Surely the solution was to give everyone their fair share, no matter how small that might turn out to be?

DANNY PARR'S STORY

Danny approached me through my website in January 2014 asking me whether I thought he might have hypopituitarism and asking what tests I thought he should take. His hunch proved correct.

I am 38. When I was 16 I began to experiment with Ecstasy eventually taking it on a weekly basis with the dosage increasing gradually until I was taking around eight pills staggered over a night's clubbing. On two or three occasions, and always on the way home from the night, I experienced numbness and tingling down the whole left side of my body, especially in my face, hand and foot. I had some weakness in my muscles on the left side and some sort of spasticity in my left hand, arm and neck. I couldn't stand, I suffered headaches, confusion and vomiting. I did not seek medical attention and the symptoms subsided after 30-45 minutes. Looking back I suspect this was due to water intoxification and pressure inside my skull.

On the third occasion (I was 17 at the time) I played soccer the following day. Early in the game I and another player collided while both sprinting at full pace towards each other. His knee hit my cheek/eye socket area. I was severely concussed, but shortly after being taken from the field the symptoms I'd had the previous night (or in fact the early hours of the morning) began again, only this time they were more severe. I also had the added symptoms of patches of blurred vision and an inability to speak, or my words coming out in the wrong order. I was taken to hospital and the symptoms lasted for hours this time, and the vomiting continued until bile was all that came up and then not even bile. I did not have any head scans and I did not tell the nurses/doctors about the Ecstasy because my parents were present. The symptoms eventually subsided and I was kept in overnight. I did have X-rays and a depressed fracture of the *zygoma* (the bone round the eye-socket) was spotted. I had an operation to lift and fix this with titanium plates a few days later.

While I was recovering from the operation I noticed I had no desire to masturbate and when I did try my erections were never full. My orgasms were weak and the ejaculation volume was reduced. This never changed. I had many failed relationships due to difficulty in penetration because of poor erections, or losing erections once I had achieved penetration, and very low libido. I did not feel any of the sexual urges I had felt before the collision. I had some testicular atrophy and if I ejaculated twice within a short period of time it would take maybe a week before I could achieve orgasm again. I saw my doctor and a urologist many times in my late teens and early twenties but it was always attributed to my brief flirtation with steroids, or to a psychological problem, so I gave up trying to get help. I also gave up on relationships for a good few years, partly out of embarrassment and partly due to the heartache of previous failures and the fear of further failure.

Another symptom was that I could not think as clearly as I used to, and had difficulty in putting my thoughts into words. I would experience a sudden onset of social phobia/panic in situations where I had to speak outside my comfort zone. Along with this came feelings of depression, irritability and anger which sometimes made me uncharacteristically aggressive and violent. I was often tired and had trouble getting up to start the day. I also had long-term, borderline high blood pressure, which was strange because I try to keep myself very fit.

I didn't consider the head injury as a possible cause for many years. Viagra arrived and I managed some form of reasonable, but not good, sex life with my now long-term partner, and have two children.

More recently I thought back to my teenage years in nightclubs, and how the clubs were rammed full, very hot, and the Ecstasy would have you dancing all night. The only solution was to drink water and I used to drink a hell of a lot of it. But, as I learnt from reading up about it, Ecstasy stimulates a hormone (ADH) that stops you passing urine – I used to go and stand in the urinal for 20 minutes and pass nothing. Basically, the water makes your brain swell, and the restricted space inside the skull means there is nowhere for it to go except downwards, exerting pressure on the brain stem. This is what made that poor girl Leah Betts collapse and die.

I began to wonder if the pressure inside my head caused by the Ecstasy had meant the heavy blunt force of the football collision had caused brain injury, and possibly hypopituitarism. However when I suggested this to my GP, who had been treating me for my depression and anxiety, he took one look at my reasonably athletic appearance and body hair and suggested that it was unlikely.

However, I still couldn't help feeling that all these problems were linked, especially as when I experimented with injecting a testosterone blend (obviously I know this was unwise) I experienced strong sexual desire and strong erections and orgasms for the first time since my head trauma. I also found that my social anxiety and panic were lessened, and I was much more comfortable speaking to an audience. Four to five weeks after I stopped taking the testosterone the symptoms came back, worse than ever.

So I persisted with my GP, who tested my baseline TSH, LH, FSH, cortisol and prolactin, which all came back normal, but he somehow omitted testosterone. I had to push for that, and when it came back at 9.7 nmol/L (the range is 8.5-35) he said 'Like I expected, it is normal.' However, I had been doing some research and found a paper that showed that the average level for men aged 85-100 is 13 nmol/L, and that for a man of my age it should be 24 nmol/L. The GP referred me to an endocrinologist, who did two more tests, which came out at 8.4 and 7.5.

The endocrinologist thought I did have a testosterone deficiency and booked an MRI scan for me, which picked up an 'area of non-enhancement' on the right of my pituitary gland. I was started on testosterone injections (Nebido) every twelve weeks and the effect has been amazing. In general I feel so much more confident and productive, and my wife is a lot happier too.

It hasn't all been plain sailing. The effect of the injections wears off after eight weeks, and once more I experience libido and erection problems along with irritability, social anxiety, and poor energy and motivation. They have reduced the interval between injections now, so that I have them every ten weeks instead of twelve.

That apart, my quality of life has improved beyond recognition. It's just a pity it took twenty years.

33 - ROYAL COLLEGE OF PHYSICIANS – SECOND ATTEMPT

Every so often I tried to get a grip on my admin. I never succeeded, but sometimes I'd find emails I'd sent long ago which had been ignored and then I would think, 'I'm not letting them get off that easily.' This is how I came to focus on the Royal College of Physicians.

I had approached the College in 2009, and I now tackled them for the second time in July 2010, writing to the outgoing president, who passed me on to his registrar, Dr Patrick Cadigan. A six-month correspondence followed. My dealings with Dr Cadigan were characterised by suspicion on my side and extraordinary charm and urbanity on his. I achieved little, and can see now how many tricks I missed.

As soon as Dr Cadigan wrote, 'our endocrine adviser comments that, anecdotally, the condition is not seen as commonly as some of the studies might suggest', my heart sank. The old tune again. I summarised the research, told him I knew about Professor Wass's study and suggested that it might be one of those results that buck a much larger trend, an 'outlier' that was statistically inevitable. As for the condition not being commonly seen, I reminded him that the research said that the general after-effects (*sequelae*) of brain injury are so much like the symptoms of hypopituitarism, that PTHP is easily missed – would he discount this possibility? I picked up his word 'anecdotally' and asked why anecdotal evidence was given preference over published research.

Dr Cadigan was too canny to voice an opinion. 'Thank you for these further very interesting comments. I would be going well beyond my own area of expertise if I attempted to deal with the issues you raise.' He said he was anxious that the College did not miss any opportunity to improve the chances of this condition being recognised and would seek advice.

He did duly ask advice – from Professor Wass – and passed on what he said, which was the old news that only one or two cases were found in 50 patients in his own study, which he hadn't published because they weren't sure how common the type of head injury they'd studied was. He didn't think PTHP was common enough to warrant inclusion in the *Clinical Medicine* journal.

I was absolutely sure by now that Professor Wass was the author of the 'new unpublished research' that NICE had used as an excuse to leave their guideline as it was, and whose name had been blacked out among so much else in my Freedom of Information request.

Perhaps this was what distracted me from the obvious retort I could have made. Why didn't I say, 'There are 135,000 serious head injuries a year. If Professor Wass is right and there are two in every fifty that means 5,400 people. Aren't they worth warning?' Also, why didn't I pick up that reference to *Clinical Medicine*? This is the journal of the Royal College of Physicians and now I see, googling, that it seeks, among other things, 'to encourage high standards of medical care by promoting good clinical practice and influencing policy through original research and articles on current issues.' It would have been the ideal vehicle to educate the College's members about PTHP. If I had asked directly, it would have been hard for someone professedly 'anxious that the College did not miss an opportunity' to refuse.

But I missed the chance. In the end all I got was a mention of the topic by the new President Sir Richard Thompson in their monthly e-bulletin. He said hypopituitarism could happen after 20 per cent of brain injuries and be delayed. Usually, he said, there was growth hormone deficiency, with increasing weight, lethargy, and muscle weakness. So far, so good. His next sentence, however, pulled me up short. 'These symptoms sound uncannily like my own, which are probably more related to stress and ageing, but this emphasises how easily this condition can be missed.'

This bluff, humorous vignette, trivialising a condition that could strike young people as well as old, robbing them of their relationships and jobs and driving some of them to suicide appalled me. It gave a double signal: it happens, but don't listen to me, it isn't very important. It was a far cry from the forceful warning I'd like to have seen.

I could not help a muffled protest to Dr Cadigan. There had been no mention of the loss of sex drive or the infertility, I said, yet these were even more common than growth hormone deficiency, which he had mentioned. Was there any way of discreetly filling out Sir Richard's account in the next e-bulletin without offending anybody? Dr Cadigan was emphatic that there wasn't. 'Dear Mrs Lane, Frankly, it would be very difficult to get any more space in the e-bulletin for this issue for quite some time.'

Three years on I am pondering my ineffectuality and trying to analyse it. It was a combination of inexperience and timidity. I was overawed by being given this leisurely, urbane treatment by such an eminent man. How much was his time worth an hour? I always had to fight the feeling that I was being a nuisance. No amount of internal talkings-to of the 'I'm doing this for Christopher!

Hard luck if it uses up their time!' variety ever erased this feeling.

There was also the sense that I had, with him and other medics, that there is a membrane of almost Japanese politeness that must never, ever be torn. Any trouble taken by the other person must be acknowledged effusively. Any disagreement has to be couched in the most tentative and delicate terms, with liberal expressions of gratitude, humility, and flattery. I was focusing anxiously on the intricate steps of the dance, when maybe I should have shouted, 'This isn't a dance' and trampled on everyone's feet.

34 - SEEDS

I spent the rest of 2010 perturbed. At home, I felt divided between my hunger to spend all my time with Jenny and baby Katherine, and my mother-in-law's growing helplessness. We were lucky to find a good carer, but inevitably she would keep alerting us to things that had to be done as Celia deteriorated, and John and I would be kept busy, paying emergency visits alongside our normal ones. It was hard to find time for campaigning.

It was difficult, too, to cope with my suspicions, which had been hardened by Sir Richard's warning in that newsletter. That, plus Dr Kearney's mixed messages, the misinformation from Dr Baldeweg and Dr Murray, NICE's 'porkies', Headway's mysterious suppression of its own research, all made me sure something untoward was going on. Of course any of these things on its own could be explained away – but together? I felt isolated, even slightly mad. Anyone I confided in tended to eye me doubtfully, and would talk soothingly about the reluctance of medics to be lectured to by a layperson and the difficulties of introducing change. One friend was angrily outspoken and told me off for my 'ridiculous conspiracy theories.' I could see how I must appear – elderly, bereaved, no doubt looking for anyone or anything to blame for Chris's death rather than myself.

I'd lived much of my life, up to maybe my mid-thirties, in a state of childlike trust towards anyone in authority. I think this innocence was first disturbed during the Falklands War. The UK media claimed that British bombs had completely destroyed the Port Stanley runway, whereas stories from the other side claimed that they hadn't. Of course I believed 'our' version and thought what liars the Argentinians were – but then after the war I found that out of 21 bombs only one had hit the runway and the damage had been repaired within 24 hours. Once you have been deceived – clearly by a government source – you are wary of believing again. I was shocked too to learn that the *Belgrano* was outside the exclusion zone when it was sunk.

When the BSE crisis began to loom, ten years on in the 1990s, and Professor Richard Lacey, a professor of microbiology who raised the alarm, was branded a self-publicising scaremonger (he even lost his university tenure), I remember thinking, quite early on, that the reaction against him was extreme. Surely someone alerting people to a public danger didn't deserve all this abuse? I suspected that there was some kind of campaign against him, which could only have come from the government or the beef industry. My instincts told me that he was right and John Selwyn Gummer was wrong, and I stopped giving my family beef.

In due course, Professor Lacey was vindicated when young people began to die of vCJD, and from then on I took the view that anyone warning the public about anything, who became a victim of hostile press, was probably right and had to be listened to very carefully.

I needed allies more than you can imagine. I was stressed, not sleeping well, and bothered by a persistent cough. I was still tormented by times when it just seemed impossible that Chris was dead. Sometimes I would catch sight of young men who looked at bit like him and my heart would stop. So now I tried to get in touch with Professor Lacey. I thought he might have good advice or at least reassure me that I was in my right mind. But I had no luck, and I guessed he must be quite elderly by then and had closed himself off from public life for good.

While googling, however, I came across a journalist called Christine Lord, whose son, also a journalist, had died aged 24 of the human form of BSE (vCJD) in 2007, only a year before our Chris's suicide. Before he died, while this poor boy could still speak, he'd said, 'Find out who did this to me, Mum, and expose them' and she'd made that her mission. She had managed to gain enviable coverage – including getting her son's story on to the BBC One programme *Inside Out*, which I found posted on YouTube, showing Andy's final, tortured days. What particularly got to me was when she spoke to camera about how she'd made packed lunches for him when he was a little boy and how she wondered now if she had been giving him the food that killed him. I felt, as her fierce, dark eyes made contact with mine through the computer screen, that she was somebody who would absolutely understand me, as I understood her.

She had a website called Justice4Andy and I reached her through that. Her home address was on some of the documents she had posted so I wrote there too, to be safe.

Her reaction was jumpy. She was particularly spooked by getting my letter in the post, and she quizzed me closely on my motives and how I'd found out about her. I had the impression that she thought I had been briefed to worm myself into her affections and spy on her. Quite early on she told me she'd been threatened over the phone and in person, and although this would have justified her twitchiness, I was doubtful at first. Could such a thing really happen in the UK in this day and age? Yet when I read her more circumstantial account of the threats in her book, *Who killed my Son?*, I did believe her, and still do.

She had found out some highly inconvenient facts and publicised them widely, which was more than enough to provoke a sinister disembodied voice on the telephone to say, 'You're annoying a lot of people, Christine. We'd like you to stop.'

It took a while for her to trust me, but she gave me the reassurance I needed, that I wasn't going mad. I had no need to persuade her that dirty tricks happened.

As time went on, we supported each other. I was able to help her by writing layman-friendly paraphrases of vCJD research for her, and by asking my scientist brother-in-law to find her a mail order gene analysis service which would tell her whether she was in the same vulnerable genetic group that she had been told Andy belonged to – a very reasonable request that had so far been denied.

Christine helped me prepare press releases ('You have to put a lot of emotion in') and introduced me to a journalist colleague, Dominic, who said he'd do a feature on local radio if I could find a patient with hypopituitarism in Hampshire or the Isle of Wight.

In spite of trying very hard to find someone suitable, I failed and was despondent, but I was grateful for my friendship with Christine.

That disappointment was followed by what seemed another dead end.

Every year since way back, my sister-in-law Margaret and I have gone to the Winchester Writers' Festival. It falls at the end of June and is nearly always a hot day, and between lectures we sit basking on grass slopes, catching up on our lives and fantasising about literary fame. We have each had some success with short stories, so it gives us a pleasant buzz of hope when delegates stand up during the opening session and say, 'Last year I was a struggling nobody, but thanks to the Winchester festival I now have

an agent, a published book, and two more in the pipeline.'
(Though now I think, be careful what you wish for.)

We generally go to the same sessions, companionably, and in 2010 we chose one by author and broadcaster Jane Wenham-Jones. Her lecture was a delight, delivered in a friendly, funny way and it made us feel as if we could ask her anything. So I asked her how to publicise PTHP.

Her reply had the spot-on promptness of Wellington saying, 'Sparrow-hawks Ma'am!' to Queen Victoria when the pigeons were defacing Crystal Palace. She said, 'Get it into a soap!'

She suggested *Eastenders* which had a head injury story coming up, so I looked up who the scriptwriters were and found some literary agencies that handled their work. Gillian Richmond looked prolific and successful so I decided to approach her through one of these agencies. I spoke to a lovely human man who sounded very sorry about Chris and said he would pass an email from me on to her. I said I'd wait for a refusal before I asked another scriptwriter (I thought they'd be cross with me if two people ended up duplicating the story) and this prompted a kind reply from him saying no, go ahead and write to the others, there was no guarantee that Gillian would do anything, and if she did, the script might not be used, 'Whether or not those screenwriters are, ultimately, willing or able to cover the subject,' he said, 'at the very, very least, people like me will hear the story. And that's something.'

I liked the 'very, very least,' it seemed to come from strong feeling.

But the months went by, and the year ended with no word. Never mind, I thought, it wasn't as though I'd really expected anything. You win some, you lose some. I thought of trying again with a different agency but I was too tired.

Sometime during that winter I looked up the health statistics website to get the 2009-2010 figures for hypopituitarism. There had been 2,032 diagnosed cases, up from 1,941 the previous year. At least that was better than the numbers going down, but when, oh when, would the number reflect the reality of incidence?

Celia had gone downhill badly over the year and didn't seem likely to survive much longer. My sister-in-law, Margaret, came regularly up from Chandler's Ford to visit, and we used to feel so depressed after spending time with her – seeing her such a shadow of the jolly, active person she used to be – that we would make a point of having a cup of tea and a nice piece of cake to cheer ourselves up. My campaign was hardly happening. I felt as if I was being extinguished, and I could hardly believe that I would ever reach and save my imaginary young man with PTHP. However, it's often in those times when you feel you are getting nowhere, that you are planting seeds for the future.

35 - THE TEST THAT DOESN'T

January 2011 was a depressing month. For one thing, Celia died. I remember us all, black figures shivering in the churchyard in the bleak winter wind at her funeral. I thought how sad her last years had been, blighted by Chris's death and by everyone's grief, and how good and patient she had been enduring her increasingly awful physical symptoms. But I must, in honesty, admit that her death was a relief to me, and I think even to John.

It was a tiring month too. Jenny went back to work and I began to childmind Katherine. I had urgently wanted to do this and am very glad I did, because it laid the foundation for a close, special relationship with her which I don't think I could have achieved in any other way. I looked after Katherine one week on, one week off, alternating with her other granny, who didn't want her to go to a nursery either. I was supported by Linda, a neighbour of Celia's who had been one of the people who had cared for her in her decline. Linda is a kind, practical, tactful person, a devout Catholic, and we couldn't have managed without her. Even so, I found it was a long day, starting at around 7 a.m. and continuing until Jenny got home, sometimes as late as 8 p.m. Of course, every other week was nominally free, but I felt guilty about my co-granny, who couldn't drive and wasn't very mobile, and I would call most days and take Katherine out to a toddler group.

There were times when I'd sit up late at the computer, too tired to do anything constructive, too dazed to switch off and go to bed, aimlessly googling. I was filled with what I can only describe as a hollow, aching, sucking feeling, as if I were a baby chomping uselessly on a dry nipple. I wanted something from the internet which I couldn't get, which it wouldn't give me.

Sometimes I googled 'Chris Lane' – just to see if I could retrieve some little bit of him that I hadn't known about. But there are a lot of Chris Lanes and the only entries about the right one were what I'd put there myself. Just reading his dear, familiar name left me hopelessly miserable. More often I googled the word 'hypopituitarism'.

Wasted time, most of it, and a sure way to a sleepless night afterwards. Yet one evening in February I was arrested by a story on an ME website. I sat forward, suddenly awake again.

The story was that of a Mrs Christine Wrightson. She described how she had suffered from rheumatoid arthritis for over 30 years, and then, in 2005, had a virus that wouldn't clear up. At first she had a sore throat and felt as if she had flu. Then her symptoms escalated to include severe fatigue, vertigo, tinnitus, blurred vision, vomiting, feeling faint, palpitations, poor circulation, and hot sweats. 'I felt at times that I was going to die.'

After private appointments with several consultants, a cardiologist thought her erratic blood pressure could have a hormonal cause and advised her to see an endocrinologist. This endocrinologist arranged a test which he said would reveal if she was lacking in either of two pituitary hormones, cortisol and growth hormone (see chapter 10).

She was told the result was normal and that she didn't have a pituitary problem. Back home she got worse and worse until she was surprised she was still alive.

A saliva test carried out privately in January 2007 showed her 'adrenals were at exhaustion stage, pointing to a pituitary problem.' She decided to complain to the hospital about the test she'd been given – the short synacthen test which mimicked the action of the pituitary gland. It stimulated the adrenal glands with ACTH, and showed whether they produced cortisol in response, i.e. were working normally. The test could show up faulty adrenals, but told you little or nothing about the pituitary itself.

This distinction reminded me of times when an electric appliance such as a kettle fails. When it stops working there's no way of telling if the problem is in the kettle itself or the plug. The only way to check is to replace the plug with one which you know is OK. If it works, it's obvious that the kettle is fine and the problem is in the socket. If there is still no action, then the problem is in the kettle. Clearly in Christine's case, the kettle was fine, and the next stage of investigation should have been to look into whether the electricity was getting through. But the endocrinologist had not done this.

The hospital would not accept Christine's private saliva test results.

After another specialist told her she had a pituitary problem she complained to the hospital again, and was ignored once more. Meanwhile she was growing more and more ill. 'I became toxic, everything I ate tasted like poison and the only thing I could tolerate was rice pudding.'

She told her consultant she thought she was going to die. He asked if she could travel – possibly, she said, if she could lie down – and he referred her to another consultant privately. She had to make many 90-mile round trips, which she bore, encouraging herself with the thought that she was helping others as well as herself. Finally, in the spring of 2008, she was given a more appropriate test, which lowers blood sugar, stressing the body, and would normally make it produce extra cortisol and growth hormone to cope. If it doesn't, it shows that the pituitary is not working. This test is called the glucagon stimulation test.

Christine's result showed she had severe growth hormone deficiency and low cortisol – in other words she had been right all along. Her diagnosis had taken three years, courtesy of the woefully inadequate short synacthen test. In August 2008 (the month Chris died) she started on hormone replacement. I was sad, though, to read, 'the consultant has said that my body has been deprived of the hormones for so long it could take years to restore full health again.'

Christine took her complaint to the Healthcare Commission and the Health Ombudsman but was turned down, and she continued to campaign, ill as she was, lobbying 1,400 MPs and members of the House of Lords, and writing to the Strategic Health Authorities (as they were then) and the Society for Endocrinologists. Three of the SHAs agreed with her consultant that the short synacthen test could not be relied upon, as did the Society for Endocrinologists. She ended by addressing ME sufferers with the words, 'I put my heart & soul into my story. I wrote it to help you. I think of you all each & every day now & forever.'

Well, I thought, leaning back stiffly from my computer screen at last. If you don't want to find something, there's nothing like using the wrong test!

The website put me in touch with Christine. She had a deep, hoarse voice with a strong Yorkshire accent, which of course I liked, being from Yorkshire myself. She sent me printouts of articles about her in the local press, and a copy of an all-important letter from the Society for Endocrinologists, which can be seen on my website. Sometimes she would ring me on my mobile while I was out shopping and I would stand transfixed, feeling as if I was being told secrets by Deep Throat. She had a firm belief that ME patients were being deliberately kept ill, though she could not say why. This reminded me that I had never received a reply from the Royal College of General Practitioners to my letter about PTHP signed by 30 consultants, despite more than one reminder from me.

I only knew Christine for a few months, but she left a deep impression on me. She was in her sixties, and not computer-literate, yet she achieved so much – articles about her illness in the local papers, her story on the website, all those letters to MPs and Lords. In a way, she was the most important contact I ever made, not just because she alerted me to the short synacthen test, but because through her I began to glean the answer to the question that had perplexed me from the beginning. I had known from the research that there must be thousands of PTHP sufferers ... but my question had always been, where were they all?

Christine was the gateway through which, one by one, these hitherto invisible people appeared, bringing with them their own horrific stories, and the stories of others. There was Jill Mizen, Christine's friend and fellow-victim of the short synacthen test, who was knocked out as a toddler when she fell from a roundabout. She was diagnosed with cortisol and growth hormone deficiency after 28 years of illness, and she became my own friend. I wrote about her and Christine in an article for the *Mail on Sunday*. Through her I met Eddie Barker who suffered three head injuries between 1972 and 2003 yet wasn't diagnosed with hypopituitarism until the summer of 2008, strangely – again – around the time of Chris's death. Then there was Amy (ill for ten years), Danny (ill for 20 years), Kenneth (ill for 40 years). All of them had been told their problems were psychological. All of them had pituitary damage.

To go back to that night when I first read Christine's story, I spent the next few days checking the research about the short synacthen test (SST). The literature confirmed that this test mimicked the action of the pituitary by stimulating the adrenals with synthetic ACTH, just as Christine had claimed, and I also found that in the 1980s there had been sufficient concern about its reliability for diagnosing secondary adrenal insufficiency (that is, of pituitary origin) to prompt the development of a different version of the test – the low-dose short synacthen test. However, it was not until later that I discovered the crucial paper – the 2003 Dorin review. For this review, three decades of research on diagnosing adrenal insufficiency was trawled through in the MEDLINE database, and its conclusion was that when the patient had *secondary* adrenal insufficiency, the test – even the marginally more accurate low-dose version – missed two people in every five.

If the short synacthen test only gave information about the adrenal glands themselves, I was puzzled as to how it could detect *any* cases of pituitary-induced hypoadrenalism, let alone three fifths of them. I wrote to a kindly consultant for help. He explained that if the adrenal glands hadn't been stimulated for a while, they responded poorly to synacthen, so the test could give information about the pituitary. 'Whether it is the best test I doubt as the insulin test seems the best.'

I spent ages trying to work out what the point of giving

the short synacthen test could be. I could understand an inexpensive test being used to whittle down the number of people you had to give an expensive test to – a sort of preliminary winnowing process – but you couldn't use the SST in that way. You would miss 40 per cent of pituitary-induced hypoadrenalism cases. So what was happening? You were giving a cheap test to people, who, if they failed it (it seemed to me) would have to have the expensive test anyway. So you ended up spending more, not less. It was nonsensical to me. Three years later, in May 2013, Professor Peter Snyder at the University of Pennsylvania wrote in an email to me, 'A Synacthen test is never helpful, so it should never be performed.' Carol Smith, one of the people that Christine's 'thread' led me to, says in her forthright way, 'I have never known anyone fail it.'

The other issue that disturbed me, even more deeply than the uselessness of the test, was the failure of the NHS complaints system. I was given a fuller account of this by Jill, who'd been a victim of it herself, and in fact collaborated in the version which is posted on line. Here was a complainant (Christine) who'd been misdiagnosed on the basis of a test which had been shown by a review of 30 years'-worth of research to be inadequate, who'd suffered dreadful symptoms unnecessarily for more than two years, and who'd finally been shown conclusively to have the illness that the dubious test had wrongly excluded. How could anyone not uphold her complaint? Yet the hospital rebuffed her with the following mad logic:

> 'This [the SST] is a definitive test used for investigating adrenal failure and these results excluded the possibility of a pituitary abnormality causing your adrenal insufficiency.'

Any normal person's reaction would be to ask how, if this test claimed to prove that she hadn't got an illness when she had, could it be definitive?

When Christine went higher and appealed to the Healthcare Commission, they cited advice from a consultant endocrinologist which (if it has been quoted correctly) I find unintelligible:

> 'That the short synacthen test, which is used for Addison's disease, is the standard test for adrenal insufficiency widely known by trained endo-crinologists in the UK would, to the best of his knowledge, not agree that your test was *unequivocally normal.*'

Quite apart from the difficulty of parsing this sentence, there is the strangeness that if you *don't* agree that something is unequivocally normal, then you're saying it's abnormal. Whatever, it was enough to make the HCC reject Christine's complaint.

When she finally appealed to the Health Ombudsman, she asked under the Freedom of Information Act for the name of the clinical adviser who had made this curious statement. Christine was permitted to know his qualifications, which were MD, FRCP (Retired Consultant Physician & Endocrinologist), but not his name. To impart this, they said, would cause 'an unwarrantable invasion of their privacy.'

36 - APPROACHES OUT OF THE BLUE

If you are walking along a country footpath and strangers keep coming up to you and telling you politely that the footpath is boring and doesn't lead anywhere, you begin to wonder whether it does. Every so often I would get unsolicited emails from consultants, telling me that PTHP was a small problem, and that everything was in hand. I have already mentioned Dr Murray's early letter of 2009 with the unsubstantiated 10 per cent figure.

In March 2011 – a bitter spring when the white blossom in our garden hung as still as if it was printed on a page – I was unexpectedly forwarded a study via the Society for British Neurological Surgeons, which Mr Peter Hutchinson, Consultant Neurosurgeon at Addenbrooke's Hospital in Cambridge, had thought I 'would find of interest.' It included 84 brain-injured patients and found that only 12 per cent of them had PTHP. When I looked carefully at the abstract it seemed to me that this low figure could be partly explained by the use of the short synacthen test (SST) to check out five patients who had low early morning cortisol. After reading Christine's story I had no trust in the SST. My email and reminders to Mr Hutchinson querying the use of the test were ignored, but after much pressing I eventually received in reply a group letter from his colleagues.

They said that overall the SST was good at assessing whether the pituitary was working. 'We have experience with many hundreds of patients […] using a SST and are very comfortable in interpreting the data.' They used the synacthen test at six months after injury to check cortisol. At twelve months they used the glucagon test to check growth hormone and cortisol. Good, I thought, because the glucagon test was the good test that eventually diagnosed Christine. I did not take in the significance of the next sentence:

'However the glucagon test can give false negative results so if there is an abnormal result then we would use a second test usually an SST to assess adrenal reserve.'

They ended by reminding me that pituitary problems that showed shortly after injury could improve over time and claimed that a normal test after a year suggested that the patient was all right.

What really strikes me now is the enormity of the sentence about the glucagon test. They were saying that, if the glucagon test suggested there was something wrong, and the SST was normal, they would ignore the glucagon test result as a 'false negative'. The idea of using the unreliable SST as a back-up test for the far more reliable glucagon test is laughable – it's like asking Pinocchio if George Washington has told the truth. Finally, by saying that a normal test at 12 months suggested there was no damage, they were ignoring all the papers that had warned that the condition could show itself many years later (those same papers that I had quoted to Dr Baldeweg so soon after Chris's death.)

Another unsolicited approach came in 2012, when Dr Dominic Heaney, a consultant neurologist at University College Hospital, London (coincidentally, where Dr Baldeweg works), wrote that though he took pituitary damage after brain injury seriously, he hadn't found any cases out of 25 head injuries, and his colleagues were in agreement.

I wrote back conceding that there were some studies suggesting PTHP was uncommon (I actually quoted van der Eerden, one of those negative papers cited so extensively by NICE and their ilk), but saying I couldn't see how all those systematic reviews could be wrong. I added that some of the tests used weren't reliable, e.g. the short synacthen test and IGF-1 levels (I did not know what IGF-1 levels were but I knew they were normal in most people with hypopituitarism!), and asked him which tests he used. He did not answer that question.

When I sent him another study that found PTHP in more than a fifth of over 200 patients across five centres he proceeded, rather to my surprise (because I had randomly sent it as one example out of many), to rubbish the paper. First he said that it wasn't in a reputable journal, then that the pituitary deficiencies could be due not just to head injury, but alcohol, anti-depressants, and seizures, and that the author (Christian Berg) didn't have a 'control' group, a similarly ill population of individuals who have suffered, for example, stroke, depression, or chronic epilepsy, but no head injury, which was 'a big problem for his work.'

I said surely all those other factors were present in head injury patients everywhere ('Don't your own patients suffer depression, drink too much and have seizures?'), so he too ought to be finding a high incidence of pituitary problems, either as a primary or secondary phenomenon. But I understood him to say that he wasn't … so it must be the tests.

He said Berg's tests were too sensitive and would show pituitary deficiencies which didn't matter as the patient had no symptoms.

I asked him repeatedly to tell me what tests he used, joking that I would find an article in a *reputable* journal that would support the tests used in the literature and show they were not oversensitive. He did not reply.

The blossom was falling and the days were getting warmer. I moved on.

37 - ELATION

A couple of months earlier, in February 2011, I had learned that Christopher's medical condition would be used in an episode of *Holby City*. I literally felt an overall tingling glow when I read this. Wow! This would spread the news to millions of people. Could it be that an exchange of five emails the previous July could have had such a fantastic effect? I looked up the scheduled date for Episode 31 and saw it was due out on 17 May. Would something happen to stop this? Would it be scrapped? I hardly dared tell people in case something went wrong, and I hugged the news to my chest for several weeks.

It was easy to distract myself because I had a looming challenge. I had to give a talk at the Child Brain Injury Trust (CBIT) conference on 24 March. I'd had a baptism as a public speaker the previous autumn at the UK Acquired Brain Injury Forum conference, thanks to Professor Barnes, but this in no way lessened my terror. A kind neighbour, a drama teacher, gave me some coaching ('not so fast! Give them time to take it in!'), and I spent a long time assembling my slides and writing my speech. Everyone said, 'Speak from cards, not a script', but I didn't dare. I dreaded being left wordless and paralysed. I nearly missed the conference altogether, only discovering by chance that I'd made a mistake about the day, and rushing off suddenly, arriving late for the pre-conference dinner.

Lisa Turan, CBIT's chief executive officer had earlier got the charity's medical committee to write a factsheet about PTHP and, as a very sensitive gesture, dedicated it to 'Christopher Mark Lane, 25/9/76 – 26/8/2008.' And now she'd invited me to speak.

I felt nervous as I took my place on the platform in front of the sea of faces, but as my neighbour Jenny had predicted, I soon got involved in what I was saying. I could not help my voice breaking as I spoke about Chris's death but recovered and went on. The speaker before me had spoken about the amygdala, the emotional part of the brain that responds to movement and sensory stimulation, and makes people act impulsively if their damaged frontal lobes can't exert control. He said, 'This is why I am pacing up and down while I talk to you, because it makes your amygdalas pay attention.'

Hearing his talk had given me an idea, and before I mounted the stage I did a brave thing. I got myself wired up with a portable microphone. Then, just before the end of my talk I said, 'And now, for the sake of your amygdalas…' and left the lectern to stand centre stage. I got a laugh, and felt I had everyone's attention as I talked about the 'silence' I had found in the NICE guideline and other websites:

> 'After two years of it, I no longer believe this silence is an accident, just waiting for someone like me to come along and notice and tell everybody. I think there is an active reluctance to encourage the diagnosis of a condition which is so expensive to treat and affects so many people…'

I ended by asking the audience to google PTHP, and if they were convinced, to push for screening every head-injured child and to be on the watch for failure to grow, weight gain, fatigue, and depression, and to be aware that there could be hidden sexual and fertility difficulties later. 'These are not nice things to have to tell a parent, but of course we wish someone had told us.' And then I thanked everyone for listening and sat down.

I got a huge, long round of applause.

But fate is always ready to knock you off your perch. I remembered that in my pre-talk agitation I had left all my belongings in my hotel room and would get charged another night, and had to grovel to reception with an embarrassing sob story. But the hotel staff were kind and let me off.

On the train home an elderly lady sitting next to me saw my conference folder and asked me about it. Of course I told her Chris's story. She said, 'I had a head injury too.' She pointed to a deep dent in her forehead. She said, 'I never had children, though I wanted them. Perhaps I know why, now.'

It must have been terrible for her to be told of such an upsetting possibility so abruptly, from a stranger, and be left alone to digest it. But I could do nothing. We got off at Euston station and went our separate ways.

38 - GULF WAR SYNDROME

In the audience at the conference there had been a solicitor from Fenton's, and my remarks about intentional silence made him advise me to talk to his colleague Mark McGhee.

I hadn't looked up Mark beforehand, so I didn't know about his success in getting a disability pension for a Gulf War veteran in 2005 – a landmark decision because the Ministry of Defence had long been stoutly denying the existence of Gulf War syndrome. This meant that when he told me, 'Yes, there is a conspiracy. I was involved with Gulf War Syndrome. That was hypopituitarism too,' my ears failed to decode 'Gulf War', which can come out as a rather indistinct guffawing sound, and I sat staring at him blankly, too overawed to ask him to repeat himself. I must have seemed very dumb. I was mesmerized by that word 'conspiracy' that he came right out with, so firmly and easily, a word which I had tended to avoid using, even in my thoughts. I was pleased that he said it, though. I thought that would be one in the eye for my sceptical friends.

Looking at the correspondence I see that the purpose of my meeting Mark was to discuss my attempts to amend the NICE guidance, but I don't know if I even took this in at the time, or if I talked sensibly to Mark about NICE. Later – three years later – I was to wish sharply that I had engaged properly with him, as he would have been an answer to my prayer.

As for whether Mark was right about the pituitary

aspects of Gulf War Syndrome, it would need a lot of reading to be sure, but I found an interesting entry on the British Gulf War Syndrome page on Facebook, a page set up by veterans for their comrades with the object of telling them about important medical tests they should take. I noticed a complaint on the forum about difficulty in persuading doctors to authorise the recommended 'Gold Standard Insulin Stress Test'. 'This is, of course, one of the most reliable tests available for diagnosing growth hormone and cortisol deficiency, which as readers will know by now are common effects of pituitary damage. Googling brought up evidence that the vaccinations given to the veterans caused this deficiency.

39 - HOLBY CITY

As May drew nearer, and with it the airing of 'my' *Holby City* episode, I became more and more on edge. I needed to use the opportunity for publicity, but suppose the episode was dropped, or the date was wrong? Would I lose credibility and would that spoil future media chances? But it was no good dithering; if I dithered there would be no chance of coverage. So I told the Pituitary Foundation (supportive again, since Kit's departure) and my local newspaper, and then, when Jon Danzig, with whom I'd made that joint complaint to the Charities Commission (being a good friend even though he felt rotten at that time) said, 'Think big, Joanna!' I tried the *Sun*, BBC Radio London, and *BBC Breakfast*. Helen Carroll covered the story with a little paragraph in the *Sun* headed 'HOLBY PAIN' in the centre of the centrefold, which was fantastic as the circulation is seven million. I got three minutes on BBC Radio London, which I wasted by babbling about my sister instead of PTHP's symptoms and other vital facts. However, best of all, it seemed, I got the offer to appear on *BBC Breakfast* the day the episode was aired.

My stomach quaked at the thought, and I was terrified that I would be so nervous that anything I said would be unintelligible. But I couldn't not do it, I had to face it like a man ... which meant I had my hair done, fretted about clothes, and made little lists to myself of the facts I *had* to get in. *BBC Breakfast* told me they had ordered a car to pick me up the next morning.

But at 3 p.m. the day before, I had a call to say they'd pulled it. Apparently they needed either the executive producer, the main storyline editor, or the series producer of *Holby City* to appear with me, and one of them had chicken pox, one of them was on holiday in Wales, and one was somewhere else far away. 'Your voice will be heard in the end,' crooned the man who gave me this bad news, 'just not this time.'

This was disappointing, but even more so was the matter of support phonelines. I hadn't thought about the need to display phone numbers after the programme for anyone affected by the issues to ring, but a friend nudged me to ask. I couldn't communicate with the series producer, Myar Craig-Brown, directly, and had to go through the publicity agency. It is common after a programme that raises an issue that may affect viewers to display phone numbers of helplines, so I was amazed when I was refused. I asked three times, and each time was met with excuses. They said the BBC wasn't allowed to endorse charities. When I pointed out that they sometimes do, with a disclaimer, the agency said they only did that for factual programmes – again untrue, because *Waterloo Road* and *Eastenders* regularly displayed links to relevant charities. I was finally given a flat refusal with no reason: 'The producer's said no and there's nothing I can do.'

However, the PTHP storyline was excellent. I wrote in my blog:

'In my campaign I've mostly concentrated on getting the facts out there, but Gillian Richmond's script communicated the emotional things – the young man's despair, his girlfriend's feelings, their joy when they heard treatment was possible. It was beautifully done ... a metaphor came to me. When someone loses, say, an arm and suffers pain in the phantom limb, you can cure the pain by placing a mirror so that the reflection of the good arm gives the illusion that both arms are there, and then the subject is encouraged to do exercises. Somehow, seeing a young man who had just a bit of a look of our son, lying on the bed and being told good news, which is so much what I wish could have happened to Chris, eased something inside me.'

By an odd coincidence, the day before the broadcast I was reading *Empty Cradles*, social worker Margaret Humphreys' account of how she uncovered the huge scandal when British children were shipped to Australia to boost the population there, often being told, untruly, that their parents were dead, and then used as slave labour or sexually abused. A dramatisation was made, very shocking and moving apparently, called *The Leaving of Liverpool*. Strangely, the BBC sat on the programme for a year, and then refused to do publicity for it, saying there was no funding for that or for helplines. Helplines, in Margaret's view (later shown to be correct), were vital because a lot of traumatized people would be watching. When Margaret herself organised publicity and found funding for helplines, the BBC said they wouldn't display the numbers because it 'wasn't necessary'. It was only after questions were asked in the House of Commons, with two MPs demanding an inquiry into the BBC's refusal, that they finally caved in.

In Margaret Humphreys' case the only explanation I can think of is that Whitehall was exerting pressure, possibly because the scandal of the so-called orphans might lay the government open to over a 100,000 crippling compensation claims. Could it be that awareness of PTHP might similarly open the way to thousands of compensation claims?

Whatever the reason, I had now worked up a good head of anger that propelled me into making a sustained fuss about the absence of helplines. I had to send my letter of complaint to Myar Craig-Brown more than once, copying in an increasing number of important people, before I had a reply about a month after the broadcast. It said, 'We cover a range of issues every week in *Holby City*, and although we occasionally give the number of a BBC Action Line at the end of an episode, we don't have the space to do this every time we air an issue. The character with pituitary damage featured in a relatively small guest story that wasn't the focus of the episode, so we didn't feel it was necessary to offer an Action Line at the end of the episode.'

I wrote a mild, sweet reply asking to be referred to the BBC's Action Line person, copying in both the Pituitary Foundation and Headway. The format of the Action Line site is a page listing recent programmes with the issues raised, plus a page with an alphabetical list of issues and links to relevant helplines such as sexual abuse, domestic violence, and rape. Clearly they could retrospectively put something in there. They refused, but suggested I contact their health website representative who agreed to include the information I suggested. The website stayed up for a couple of years but was then taken down on the grounds that they were duplicating other health websites.

Raising awareness is like writing on sand. The tide comes in regularly and you have to write it all over again.

40 - THE SHINY SWORD

Seeds planted long ago do sprout sometimes.

In early 2009, when advice was still raining in on me from all sides, I had followed up a suggestion to write to the Army, shortly after the scandal over Snatch Land Rovers. These were combat vehicles, designed for use in Northern Ireland rather than Iraq or Afghanistan, which offered scant protection from landmine blasts and were notoriously called 'mobile coffins', yet soldiers were using them in desert terrain because they were given nothing better. There were many needless deaths. I wrote to Lieutenant Colonel John Etherington, Clinical Director at Headley Court Rehab Centre, attaching my list of research papers, and adding sympathetically that I had been shocked by the scandal and hoped that, at the very least, head injured soldiers could receive proper treatment afterwards.

He replied in June the following year. I have the letter in front of me now, headed with its symbol of a jewelled crown presiding over an eagle with spread wings against crossed swords and an anchor. It is one of the few letters I have had from state organisations which make me feel good. Anything on cream paper with a portcullis on top, for example, triggers queasiness. It was a human, straightforward letter. He said '[we are aware] of these potential complications, but I appreciate your concerns and I will pass this on to the neuro rehabilitation team at DMRC so that they can review their policies […] Thank you for your consideration regarding wounded and injured service personnel.'

It was clear that I wasn't telling them anything new, so I do not know if my information had any direct effect. However, I have a sneaky hope that it did something, because in July 2011 I discovered through an FOI request that an army hospital in Surrey was screening all head injury patients routinely for PTHP, and later still I learned that this practice had been extended to Queen Elizabeth Hospital in Birmingham, which is the first port of call for the wounded.

This was great news. It also put into my hand what I hoped would be a nice, sharp sword, as shiny as the ones adorning Colonel Etherington's letter. I could now ask, 'Why are soldiers *screened*, when civilians aren't even *warned*?' Surely nobody could wriggle out of that one.

I told my MP (Richard Ottaway, now Sir) about my FOI request, remarking that the news about screening soldiers was excellent, bearing in mind we were talking about a condition that could lead to suicide, and which was treatable. I asked him:

'Why is there this disparity between how we treat our soldiers and our civilians?

Secondly, if the disparity is not considered acceptable, what is being done to address it?

I am beginning to wonder if a question in the House might not be the way forward. What do you think?'

Unfortunately, this was far from the killer weapon I had dreamed of.

I first wrote on 8 July. He asked to see a copy of my FOI response, which I sent. Then he wrote to the MOD for confirmation and sent me a copy of their reply. That done, he seemed to feel he had fulfilled his duty.

It was now mid-August. I had to crank the wheels into motion again. 'Now that we have established this fact [that soldiers were being screened] may I refer you back to my email of 8th July…?'

I waited a month, and then in mid-September sent a reminder. This was the third time I had written the identical words about disparities and anomalies.

By 2 October I had still had no reply and had to prompt him.

In November, Richard Ottaway forwarded me a reply from Earl Howe, the Minister responsible for quality at the Department of Health, which was in no way worth the long wait. The old standby reply about NICE's independence was trotted out once more. NICE seems to have been set up like this precisely so that the government can stonewall protest in this way.

The letter said screening was expensive and the military should have priority. I had not asked for screening. He did not explain why *warning* patients, which was what I was asking for, was expensive. He told me that the NICE head injury guideline was due to be updated soon anyway, which I knew, but I also knew that they had said they would not include PTHP in it.

I replied via Richard Ottaway answering these points, and meanwhile kept gently prodding him to ask a question in the House of Commons. Nothing happened until a chance conversation with a friend triggered a sequence of events that ended in the most useful outcome I have ever had from the Parliamentary process.

My friend remarked that Tony Blair's former adviser Alastair Campbell had recently been doing a lot of campaigning on issues such as mental health and depression, and so she suggested writing to him.

The events of the Iraq War meant I didn't feel kindly towards him. However, I thought 'Well, I'll try anything' and wrote to him. The young football manager Gary Speed had just committed suicide, and I knew that he'd had a head injury in 2004, and also that repetitive concussion could cause hypopituitarism, so I brought that in too. This was early December.

To my amazement Alastair wrote back within the hour!

'Thanks for getting in touch. This is not something I was aware of. All I can recommend is that following Gary Speed's death, without in any way prejudging what may have happened, you seek to step up your campaigning activities. You clearly know what you are talking about and present your arguments very well, so just keep going. Send something similar to members of the health select committee and to the Parliamentary mental health group. It is frustrating when people don't reply but you just have to keep on keeping on.

I'm sorry I can't get more directly involved but I am at the outer end of my limits on time and commitments at the moment.'

The phrase 'keep on keeping on' arrested me sharply. It took me back to Chris's hospital bed when he'd had his accident as a little boy. I used to hold his hand and say, over and over again as he lay there unconscious, 'Just keep on keeping on my darling, keep on keeping on.'

I did everything Alastair said, researching each individual member of the health select committee and the mental health all-party Parliamentary group (MHAPPG), and trying to find a 'hook' for each one on which I could hang my letter. This was my equivalent of saying, 'Yes you! The man in the brown hat in the back row!' which I hoped would save my letter from being dismissed as a circular. If they were doctors, as I discovered both Sarah Wollaston MP and Dan Poulter MP had been, I used that. If their careers showed a particular concern for young people, I emphasised that most head injuries happen to people under 24. If they had children themselves, I said that as a parent I was sure they would understand what we had gone through when Chris died. And so on. My research turned up interesting items.

For example, I found a startling cross-connection between the two committees. Dan Poulter (Health Select Committee) had saved the life of Guy Opperman (of the Parliamentary Group) by recognising that Guy's headache and nausea might be brain tumour symptoms – as in fact they were – and insisting he went to hospital by ambulance. I discovered too that Dame Anne Begg (of the same group) had been a wheelchair user since 1984 with a degenerative disease, and was still managing, despite being in constant pain, to have a busy and successful career as MP for Aberdeen South. I felt she might be sympathetic and in fact we did maintain a correspondence about PTHP for a while, during which she gave me helpful strategic advice, besides writing to the Scottish Health Minister for me.

But the real star, with whom I had nothing in common except motherhood, was Valerie Vaz, Labour MP for Walsall South. I had hardly posted my letter to her – which I did in early January 2012 – when she swung into action. By the end of that month she had written to the Department of Health, to the Chairman of the Football Association David Bernstein, and asked six written questions in the House (all of which received fob-offs).

And on 27 February she tabled an Early Day Motion (EDM) about PTHP. A good result.

Interestingly, after I had written to the Health Select Committee, my MP, Richard Ottaway, showed signs of life at last. He wrote in January inviting me to make an appointment. I saw him in early February, and he followed this up by asking two written questions of his own in the House, one on 28 February and one on 12 March. He even expressed dissatisfaction with the answer to his first written question and wrote, off his own bat, to Paul Burstow, then Minister of State in the Department of Health.

However, when I ask myself what came of all this activity, the answer is, very little. The baseline is that 32 more people now know about the risk, who possibly didn't before, and you never know, that information may prove vital to them personally one day. A second consequence was that the Early Day Motion gives me credibility when I email new people. At least it shows that PTHP is a real enough issue for seven MPs to sponsor the motion and twenty-three to sign, though I've read that only an EDM signed by more than 200 people has any influence; the rest tend to be dismissed as 'parliamentary graffiti'. And thirdly, it is an official record, a marker that can be pointed to later ('As long ago as 2012 this issue was raised, and now, ten years later, nothing has been done').

Other than in these tenuous ways I did not feel much had moved forward. The letters I received from the Earl Howe and Paul Burstow, and the answers to the written questions, were so much useless verbiage.

The letter from Paul Burstow in April is the only direct answer I ever had to my question about disparity. He said that PTHP was rare, and severe head injuries happened more often in the army, and this justified not extending routine screening and advice to the NHS.

Nothing he said was true or to the point. PTHP of course is not rare – only its diagnosis is. Soldiers may suffer a higher *percentage* of head injuries, but in actual numbers the head injuries suffered by civilians are many, many times more. I wrote back that the government had consistently failed to address the right of this large section of the population to be told that they were at risk. I said that the decision to warn or not to warn should not be a local one (as he'd claimed), as it would clearly be most unfair for one postcode to be given life-saving information and not another. I challenged him to explain the rationale behind this denial of a basic right to so many people.

I received no reply.

The government is impervious both to fact and to reason. If you write telling them that they need to act, for a reason as obvious as that an elephant is not a kangaroo, they will still reply that regrettably, until it has been definitively proved that an elephant is not a kangaroo, they can do nothing. Their replies will be polite, lengthy, and boring. In fact the politeness, length, and tedium will vary inversely with the simplicity of the message, which is 'We are bigger than you, and we'll do what we want.'

The only language they understand is massive negative publicity, which is hard to arrange, because the verbiage gets in the way. My experience over these past six years has taught me that as an instrument of stealthy oppression, dense parliament-speak can hardly be beaten. It's hard for the injured party to get help because other people have to read a host of mind-numbing screeds before they can even understand what's happening. I wonder how many appalling miscarriages of justice have trotted through like armadillos, nose to the ground, protected from public awareness by an impenetrable carapace of words?

My brief encounter with Alastair Campbell came into its own later. In my thank you email at the time I said, 'If I am still hammering at doors in a couple of years' time, I would like to think, with your permission, that I could contact you again?' He didn't answer, but I did contact him again, later that year in September, and again was to receive real help.

41 - 'YOU WERE BRAVE'

When I made my next foray into the brain injury world in July 2011, the same month as the good news from the Army came, I felt that people were starting to take notice of PTHP.

I was lucky to get a place at a seminar held at a brain injury rehabilitation centre in Northamptonshire, a beautiful building set in peaceful green grounds, where I imagined anyone with a brain injury might feel soothed and safe. Among the speakers was Dr David Henderson-Slater a consultant in Disability Medicine at the Nuffield Orthopaedic Centre, along with Professor Derick Wade and Professor John Wass.

Dr Henderson-Slater's talk was energetic, clear, and well delivered. I was heartened to hear him mentioning pituitary problems early on.

But only for a moment. Pointing to a slide of a comically overweight Hell's Angel in leather gear and studs, he said, as I recall, 'You can see this chap is on the porky side, and that brings me to a possible consequence of brain injury – hypopituitarism. My own findings suggest this is rare, though I believe there is a dubious Turkish study that suggests a 30 per cent occurrence...' and he moved swiftly on.

I could hardly believe it. I seethed silently until question time and then could not help leaping to my feet, neck throbbing, beginning politely enough with, 'I was interested that you mentioned hypopituitarism' (that bothersome word, so hard to pronounce), but getting more and more heated as I went on. I said that it wasn't a solitary Turkish study that said the incidence was high, but many, many studies, and Headley Court the military hospital was screening soldiers, and I didn't think they'd be doing that if it was rare, and it wasn't just weight, it was sex ... Dr Henderson-Slater said then (which is true) that hypopituitarism is common during the acute stage of brain injury and often settles down. But not always, I said, quoting the Berg study of 246 unselected patients of whom 20 per cent were diagnosed.

'Ah, but how long after the injury?' asked Dr Henderson-Slater very sharply.

'Twenty-four to thirty-six months,' I said – hoping to God I was right.

'May I ask who you are?' he said, more sharply still, so I said my piece about Christopher, at which point the Chair suggested we moved on.

At coffee time a couple of the delegates came over to me. One of them said she'd read the Berg study and the other said I was brave to speak out. This told me two things – first that people were starting to be aware, and secondly, that if they thought I was brave, it perhaps meant that those with NHS jobs to worry about didn't feel comfortable mentioning the topic. I had by then read several stories of whistle-blowers being treated harshly.

When it was time to go I went to my car, took out my phone, and anxiously checked the post-injury times of the Berg study – it was 12 months +/- 6, so I'd been a whole year out! I was afraid it might be a slip that could be used against me and thought I'd better email Dr Henderson-Slater.

This I did as charmingly as I could, easily done when you have time to choose your words. I confessed to quoting the wrong figures adding, 'However they were well past the acute stage, so the study still supported my point.' I admitted that consultants typically did more to help people in a single month than I'd done in my whole life, but if they described PTHP as rare and didn't spell out the consequences – weight gain was minor compared with loss of sexual drive and infertility – then people like our son would continue to be missed.

To my relief he answered affably, and we had a friendly exchange in which we became 'David' and 'Joanna' to each other. It was perhaps wrong though to call it an exchange, since it consisted on his side of long explanations as to why it was difficult to know which tests to use, and which patients to test (he believed he did more tests than his colleagues), and on my side, I reiterated that I was not campaigning for screening. In my final email I said I wasn't qualified to make those decisions: my campaign could be summed up as, 'Warn patients, families, and GPs' and 'in pressing for this I am on equal terms, because it is an ethical matter. The patient's right to know about his or her condition and its risks is enshrined in medical ethics. When one says that pituitary deficiencies "unquestionably" occur [as Dr Henderson-Slater had just admitted], on what grounds can one possibly argue that the patient should remain in ignorance? Just a few words might have saved our son.'

He did not answer this point.

My correspondence with him had a brief sequel three years later when a colleague of his gave a talk at a workshop in Oxford and I asked him some probing questions about PTHP. The intervening period had still not taught me how to do this without sounding aggressive, so afterwards I wrote my usual conciliatory email. To my surprise I got a reply not from the speaker himself, but from Dr Henderson-Slater addressing me (alas!) as 'Mrs

Lane'. He said that as the tests for GH deficiency were unpleasant and dangerous, his team were advised by the endocrinology department to be guided by IGF-1 levels (insulin growth factor 1), and despite years of testing head injury outpatients who had unexplained fatigue, he had yet to find a single hormone-deficient patient.

I knew from our earlier exchange that by 'unpleasant and dangerous tests' he meant the insulin tolerance test. I also knew that in the past this test had not had nearly such a bad press as it was getting now. I sent a reply quoting research that in up to 65 per cent of patients with growth hormone deficiency, IGF-1 levels were normal, 'and this may explain your lack of success in picking up cases.' I said that though the insulin tolerance test could be unpleasant and risky, the glucagon stimulation test and another, arginine-based test, were relatively tolerable, even if not quite so reliable. I wondered why he didn't give his patients these? I conceded that I knew nothing about the funding issues he faced and the difficulty prioritising, but 'I do think head injury patients have a right to be warned, and would be grateful if you could confirm that they are.'

He did not reply, so I assumed that they weren't. But afterwards I thought that he had helped me by divulging the test he used, which he hadn't needed to tell me.

In connection with this, I remember an 'insider's view' I got some time later.

A friendly head injury nurse confirmed my growing impression that even sympathetic consultants had their hands tied by budgetary constraints and pressure from big pharma and their bosses. 'They don't really get so much of a say,' she told me, 'Not unless they're prepared to risk their livelihoods.' But that's a big ask.

42 - THE PEOPLE OUT THERE 2

In 2011, I'd had an email from Henk Griffin, a youngish American man living in Amsterdam (see chapter 24). His story highlighted the stress of having one's illness ignored, but what I didn't expect were his kind attempts to comfort me. When I said how I thought Chris must have suffered from not being 'allowed to be ill', he talked consolingly about societal pressures to be positive. 'Plus men feel they are not men if they speak of their problems'. He said, 'I actually have a number of replies to "How are you?" that allow me when I am having bad days not to tell the truth while at the same time not lie either. Your son may not even have been looking for sympathy or understanding … I think men tend to have feelings more of isolation and loneliness. Obviously there is not anything more you could have done and I am sure he appreciates what you do now in his memory.'

I wanted to know if Henk had ever had a head injury. He said that meningitis and encephalitis could cause hypopituitarism and he suspected he'd suffered one of those, but his doctor leaned more towards head injury.

'I have hit my head countless times. Was in bad car accident as kid, always split my head open on something until about twelve, swam into end of pool multiple times, fell out of van when going around a corner, as bicycle courier car pulled in front of me to park and I went into back of car

215

> twice but wearing helmet which helped, and was
> beat up about the head twice, was tackled badly by
> group on ice playing game with unconsciousness ...
> so certainly enough head injury possibilities.'

Well gosh, I thought, taken aback by this almost cartoon-like sequence, no, head injury couldn't be ruled out.

I found it comforting to be in touch with him. John and I visited him in Amsterdam in the freezing winter. The plan was that he would make us a pizza, something he was skilled at, but he had broken his leg when we came so he couldn't. Osteoporosis is one of the many possible side-effects of hypopituitarism – there seems to be no end to the ways it can damage you. It felt good to meet him even in these unfortunate circumstances. We were impressed by the immense orderliness of his flat, and the way he could tell us from his bed exactly where to find a particular flavour of tea on his kitchen shelf, without being able to look for himself. I liked his slightly strange English – although he was a native English speaker, born in Maine, he had been speaking Dutch for so long that his sentence structures had become Germanic. He wrote to me afterwards that I reminded him of an aunt he was fond of, and I liked that too.

Something else he told me had resonated when I thought of our son. I'd been puzzled that whereas most websites gave intolerance of cold as a symptom of hypopituitarism, with Chris it must have been the other way round, because otherwise he surely would have mended his central heating. But when I asked Henk he said his own normal temperature was very low and he could immerse himself in the sea for long periods without a wetsuit and without getting hypothermia ('Surfers think I am extreme and a cool dude ☺'). Some hypopituitarism websites corroborate low temperature tolerance as a symptom.

That same year, I had an email from a mother whose son had hypopituitarism, and had only been diagnosed because, as a nurse, she recognised his symptoms and insisted the doctor check him out. Her general complaint was, 'It is so difficult to try and tell doctors "I do not think you are delivering the right level of care" or "I think the opinion of an expert in this area is required." The years of pursuing his care through mental health have been ridiculously difficult and wearing, but I thought that physiological problems would be easier as we are fairly able and informed, but unfortunately I was wrong and I feel that here we go again. I am compelled to be Mrs Angry all the time, having to fight everybody.'

In a way I could see she was worse off than I was. I am Mrs Angry too, but I don't have the ever-present pain and stress of seeing my child neglected and knowing that I have to keep fighting continuously or he will suffer.

At the very end of 2011, I found an email in my inbox that made the whole year worthwhile. It was from a man in his early thirties who had been searching for nearly a decade to discover what was wrong with him. At last he'd seen Headway's information – the information I'd fought so hard for them to display – and the word 'hypopituitarism' jumped out at him, and all the pieces of the puzzle seemed to fit together. Now, at last, I had what I'd yearned for – proof that Chris's tragedy had helped to save someone else. Something good had finally come out of his death.

Despite being fobbed off with two normal synacthen tests, he got himself referred to Dr Kearney, my love-hate figure, and she diagnosed him properly. I was pleased to read, 'Dr Kearney is amazing!' and 'Dr Kearney doesn't think much of the short synacthen test' and 'she is so methodical, clear and organised and does stuff properly.' I couldn't help feeling thankful that he was in her hands.

As I hypothesised about the pressures that could be exerted on a person who cares about her patients, I wondered what I would do if I was made to understand my funding would be cut, and my patients suffer, unless I did what I was told.

It had been a hard year, 2011. The childminding had been tiring, I was still having broken nights when nursery rhymes would go round and round in my head – '*Wind* the bobbin up, *Wind* the bobbin up' – and I would sit suddenly bolt upright in bed, absolutely unable to bear the thought that Chris was dead. From August onwards I had suffered a persistent cough which dragged me down and was to last until the following summer, until I was sensible and saw a specialist about it.

Feeling low, I followed my yearly ritual of looking at the health statistics website and I saw that the pitiful rate at which the numbers of diagnosis were increasing was just the same as it had been before Chris's death. But at least I was in touch with real people now. That was something.

43 - ANOTHER SEED SPROUTING

I was still trying to find a PTHP sufferer to speak on Radio Solent and eventually it was my childminding that opened the way. By January 2012, Katherine was two years and two months old, an energetic toddler with a love of the technical. Remote controls, mobile phones, and calculators fascinated her. It was literally child's play to her to put a call through to radio host Dominic Blake when I wasn't watching, and that revived our dialogue.

I decided to have one last try to find a patient in the Portsmouth area, and I remembered that the neurosurgeon Mr Tony Belli, who had let me come to his seminar, was based at Southampton General and must have referred his head injury patients to a local endocrinologist. A few moments on the internet brought up the name of Dr Partha Kar, and without much hope I emailed him.

Imagine my surprise and joy when within exactly six minutes he responded that hypopituitarism was 'very close to his heart' and he would be keen to raise its profile, and was delighted to be asked.

I passed on the news to Dominic who recorded an interview with him and a patient of his who was willing to be a case study, and I drove down to Portsmouth to be interviewed live. Dominic led me up to the studio, where he pottered about in a disarmingly domesticated way, making me a mug of tea and chatting, while I looked out through the floor-to-ceiling windows at the Spinnaker tower and the pale, early morning sea.

I had four minutes sometime between seven and eight

o'clock, answering a few questions from another pres-
enter, so it wasn't nearly such an ordeal as the *Woman's
Hour* interview, and most of the time I was listening – not
just to all the other news items, but to Dr Kar's interview
and his patient, who called himself James Smith.

James's story was shocking (see chapter 44). What
particularly struck me were his repeated suicide attempts
and his belief that without diagnosis he would probably be
dead.

Here was a story I would be able to quote in my
campaign. I felt that James's courageous opening up
about his suicide attempts gave me a weapon. The man
who was helped by Headway's hypopituitarism entry had
said, 'Sometimes you feel there is just no way out and
taking your own life is the only option', and I felt sure
from the suicide figures after head injury that
hypopituitarism made you want to kill yourself, but I had
never been able to argue this before, because the only
example I had was Chris, and with him it was all
conjecture, no proof. After the broadcast Dominic chatted
some more: comic anecdotes which I've now forgotten,
about public figures, episodes from his life. I remember
thinking how vital it is for our society to have honest
informative journalism, and that he represented what was
best about it. He voiced his opinion that PTHP was
suffering from 'intentional neglect' and that gave me
strength too. If Dom could see it, from outside as it were,
it must be true.

Christine Lord came to the studio presently, and we
met for the first time. We had a good hug and went for
coffee in the shopping centre and talked. All my internet
impressions of her were fulfilled – a warm, honest, down
to earth, energetic presence. I felt so hugely grateful to her
for making the broadcast possible. After meeting

Christine my next port of call was Queen Alexandra Hospital where Dr Kar worked. I had learnt already that he would be too busy to see me, but I'd found out from his secretary that he liked wine, so I'd brought him an offering (not just wine but an Easter egg and some flowers) to say thank you for the broadcast. I hoped that he would not get into trouble in some way for publicising PTHP.

44 - JAMES

I arranged to meet James, the head injury survivor from the radio programme, in a café in early April. It was a sunny day. He was dressed in black and looked macho and healthy in dark glasses. He had a breezy Aussie air about him, from his years spent down under. He opened up about his medical history in a frank, friendly way. His hypopituitarism had remained undiagnosed for five years, and although he'd had neuropsychological treatment for his brain fog and depression, and relaxation therapy for his supposed post-traumatic stress disorder, these had been completely ineffectual. He discovered that he was infertile, and this, plus his head injury, should have rung alarm bells but no, he was given the one-size-fits-all standard treatment of diet and exercise which brought no permanent benefit. What saved him in the end was a curious symptom: he bruised easily. 'I used to come up in great welts at the slightest thing.' His fibrinogen levels (fibrinogen is what helps blood to clot) were abnormal.

James's GP suspected fibromyalgia, but he wasn't entirely convinced. He gave James a thyroid test which came out low, and referred him to Dr Kar – and at last James's long search for the right diagnosis was over. By the time we met he had only had testosterone replacement, which had helped enormously, but he did not recover from his brain fog until he was given growth hormone – after a big fight – a year later. We kept in touch. James gave me a lot of useful advice about strategy and how to organise my priorities, which to some extent I absorbed.

He must have been frustrated, though, at my failure to carry out the excellent but ambitious plan he made for me, as follows:

> 'I Joanna Lane intend to spend the next three years driving at least ten thousand undiagnosed pituitary suffers in to the correct medical diagnosis and care program. I also intend to get at least one formal process adopted by the NHS that assists my goals. Finally I intend to raise awareness with the general public and in doing so, raise at least £100,000 for charities connected with Pituitary issues. I will do this working in partnership with the Pituitary Foundation or by setting myself up as a stand-alone charity.'

I can't excuse myself. I haven't saved 10,000 undiagnosed pituitary sufferers or got a single formal process adopted by the NHS, or raised £100,000 for pituitary charities, or set myself up as a stand-alone charity, and I hate to think how many people's lives haven't been changed that could have been, if I'd managed to do this. It's just ... people tend to do what they're good at, and my forte has always been words, not deeds, and I've tried to fit everything in with being a good grandmother, mother, wife. It's difficult to overcome a lifelong fear of committees and organisations and a reluctance to grapple with the unfamiliar when you're in your sixties, though I wish that I had. However, recently I've had a wonderful offer of help to start up an organisation and do all those things, so maybe in time – though after James's deadline expires – things will be better.

One thing James and I did do together in July 2013 was to concoct a letter for the *British Medical Journal*

(BMJ) website, protesting at how doctors fail to recognise head injury as a risk factor for suicide and describing James's experience. The letter has had fifty-four 'likes' (one of them mine) so that means fifty-three doctors may have had their eyes opened. Perhaps these tiny drips, if there are enough of them, make ripples that spread out to cause an eventual wave.

JAMES 'SMITH'S' STORY

I'd been out with clients on a corporate entertainment evening and I guess I decided about midnight to pack everybody else off in a cab and send them home. I was walking to a cab station, some lads saw me and decided to rob me. I was hospitalised for nearly two and a half weeks, three weeks: broken ribs, nearly lost my eye, and severe head trauma. With that three weeks the visible side could be quite identified and I healed reasonably quickly, but when I was discharged, that was it, I was simply discharged, fed into the system, no real after-care, and I guess that's when I started to, er, fall way behind where I thought I should be in terms of recuperation – not being able to get up, not being able to go to sleep, not being able to talk properly. I totally went into my own shell, became fearful of pretty much everyone and everything, you know, even the phone ringing was a nightmare for me, couldn't face a thing. I tried to take my life two or three times, and that was after weeks and weeks and weeks of just continuing negative thoughts. I'm still working my way through the whole recuperation process, but some light, a big part of light, was when I stumbled across my endocrinologist and within moments of talking to him he quickly identified what one of the problems could be. During the attack I received head trauma which affected my pituitary gland and my pituitary gland is now almost defunct, completely dead. Now that gland produces major chemicals which basically enable a human to function so the treatment is to substitute some of those chemicals, hormones, and immediately after receiving those you start to feel better. If I hadn't received help I guess I'd be no further forward, and probably – I hate to say it – maybe even dead. I don't think I would have survived the continual frustration of going through the process, going through the machine that is the NHS, getting no further forward every day. Anybody that's had a head injury should be discharged from hospital with a clear plan to look at their blood tests, look for signs of this problem, a survival plan if you will. The reality is if you don't get that clear understanding, the knowledge of what's going on around you – what's happening, how it's happening, why it's happening – your life turns upside down. Everything you've ever earnt, worked for, built up in your life leaves you and you can't understand why, and ultimately that causes a lot of people a lot of stress, and it caused *me*, particularly me, to want to leave it.

45 - CAMBRIDGE

If Dr Henderson-Slater's joke about the 'porky' motorcyclist, and my experiences with Professor Wass and Professor Wade, had made me suspect that I would get little help from Oxford, maybe symmetry demanded that I should learn the same about Cambridge.

In January 2012 I went to a free conference at the Oliver Zangwill rehabilitation centre in Ely. This little town is picturesque, and on that crisp, sunny, winter's day I enjoyed the great cathedral and the bright water, the old buildings. The rehabilitation centre is on higher ground, away from the quayside, modern but comfortable. It forms the next stage when severely head-injured patients get referred from Addenbrooke's Hospital in Cambridge. I was grateful to the rehab centre people for letting me come, and I was glad I had, because I met a personal injury lawyer there with whom I'd corresponded in 2009 about testing. That day she told me that she had referred fifty of her clients to their GP for endocrine checks and not one of them had been diagnosed with PTHP, even though you would expect about ten or more among that number. She thought GPs didn't know the right tests to give, or when to give them, or how to interpret the results, and I guessed she was right.

Her information reminded me that the Royal College of GPs had refused to inform GPs. Christine and others only succeeded because they had the funds to keep looking, and they were the 'lucky' ones, the four per cent who get diagnosed.

We all settled down to listen to the lectures. I had overcome my fear of raising my voice in public, and was now quite bold – though not always very articulate – about asking questions from the floor. When I asked a question about PTHP, however, one of the consultants, Dr Judith Allanson, who works with brain rehabilitation, smilingly hushed me and said, 'We're coming to that in the afternoon.'

Later, we heard from Tim Lodge, who had suffered a minor head injury with devastating consequences to his mood, memory, and mental function. It turned out that he had pituitary damage.

In 2009 he was knocked off his bike on the way home from work. He didn't think it was serious and after a hospital check-up he went home and expected to be back at work in a few days. Then he suffered from head swelling and headaches, and tests showed he'd had a brain injury. He suffered depression, attempted suicide, and had problems with speaking and interacting with his family. He could no longer do things like jump-starting a car, which had been second nature to him as an engineer. He couldn't control his moods. His accident solicitor recommended the Oliver Zangwill Centre where he was taught about how the brain works. He hoped this would help him understand what was wrong, because unlike other patients whose scans had shown specific injuries, his own scans hadn't shown up anything. But later, specialists told him they believed his brain had rotated during the accident and caused pituitary damage.

He talked movingly about his temper flares after the injury and how his poor little daughter 'wanted her old daddy back'. And how, thanks to the Oliver Zangwill Centre, she had him back, and how he'd made a good enough recovery to go back to his old job in engineering design. But even though his scan had shown nothing, which to me implied strongly that his pituitary damage must have been the main thing wrong with him, he did not speak of the effects of the hormone replacement (Growth hormone replacement, for example, would have had a direct impact on his depression and suicide risk.) Instead, his focus was all on the psychotherapy he'd received, on how to cope with his emotions, particularly anger, and how helpful it was to be told that your mood changes were not your fault. The subject of PTHP was not mentioned. He did not even talk of receiving replacement hormones, but I confirmed afterwards with Dr Bateman, the CEO of the rehabilitation centre, that he had. When I protested that such an important aspect of his therapy had been skimmed over, Dr Bateman shrugged and said, 'I didn't write the script.'

My most far-reaching discovery that day was that a guideline on head injury rehabilitation was due to come out in 2013, prepared by the Scottish equivalent of NICE, called SIGN. Would it include PTHP, I asked? The speaker said no, he didn't believe it would.

Later I had a chat to Dr Allanson, who had hushed me earlier, about my plan to write to the Royal Colleges again, this time with signatures from as many consultants as possible, and she was very pleasant and agreed to help me with my draft letter. She said there was still disagreement about the diagnostic tests for PTHP, which was causing delay. I could not understand why there should be delay: it was not as if hypopituitarism was a newly discovered complaint or as if the diagnostic tests were not described in standard medical textbooks. However I did not say this and thought I would email her later.

I went home determined to clarify with her what was

happening with the diagnostic tests, and to investigate the Scottish guideline. But despite her smiles and promises, she did not answer my emails, even though I sent three, in one case because I was specifically referred to her by her colleague Dr Kirker, who had helped me so much in 2009. I expect she was wary of getting into a vexatious and time-consuming correspondence, as I must admit ours could have turned out to be.

46 - SIGN

Two supportive consultants helped me draft the letter to the Royal Colleges. We sent copies off in March, addressed to each college individually. It was ignored by the Royal College of General Practitioners, as might have been expected, but it brought a few good things. The then president of the Society of British Neurosurgeons responded warmly and told me that the society would develop a PTHP guideline (however this so far remains unpublished), and Catheryne Waterhouse responded on behalf of the Royal College of Nursing Neurosciences Forum Committee with a promise to write a paper for the *British Journal of Neuroscience Nursing* (a promise she kept).

Thirty-three consultants and charities signed, and whenever I was told that PTHP was an insignificant problem, it was a comfort to look at that list and remind myself that all these professionals agreed it was real and needed to be tackled. It was to them I turned when I needed support in my dealings with the Scottish guidelines people.

At first, I was optimistic. For a start, I naively expected that the Scots might feel sufficiently antagonistic towards the English to include PTHP, just to spite NICE. Secondly I thought that as the guideline was designed to deal, among other things, with the *long-term* emotional consequences of brain injury, and its title was specifically 'Brain Injury Rehabilitation for Adults' – with no caveat that it covered the acute stage only – nobody could possibly argue that PTHP didn't fall within its remit.

I could not have been more wrong. I corresponded for just over a year with their programme lead, Dr Roberta James, yet even backed by that wonderful group of sympathetic consultants I achieved nothing except that Dr James suggested I apply for a separate guideline exclusively about PTHP. This proposal, so similar to NICE's, left me about as sceptical as the gingerbread man should have felt when the fox offered him a ride across the river, but all the consultants thought this was a good idea, so I went through the motions. Dr David Shakespeare of Lancashire Teaching Hospitals, who had already done so much to inform GPs in his area, showed me how to fill in the necessary forms. But I went on pushing for a brief insertion of around fifty words on PTHP into the main guideline, where they logically belonged. This seemed such a small 'ask', which no observer would believe could cost much in either time or money, that I hoped their refusal – inevitable as I was sure it would be – would demonstrate publicly how little they wanted PTHP patients to be diagnosed.

This request again was signed by the group of consultants, and Valerie Vaz MP, who had helped me so much before, also wrote to the Chairman, Keith Brown, on my behalf.

When, as I expected, they refused, I went back to Alastair Campbell, reporting their refusal, who commented, 'Bizarre they won't.' He advised me to contact Johann Lamont, the then leader of the Scottish Labour Party. When she did not reply he said he would have a word with her office, but if he did it didn't lead to anything. His next advice was to try the Labour health spokespeople Richard Simpson and Jackie Baillie. Through Jackie Baillie I got a question raised in the

House, asking whether the guideline would refer to PTHP.

The answer was, 'While recognising that post-traumatic hypopituitarism is an important topic, SIGN is unable to include it in the remit of this guideline. A proposal to develop a separate guideline on this topic has been received and it is currently being assessed for inclusion in the future Healthcare Improvement Scotland work programme. (November 1, 2012).'

I knew I shouldn't have applied for that separate guideline. As I expected, nothing came of the application.

The only thing left was to salvage some publicity from it all, and Eleanor Bradford gave me a few minutes on Radio Scotland. The summons to speak came while I was out rambling with our walking group in Kent and I had to rush to Chatham public library and plead with them to let me use a phone in a quiet office, which to my enormous gratitude they did. The last radio slot I'd had, on Radio London, I hadn't managed too well and had run out of time before I'd said all I needed to, so now I gabbled my piece out in such a rush that there was some extra time, marked by an awkward silence while neither I nor the interviewer could think of anything to say. Next time I'll get it right.

Natalie Walkman's article in *Scotland on Sunday* (28 October) almost certainly had more impact. I asked Alastair if I could quote his 'bizarre' comment – so important for highlighting the irrationality of SIGN's decision – and he kindly crafted me some sentences, which I included:

'Alastair Campbell, an Ambassador for Time to Change, the campaign aimed at changing attitudes to mental illness, said, "I hope Alex Salmond's team takes another look at this, and includes PTHP in the new SIGN guidance. I find it bizarre that PTHP has not been officially recognised as a condition which could be suffered by anyone who has a head injury. At the very least, anyone who could suffer from this should be tested for it to ensure they are given the appropriate care. As someone who has had depression, and still does from time to time, I worry that people who do not understand depression fail to treat it as a genuine illness. There are several studies now which link this to depression and that should be recognised. If not then there has to be a proper explanation as to why it is being excluded.'

Scotland on Sunday has a circulation of around 46,000, so I hoped that meant that at least a few more thousand people had been warned about PTHP. Natalie later wrote a second article headed, 'Brain surgeon condemns NHS head injury decision as incomprehensible'. The brain surgeon was Mr Patrick Statham, from Western General Hospital in Edinburgh, whom I had approached because Natalie had told me she needed a Scottish expert for comment. He is a straightforward, forthright person and it was lovely to be able to quote him saying phrases like, 'so daft it's incomprehensible'.

There had to be a proper explanation as to why it was being excluded, as Alastair had said. I tried quite hard to obtain such an explanation but never, in all the verbiage I received, found any that made sense. I was back in the same world of crazy logic inhabited by NICE. For example, you might think if the chair, Dr Keith Brown, wrote that a guideline's purpose is to provide doctors with the best evidence to diagnose and treat, he would continue, 'so it's vital to provide doctors with the PTHP evidence so they can diagnose and treat that.' But no. It was followed by the usual bland refusal. 'The [guideline's] priorities […] are effective referral from acute or primary care to specialist service', he says, just as if referring patients to an endocrinologist didn't come under that umbrella, or as if professionals who are in the dark about PTHP can still somehow magically manage to make that referral.

As in my dealings with NICE, two things stood out from this campaign. One was the Scottish MPs' excuse that SIGN was independent of the government so they could not tell them what to do – now where had I heard something like that before? – the other thing was that SIGN would not tell me the names of the individuals who were developing the guideline.

Dr Peter Brambleby, an honest and outspoken public health doctor who had signed my letter, was particularly incensed by this secrecy, for which the only excuse SIGN could offer was that it protected the group from being badgered by pharmaceutical salesmen. But SIGN would not budge. I could not let it go at that, and asked Dr Brown to pose two questions to the group which they could reply to anonymously if they wished: what steps had they taken to make sure that the guideline would get PTHP patients referred to the right specialists (endocrinologists), when those making the referral would have no idea the PTHP existed; and – to put it simply – did the group want PTHP patients to be diagnosed?

I felt they could only answer 'none' to the first. As regards the second, they could hardly say openly that they didn't want PTHP patients to be diagnosed – and if they replied 'yes' I could say, 'Why aren't you mentioning them in the guideline then?'

But of course what I got was a whole lot of guff that didn't give a straight answer to either question. The gist was: we would need to do a lot of literature-searching, which we haven't time to do. But we know [without literature-searching apparently] that your figures are wrong and your evidence is sketchy and poor quality. Some of us have never come across this condition [so clearly it doesn't exist]. And anyway, you said nothing at the initial consultation stage, so hard cheese. It was bad luck that by the time I heard about the proposed guideline, the consultation stage was already over.

The only positive thing in the letter was that a group member had suggested mentioning PTHP in the recommendations for further research, 'and I think this is something we could do'. Although I replied saying, 'yes please,' the sixteen 'Recommendations for further research' remained entirely devoid of anything about PTHP.

The whole episode made me think about individual responsibility. I had corresponded with so many people at NICE and so many people at SIGN that I could not believe that most of them didn't have an uneasy feeling that their actions were perpetuating terrible suffering for thousands of their fellow Britons. But nobody stood out of line, nobody protested.

Would I have been any different? Like most people I am bombarded daily by email petitions about injustices – companies who won't pay out compensation to injured employees, women who are condemned to death because they have complained about rape, mothers of soldiers who are denied information about how they died, and so on, and sometimes I go so far as to sign a petition or write to my MP, even give money occasionally, but mainly I do nothing. There are too many injustices. You can't do everything.

But then I think of this well-known quotation, which puts its finger on the problem.

'First they came for the Socialists, and I did not speak out because I was not a Socialist.

Then they came for the Trade Unionists, and I did not speak out because I was not a Trade Unionist.

Then they came for the Jews, and I did not speak out because I was not a Jew.

Then they came for me. And there was no one left to speak for me.'

Pastor Martin Niemöller

When our public institutions, whose remit is to protect people – whether their health, or their property, or their rights – start to flout their own rules, it is a disaster for everyone. It is no good thinking, 'PTHP doesn't affect me,' because even though you may be lucky enough to be right, the failure of the *institution* will almost certainly impinge on you, in one way or another. It has stopped protecting the people it should be protecting. We are all at risk.

Even though SIGN's decision did not surprise me, I felt very low. Nevertheless, I went on trying to milk the opportunity for all it was worth, and when some of the consultants who had signed suggested writing a letter of protest to the BMJ I enlisted their help once more. The preliminary debate about the wording was interesting in itself. One consultant withdrew from the venture saying, 'I have a bad feeling about the BMJ.' Other consultants wanted to water the wording down to make it more conciliatory, but Dr Richard Fitzgerald, consultant radiologist at the Royal Wolverhampton (to whom I owe a lot), said, 'Timid verbose letters never achieve anything' and we stuck with the stronger version.

The BMJ is obliged to post any letter which is not libellous or obscene on its website so it did appear there. However, a letter signed by so many consultants might have been expected to appear in its print version too, and this did not happen. The consultant who had a bad feeling about the BMJ may have been right.

I am pleased at least that the letter has racked up 61 'likes' since it was posted. More ripples?

47 - SOMETHING GOOD AT LAST

There have been times when I have been tempted to forget about PTHP completely, and move on – go back to learning languages in my spare time, pick up the interests that I dropped, the friends I have neglected. I feel sometimes like a weary horse, stumbling to the ground, almost collapsing, yet being urged on by an implacable rider, and I wonder, 'Who is this rider? Why can't I stop?'

A friend thinks the rider is guilt, but I'm not sure. Guilt makes you want to curl up and die, not act. The force that impels me seems more like the one that drove Julie Ward's father to spend two decades of his life and more than £2m on discovering how his daughter died and trying to bring the killers to justice. Or like what drove Charles and Ann Ming whose daughter was murdered, to institute, single-handedly, the reform of the double jeopardy law. Revenge, then? But even that seems not quite to fit. It seems more like love – your child has gone, but the love you feel is still there and needs somewhere to go. What motivated Christine Wrightson to expose the short synacthen test was that she didn't want anyone else to go through what she had, she wanted to make the world safer, and I feel that too. Anyway, the rider – whoever it is – digs in his spurs and I have to go on.

Often, though, when I have felt particularly tired and low, extraordinary opportunities have opened up through such random chance that if I believed in an afterlife I would think Chris was nudging events from above. One instance was my granddaughter Katherine playing with my mobile and phoning Dominic Blake, without which the Radio Solent programme would not have happened. Another example is what came about in July 2011, in the midst of my depressing correspondence with SIGN.

I was plodding downhill along an overgrown footpath at the side of a field with the rest of our walking group when I met Lynne Wallis. We talked, as strangers do, passing the time, with no thought of ever meeting again. The fluid composition of our walking group, which has no membership and whose walks are open to anyone to come along for free, at whim, at any time, makes future meetings particularly unpredictable, and encourages the same confessional urge that prompts people to unburden themselves to fellow passengers on long train journeys.

I cannot remember what my first impressions of Lynne were, except that she struck me as unusually open, someone who would say what she was thinking without much inner censorship. I liked her voice. She told me she sang jazz in pubs, so I guessed her singing voice must be attractive too.

The confidences we exchanged were superficial at first. She told me she had done her knee in skiing in Switzerland, and I told her about the big toe joint on my right foot, which I had wrecked by wearing boots that were too small on the Tour de Mont Blanc. Then, by degrees, we dived deeper and she told me about her brother who had been a drug addict and died of an overdose, and I told her about Chris.

She is one of those rare people who can talk well and listen too. I went on and on telling her about Chris, for maybe ten minutes, and at the end she sprang a surprise on me. She was not only a jazz singer, which she did part-time, but a freelance journalist, and she thought she could get Chris's story into the *Daily Mail*.

Ah no, I said regretfully. They wouldn't publish anything about him now, four years on. I'd had my *Woman's Hour* interview and my *Guardian* article, and that was my lot. But she wasn't convinced, and I was willing to try. So we exchanged email addresses.

And that was how the funereal tempo of my correspondence with SIGN was suddenly, temporarily, blessedly, exchanged for exhilarating salsa rhythms. Within two days she'd had interest from the *Daily Mail*'s health editor, a few hours later the editor had commissioned her, then she needed some scanned photos of Chris ('Can you ping me over some pix?'), then someone from the *Mail* visited to photograph them in situ. Then she needed some phone numbers – endocrinologists, Chris's counsellor, would his girlfriend speak to her? – and she needed to contact James who had spoken with me on Radio Solent ('Just spoke to jAMES [sic] – he's in Egypt so I kept it very brief!'). Then she sent me a draft, then another ('Read this version, it's better'), then a brief, 'Think they like it!', and finally a jubilant crow, 'They like my story a lot, never had such praise from them before.' The actual words of Justine Hancock, the *Mail* health editor, were, 'Very strong piece, a great get', which caught my fancy. 'A great get, a great get,' I said to myself, rolling it about on my tongue.

Then came the hard part. Lynne showed me her draft again, now covered with around thirty comments and questions from Justine. This was my initiation into how journalists work.

It took us a long day and a half to go through everything. I was impressed by Justine's thorough, probing questions. The *Mail*'s performance is not always so impressive. In fact, it was around then that their online version (a different operation from the print version) attacked the Olympics opening ceremony for its political correctness, remarking on 'the absurdly unrealistic scene [...] showing a mixed-race middle-class family in a detached new-build suburban home [...] but it is likely to be a challenge [...] to find an educated white middle-aged mother and black father living together with a happy family in such a set-up.' The article was swiftly removed but it annoyed Dr Kar enough to make him say no when Lynne asked him for a quote. Not one to hold back, she called him churlish and he retaliated by asking me to have a word with my colleague. When Lynne read the offending article, which was still available online in someone's blog, she saw his point ('felt awful when I read it. Arseholes!'), wrote to him, and I believe they made peace.

So finally, some thirty emails later, after all the ructions and point-checking, everything was settled. James had told his story, Mr Belli had bravely pointed out that there were a million undiagnosed PTHP sufferers in the UK, the Pituitary Foundation's medical committee chair, Dr Newell-Price, had confirmed the limitations of the short synacthen test, Headway had commented, Dr Joanne Blair from Alder Hey had given her opinion. Now all I had to do was to wait for Tuesday 7 August.

I felt sure something would go wrong. It all seemed too good to be true. I could hardly sleep the night before it was due out, and when the morning came and I bought the *Mail*, I opened it with thudding heart, steeling myself against disappointment.

But it was there, just as it should have been, reaching – I hoped – a readership of one and three quarter million. I kept a beady eye on the readers' comments posted, hoping for one that would say, 'At last I know what is wrong with me!'

One reader criticized me for exposing Chris's private life: 'What has happened to dignity?' Another said, 'This is a really old story, I first heard it discussed on Radio 4. What child hasn't had a bash to the head.' But this, perversely, cheered me. Even three years later, someone had remembered my *Woman's Hour* broadcast. Another was sceptical, saying, 'If one bash can do that, then what is the frequency of impotency in boxers whose profession involves being bashed on the head often?' Boxers DO get pituitary damage, there's research to prove it.

But there were two comments of the kind I was looking for.

Jenny from Saltburn wrote:

'I have found this very interesting as I have suffered from depression since I was a very small girl and when I was 6 I fell and bumped my head severely enough to lose consciousness for a moment and needed a stitch. I am a woman and so can't comment on impotence but I have had some issues in that area, and I infuriate people by never feeling cold ... Will definitely be reading more into this. Thank you, and RIP Chris xx'

Oh bless her, I thought, touched by the 'RIP' and the kisses, and her generosity in opening up online. Another sick person who thought about others.

Lori S of Belvedere, Kent posted this comment:

'I have severe depression. I suffered concussion and a head trauma ... and 7 years later I was diagnosed as having depression and was put on my 1st set of anti-depressants. The depression only ever worsened over the years and I have been put on 9 different anti-depressant meds in the years gone by....all to no avail sadly. Like the people in this article and others that have commented..... I've suffered similar side effects (extreme fatigue and never feel the cold). I'm definitely going to research into this more now.......'

Jenny and Lois were my answer to the critic who wondered what had happened to dignity. I knew Chris would have cared so much more about making people better, than protecting his posthumous reputation. But how would Jenny and Lois fare in their hunt for diagnosis? Would they be fobbed off with useless tests such as the SST?

48 - EFFECTS

Exposure in the press taught me how careful one has to be. I had to say a few sorrys after the article came out. One was to Lisa Turan at the Child Brain Injury Trust (CBIT) who readers will remember had originated a leaflet dedicated to Chris and let me speak at their conference. I should have listed her charity as one of the helplines at the end of the article, but for some reason the idea didn't enter my head, and I named only Headway and the Pituitary Foundation, whose help had been much less spontaneous. Luckily Lynne was able to insert CBIT into the list in the article's online version. Then there was Valerie Vaz MP who had given Lynne a long interview and was understandably offended that her name didn't appear. This was not Lynne's fault. I wrote to Valerie explaining that I'd seen the draft which she had featured in, but it had been edited out.

Then I had a gentle email from one of Chris's friends ('I was quite surprised that it was about someone I knew…') and I realised I hadn't warned them. This was horrifying. How could I not have? My only excuse was that everything had happened so hectically and fast. I set about apologising and explaining to them all. I hope they understood.

Lynne had told me there might be follow-ups, and in fact she had an offer from *best Magazine* to write the story again, this time focusing on the human interest side. Go for it, I said. She warned me she would have to sensationalise it and pack it with emotion and that she wouldn't be responsible for the headline, and I said, 'Fine'.

When it came out it had a huge headline: I WISH I'D BEEN A BETTER MUM. It was exactly true, I did wish I'd been a better mum, but somehow, in print ... but hey, the news about PTHP was reaching another 200,000 readers, and at least the title was better, marginally, than SEX SHAME FROM THE GRAVE.

The most valuable and lasting legacy of the *Daily Mail* article was that I became friends with Lynne. There was probably some initial calculation on both sides: I needed access to her talent, to get the news out there, and she may have seen me as a source of future stories (though I discovered her to be the least calculating person I've ever met). But just as scientists can grow living organs by coating a synthetic scaffold with stem cells, so it is possible for a real relationship to grow from somewhat schematic beginnings. By the time we had done a few more walks together and exchanged several indiscreet confidences, and laughed a lot, and got slightly drunk, and by the time I had come to a few of her gigs and listened to her singing 'Summertime', I felt as though she was securely my friend, and I hers.

49 - EDDIE'S STORY

When I looked at the diagnosis figures for 2012 I was, as usual, disappointed. There were 2,222 cases, which was an increase of only 79 from the previous year, in fact a smaller increase than the year before. I felt despondent. Where, oh where, were the tens of thousands that there should be?

I had a private measure of my own, however, which was based on the number of diagnosed people who'd written to me each year.

This graph went as follows:

$$2008 - 0$$
$$2009 - 0$$
$$2010 - 0$$
$$2011 - 4$$
$$2012 - 9$$

Another straw in the wind were those recent conferences, where people I chatted with at coffee time knew about PTHP, whereas earlier nobody had seemed to. Despite the depressing figures, I had a sense that something was shifting. I couldn't allow myself to feel too exultant, but I was cautiously optimistic.

Over the course of 2012 I 'met' five new people: James, who spoke with me on Radio Solent; Jill, who was Christine Wrightson's friend; Eddie, who was Jill's friend; Catherine whose story is in chapter 19; and Julian, an editor. Jill and Eddie had the most impact on my life. I featured Jill's story in an article in the *Mail on Sunday* that was eventually published in 2014 (see appendix 2).

Over the past four years Eddie has written me roughly eight emails a day, which comes to around 12,000 and rising. He has sent me his medical story, links to research that interests him, photographs of himself, his family and house, links to pop songs he likes, silly jokes which make me laugh, other jokes which don't, a sad email recalling his baby son David's death (to show he understood about Chris), complaints about his patient wife Sue's smoking habit, nightly 3 a.m. rants about certain medics, and in short, anything that comes into his head. His spelling is eccentric and it has taken me a while to achieve automatic mental translation of 'coursed', 'angels', 'no how', and 'shore' into caused, angles, know-how, and sure. Sometimes I can hardly believe that anyone can read 'sure' in other people's emails so many times and still not notice … but then, my pedantic accuracy sometimes riles him too ('Go on Joanna, make a spelling mistake for once in your life…') He is a brave, honest, kind person and I have learnt a lot from him, not least what happens when you complain about the NHS.

Eddie didn't have a proper education. He was born in Leeds, and was taken into care at a young age because his parents couldn't cope with their large family. He seems always to have been loveable. A seaside guesthouse manageress wrote to Eddie's care home after hosting a group of boys from there, saying what a 'grand lot of lads' they were, and how she and her husband had taken 'a great fancy to one little boy Eddie Barker and would like to have him stay with us sometime' with his brother.

But sadly Eddie went off the rails in his teens, had to sleep rough, got caught joy-riding and was sent to a borstal in Reading where he suffered horrible abuse but at least learned how to weld. After that he met Sue, who, though only sixteen at the time, was his salvation.

They got married and the welding came in handy because he made a living repairing and trading cars. His friend Ray told me that Eddie had been a brilliant mechanic before illness struck him down. In fact over the years he became a wealthy man – but then had to sell his three Rolls-Royces, and most of his other assets, to fund his desperate and costly search for diagnosis.

In 1972, while working as a truck-driver, Eddie injured his head in an accident, and in 1985 he fractured the base of his skull when he suffered a violent assault. It is a measure of his physical resilience that he survived these injuries without apparent ill effect. However, in 2003 he intervened in a bar fight in Spain, and a Russian doorman held him in a choke-hold which cut off the supply of blood to his brain for several minutes and made him pass out. After that he was never the same again.

He had headaches, neck pain, dizziness, vertigo, tinnitus, and deafness in his right ear. He attended a clinic specialising in dizziness and balance issues, but they could not help him. He was still suffering the same symptoms two years later, plus face pains, inability to sleep, and tingling and numbness in his hands. He was then diagnosed with Ménière's disease. His GP of 30 years, an old family friend, suspected thyroid deficiency, which was confirmed by testing. Eddie began to take thyroxine.

Eddie's experience as a mechanic meant he saw his body as a kind of engine. Somewhere there was a fault that needed to be diagnosed, and he spent money at one private clinic after another, looking for the super-mechanic who would pinpoint and fix it. Now that he had been diagnosed with thyroid deficiency, he began to think that this super-mechanic might be an endocrinologist.

A BUPA test showed his thyroid stimulating hormone (TSH) levels were borderline low. TSH is produced by the pituitary gland, so low levels can be a sign that the gland is not functioning as it should. So he went to the North Manchester General Hospital and asked consultant endocrinologist Dr Mark Savage to examine him. Dr Savage gave him the short synacthen test and told him, with no apparent misgivings or reservations, that the result was normal and therefore excluded hypopituitarism.

Eddie, who had now been suffering almost unendurable symptoms for four years, was not satisfied. He was now experiencing heart problems (atrial fibrillation), chest discomfort, depression, and chronic fatigue. He got himself referred to Professor Julian Davis at Manchester Royal Infirmary, who had an international reputation and had held all kinds of eminent positions in the Society for Endocrinology and other august institutions. Surely he would know?

Professor Davis wrote to Dr Savage in 2007 saying:

'This man has sought yet another opinion about his endocrine status. For whatever reason, he was quite keen to come to the MRI and I hope that this will be okay with you. I rather doubt that we will progress matters much further, however.'

Professor Davis gave Eddie another short synacthen test, told him the result was normal, and sent him away. He refused Eddie's request for a more reliable test even though Eddie tells me he offered to pay for it.

Eddie's GP received this letter after the appointment with Professor Davis:

'We have explained to Mr Barker today that there are no signs of an underlying endocrinological problem to explain his many symptoms. I understand the patient has recently been given a diagnosis of chronic fatigue syndrome [...] We do feel that this may be a more appropriate diagnosis and that there may well be an element of psychosomatic or depressive problems that are contributing to his current state. The patient did not seem convinced of this suggestion and I am concerned that he may go on to undergo further investigation and medicalisation of his symptoms. I wonder if the patient may benefit from a psychological therapy, such as cognitive behavioural therapy.'

In other words, Eddie's problems were all in his head, and he was to be discouraged from searching for a physical cause.

The letter was hugely damaging because it stymied Eddie's chance of an open-minded opinion from other physicians, and even more damaging because his wife Sue believed it (as why shouldn't she?) and withdrew her support completely. This reminded me of Phil's story in chapter 19, where he says his wife 'turned into some kind of monster'. Sue would no longer write letters to hospitals – support that Eddie could hardly manage without. He was left isolated and ill, with those who loved him convinced his problems were in his head. Luckily he had the moral strength to 'undergo further investigation and medicalisation of his symptoms', in defiance of the letter, though he had to change his familiar and trusted GP to do so.

In 2008 he managed to get referred to Dr Kearney at Salford Royal Hospital, who, just as she had with my other correspondent who'd been alerted by the Headway page, investigated his symptoms properly. He was given the glucagon stimulation test and the arginine test and found to be lacking in growth hormone and the pituitary hormone that stimulates the adrenal glands, ACTH. In short, despite Dr Savage's and Professor Davis's findings, he had hypopituitarism.

Eddie was at last given hormone replacement, but the years of delay had harmed him. Untreated hypopituitarism leads to heart trouble, and by now Eddie's atrial fibrillation was so bad that he had to have two pacemakers fitted in succession, which has made him pacemaker-dependent for the rest of his life. Another of the effects of prolonged growth hormone deficiency is weight gain, and Eddie's increased girth split his rectal muscles causing back pain and leg problems.

Hypopituitarism is only one of many complications of head injury. Another is an inability to breathe when asleep (sleep apnoea), which happens to around 10 per cent of survivors. When Eddie was eventually given a polysomnograph to record his breathing overnight, it showed that he could not sleep for more than two minutes at a time before waking up gasping for air. This is why every morning when I came down to my computer I'd find desperate emails from him sent in the small hours, full of despair at his tremors, tinnitus, and pain, and how nobody seemed to care. It is no wonder he suffered from fatigue.

It took until 2013 – ten years after the first appearance of his symptoms – for him to be diagnosed.

When Eddie got in touch with me he had made a complaint against the Pennine Acute Trust, for whom Dr

Savage worked. One would have thought this complaint was unanswerable. Here Eddie was, suffering from a condition to which the Trust should have been alert, as it happens after one in three head injuries – and especially so because the basal skull fracture of 1985 put him at particular risk – yet all they had done was give him an unreliable test, incorrectly inform him that the result excluded hypopituitarism, and 'diagnose' him with chronic fatigue syndrome. His subsequent, correct, diagnosis was clear demonstration of how negligent they had been. Yet he got no acknowledgment or apology.

I decided to help him write his appeal.

50 - EDDIE'S APPEAL

I made this decision instantly, out of deep indignation, and never regretted it, but there were times when the stress it caused was severe. I was back in the hateful world of NICE and SIGN, the world of long, dense letters informed by crazy logic and denial.

The Ombudsman's letter that summarised the Trust's answer to Eddie's complaint was a case in point:

'The Trust provided the results of a short synacthen test performed in December 2006. This test looks at adrenal function and would identify a problem with the pituitary. Our adviser confirmed that the result was normal, in line with the Trust's response, and that "this test plus the raised TSH levels excludes an underactive pituitary condition".'

The human being who wrote these words *must* have known this was nonsense. How could someone blandly assert, 'this test would identify a problem with the pituitary' when there *was* a problem and it *hadn't* identified it? And how could anyone say that Eddie's high level of thyroid stimulating hormone, or TSH, excluded a pituitary condition? It frequently happens that parts of the pituitary still work fine while others fail, so Eddie's TSH level – even if it had been rocket-high (and it had been low two years back, as the Trust knew) – wouldn't prove anything about the rest of the gland. The Trust was, in my view, taking advantage of Eddie's non-medical background to suggest that it could – like a dodgy garage duping a non-mechanically minded car owner with jargon.

This disingenuous missive was in reply to Eddie's complaint about Dr Savage, who was the first of the two endocrinologists to use only the short synacthen test. Before Eddie made his complaint about the second endocrinologist, Professor Davis, with my input, he received shocking news.

It was proof that the Ombudsman had lied to Eddie.

In reply to his Freedom of Information request, Eddie received a copy of the report of the clinical advisor, a kidney specialist named Dr Richard McGonigle, which ended with:

'The short synacthen stimulation test is not entirely normal as indicated by the Trust.'

Yet Eddie and I had in front of us, on our screens, the Ombudsman's words: 'Our adviser confirmed that the result was normal in line with the Trust's response.'

My faith in the institutions of our supposedly democratic country had been deeply undermined already, but I still believed that organisations like hospital trusts and their regulators acted with some respect for procedure. I could hardly credit that they would be so bent on pursuing their own agenda that they would stoop to a downright untruth.

But it was no good wringing my hands, we had to get on, making best use of this new weapon. Accordingly, Eddie's complaint about Professor Davis contained the following statements:

- That Eddie now knew the SST result had not

been normal but borderline low.

- That the SST was known to miss two in every five patients with pituitary problems.
- That Professor Davis had had the option of using more reliable tests and had been negligent in not doing so, in view of Eddie's symptoms and his high risk status after his head injuries.

I do not think the Ombudsman could make an adequate response to this email. Instead, via one of their assessors, Rob Bancroft, they said that Eddie's complaint was out of time, even though on the phone they had granted him an extension, advising him to approach the Trust again.

I wrote pressing for an extension on the grounds that Eddie hadn't known until that May that he'd been misinformed about his SST result, and that although by now the Ombudsman was claiming that their advisor had looked at the wrong document by mistake, this was beside the point, because the SST result *was* abnormal, just as Dr McGonigle had said.

At the start of the SST the patient's cortisol level is measured, to give a baseline to refer back to after the adrenal glands have been artificially stimulated. This is called the basal cortisol level because it represents the natural state of the patient before medical intervention. If a patient's basal levels are in the range 83-497 nmol/L on more than one occasion – 'upon repeat determination' – it means that he or she should be given the insulin stress test or equivalent. Articles by two eminent doctors confirmed this. Eddie's basal readings were in this range. They were 402 nmol/L for Dr Savage's test, and 337 nmol/L for Professor Davis's a few months later. He was visibly slipping down the scale and as the literature made clear, he should have been given the insulin test.

The Ombudsman, via a Mr Harrigan this time, sent a reply demonstrating such wilful stupidity that it took my breath away. He chose to interpret the words 'on repeat determination' as meaning 'when measured a second time 30 minutes later' during the test, when chemical stimulation had made them rise.

Mr Harrigan was behaving as if he didn't know the meaning of the word 'basal'. I noticed he avoided that word in his letter, using only the phrase 'serum cortisol value'. I even took the trouble to email one of the authors, Professor Snyder, to get him to confirm what he meant, which he obligingly did, ('I mean a repeat basal cortisol at 8 a.m. on a subsequent day').

I relayed Professor Snyder's reply to Mr Harrigan, adding that I had been dismayed to read recently that while the Mid Staffordshire debacle (when neglected patients were so thirsty they had to drink water from flower-vases) was building to its shocking crisis, the Ombudsman had not upheld a single patient complaint. I hoped that they would do better in Eddie's case.

To my feelings of despair about our country was now added the familiar phenomenon of taxpayer's rage. It was almost unendurable to think that John's and my money (and the money of most of the people who will read this book) is being used to pay people to sit at their desks day after day spending their time and brains on denying justice to the public in every conceivable way. Far better, I thought, to disband the Ombudsman altogether and say frankly, 'If you've been treated badly, get used to it chum. There will be no redress for you.'

The correspondence continued, with the solicitors Irwin Mitchell taking over.

Meanwhile Eddie continued to suffer not only severe physical symptoms but the constant anger and frustration that he has not been heard, and has not been given justice.

51 - JUDICIAL REVIEW OF NICE

In October 2012 I heard Bill Braithwaite QC speak at a head injury workshop, saying how the mere threat of a judicial review could frequently make public bodies behave themselves, and that he would often act without charging a fee if it was a case of say, forcing local councils to fulfil their statutory duty to provide proper care for brain injury survivors. I pricked up my ears at this, and wondered if it might be the way to deal with NICE. I liked the fact that Bill Braithwaite always acted for the patient and never for the defence (which was usually a hospital) and I trusted him. When I asked his advice – he is a genial, approachable man – he referred me to Louis Browne of Exchange Chambers, a Treasury Counsel.

Louis seemed interested, and said I'd need to find two world experts on PTHP, get a charity on board, and find a PTHP sufferer who was on benefits and eligible for legal aid. I should then approach his friend Mathieu Culverhouse at Irwin Mitchell Solicitors.

This is the point where I might have stepped back and googled all the possible legal firms, to see who had the best record. But I was scared of the whole legal scenario. I thought of it as a stressful ordeal that would devour my time without necessarily achieving anything. I decided to pick this fruit that seemed to have fallen so easily into my hand, do what was necessary, but not invest too much of myself. Even if it failed, I reasoned, it would be a good peg for publicity.

I found my two world experts without much difficulty, and out of the possible charities, the UK Acquired Brain Injury Forum – in the shape of the steadily supportive Professor Barnes – agreed straight away, and so did the Child Brain Injury Trust. I was not surprised to be refused by Headway and the Pituitary Foundation.

Finally, I needed someone on benefits, and that meant lovely Eddie, who of course agreed. I wasn't sure if he would have the necessary 'standing' (i.e. had suffered personally from NICE's omission through receiving inadequate care), because he'd had his brain injuries before even the earliest version of the guideline came out, but Mathieu assured me that he did, though a more clear reply might have been, 'whatever the facts, the Legal Aid Agency may well argue that he doesn't, and I would advise you to apply as quickly as you can, so that if they say no, you can find somebody else.' But I thought I had all my ducks in a row ready for January when the revised guideline was due out.

I was still angry with the Ombudsman for the way Eddie had been treated, and Mathieu said they would consider taking them to judicial review as well. I worried, however, about being timed out.

All that happened at our first meeting in July 2013 was that a legal aid form was produced which Mathieu's trainee promised to handle. I asked what would happen if Eddie wasn't granted legal aid, and was told that there were other options. Though unfortunately I didn't ask what these were.

Following that meeting there was a long silence, though Mathieu promised to write to the Ombudsman about the discrepancy between what their advisor had said, and what they'd said he'd said.

The three months' time limit on Eddie's judicial

review of the Ombudsman quietly came and went, and nothing happened about his legal aid forms. I fretted, but kept quiet, hampered by the fact that Irwin Mitchell were acting 'for free' so far, and that I had to be polite to them if they were going to act against NICE. I reasoned that if no action was going to be taken against the Ombudsman, then Eddie could not apply for legal aid against NICE until the guideline came out minus the PTHP information, and that meant four more months, so there was nothing I could do.

At least it seemed a good sign that Mathieu drafted a letter to the Ombudsman inviting them to 'reconsider Mr Barker's complaint' in the light of the Freedom of Information revelation. However the letter wasn't sent until the end of August, when I'd chased it.

The Ombudsman replied on 4 October. They had decided to brazen it out. Their reply confirmed my impression that they were an organisation free from any regulation whatsoever. They had concocted a strange rigmarole in which their advisor had, by mistake, looked at the result of a privately performed short synacthen test instead of the one performed by the Trust. They said that the Trust had then sent the Ombudsman the right document, which they had passed on to the advisor. Attached to their letter was what they claimed was an email from the advisor saying, 'the enclosed synacthen test is normal.'

But Eddie had never had a short synacthen test carried out privately.

Eddie and I told Mathieu this. I added that, with regard to the emails that purported to prove their story, 'nothing is easier, if you want to make an email look older than it is, than to import it into a word document and amend the date. There is even a telltale formatting feature that is consistent with this having happened here.'

Mathieu asked what the tell-tale formatting feature was. I replied that it had an isolated page number instead of the usual 'page 1 of 1' you would find at the bottom of an email.

A month later in early November, he asked the Ombudsman to send copies of the two documents that had supposedly been confused. The Ombudsman obliged by sending a copy of the short synacthen test performed by the Trust, and the results for a salivary test performed for Eddie by a private clinic in October 2006. These two documents are displayed on my website so that readers can judge for themselves how likely it would be that one would be mistaken for the other.

In short, the Ombudsman was claiming that when the advisor said, 'The short synacthen test result is not entirely normal' he meant, 'The Red Apple Clinic cortisol day curve test is not entirely normal.' I thought that if the advisor could make an error like that it was hard to imagine him lasting five minutes as a doctor, let alone as a clinical advisor to the Ombudsman.

Even if such an absurd mistake could happen, there was the very material fact that if it had, the next step on discovering that the advisor had made this mistake would have been to amend the report, which was the official document summarising the case for posterity. Yet the report hadn't been amended. And finally, the baseline cortisol level recorded during Eddie's short synacthen test *was* borderline/low, just as the advisor had said. No emails could change that.

I expected that since Irwin Mitchell had been kind enough to write the letter in the first place, they would follow it up. I wrote saying the Ombudsman was like a four-year-old who says he didn't eat the chocolate when you could see the stain round his mouth. How were they going to reply? Two days later I asked again, but got no answer until Eddie and I took part in a telephone conference with Mathieu in early January, when I repeated my question. Mathieu said they could not take the correspondence with the Ombudsman any further. He said, 'We've asked the PHSO for an explanation, they've supplied what we call the "remedy". There's not much more we can do.'

'But … but,' I said, blood rushing to my face, my thoughts whirling in that incoherent emotional state that comes with the sudden understanding that somebody you thought was on your side, isn't, 'but their explanation is blatantly untrue!'

At that point I should simply have withdrawn and, late in the day though it was, looked for another solicitor. Others, including Christine Lord and Jon Danzig, had advised me to go elsewhere. But I felt I was 'in too deep' and couldn't choose another solicitor now. 'Are you still interested in doing the Judicial Review of NICE?' I asked, and Mathieu said he was, so I hung on.

52 - THE SLOW BOIL

The updated guideline on head injury was duly issued in January 2014, unsullied by any mention of pituitary damage. The date of publication was 22 January, which meant that the window for bringing a judicial review would close, three months later, on 22 April. Four months back, Mathieu had told me he had put the date in his diary and asked me to contact him as soon as possible if there was an issue, as they would need to act quickly.

I did of course contact him the minute the guideline came out, although I received no reply. I emailed Louis Browne, the barrister, several times, and to his credit he always replied kindly and promptly. I wrote long emails to Mathieu and Louis about various issues that worried me. I got a response from Louis expressing general helpfulness but that was it. A whole month later, on 28 February, Mathieu emailed to say that Louis and he had agreed to draft a letter to NICE 'pointing out where we say they have gone wrong and why'. I spent hours working feverishly on this draft

NICE's solicitors wrote back 'vigorously defending' themselves, as Mathieu put it. I read their letter with a thumping heart, almost too angry to take the words in.

The three pillars of their defence were, first, the familiar chestnut that hypopituitarism was a long-term effect and lay outside the scope of a guideline for the acute stage; second, that Eddie's claim was a scientific not a legal dispute; and third, that he had no standing. They made the further points that warning people would worry them, and that such illustrious bodies as the Association of British Neurologists and the Royal College of General Practitioners had not raised any objections during the consultation phase.

Their paragraph about hypopituitarism not belonging in an acute guideline deserves to be quoted:

'Symptoms of hypopituitarism necessarily do not appear on the timescale covered by the Guideline, or anything close to it. First, the pituitary must suffer harm. Then that harm must lead to a reduction in the production of hormone, which in turn must lead to a reduction in the level of hormone in circulation. Finally that reduction must lead to a medically observable effect. A timescale of months may be expected...'

I knew there was not an atom of research to support this assertion, and emailed Professor Thompson asking for his comments. His splendid reply began, 'Dear Joanna, Once again NICE have not researched this issue' and went on to cite numerous papers dating from 1969 which confirmed how quickly pituitary injury could show itself. 'A [...] daily assessment of 100 patients with traumatic brain injury showed that' [and here his indignation expressed itself in capitals] 'EIGHTY PER CENT HAD SUBNORMAL CORTISOL LEVELS AT SOME STAGE DURING HOSPITAL ADMISSION (Hannon MJ et al JCEM 2013).'

He ended, 'It seems that NICE are acting in a deliberately delinquent manner in ignoring expert opinion – I wish you luck with the judicial review.'

I was jubilant and thanked him effusively. 'This will

really blow NICE out of the water,' I wrote. But NICE is a vast, tough old steamer which takes a more deadly mine than the patient, truthful observations of scholars to explode.

I sat up the whole of the night of 25 March writing my observations on the letter, which Mathieu had asked for. I quoted Professor Thompson's email and answered the absurd point that warning patients would worry them. My urgency was fuelled by the belief that I was giving Mathieu and Louis valuable ammunition in the fight. My answer to the objection that patients would be worried by being warned about PTHP and go to the doctor every time they felt headachy or tired was to invite NICE to look at the issue retrospectively:

'By omitting to warn patients of a life-wrecking yet treatable condition – something that one in three of them will experience – NICE has indeed spared the feelings of approximately 1,350,000 people since their 2003 guideline came out. These people have been saved the mental discomfort of fearing something unpleasant (though treatable, never forget). And approximately 300,000 of these tenderly treated people have been afflicted with a terrible debilitating condition which may well have destroyed the marriages and jobs of many of them, and driven some of them to suicide. Bravo! What a brilliant choice of the lesser of two evils!'

If they feared that patients would be disturbed by being warned, why did the existing discharge letter warn about seizures? Perhaps they should stay silent here too, because they might disturb the mental peace of the 93 per cent who wouldn't have that symptom.

As for Eddie's standing, I repeated all the points that Mathieu had made to me, that the concept (of whether or not someone had suffered personally from NICE's omission through receiving inadequate care) was broad and could here even apply to anyone at risk of having a brain injury in the future … i.e. anybody at all. I pointed out that the UK Acquired Brain Injury Forum was supporting the case and represented many people with past brain injury, around a third of whom must have undiagnosed pituitary damage.

I will not describe every claim and counter-claim but I believe that I demolished every single point that NICE's solicitors made. Neither Mathieu nor Louis acknowledged receipt of my long document.

The silence from Mathieu and Louis remained unbroken until 16 April, which was the day after Eddie's application for funding was turned down by the Legal Aid Agency (LAA). The LAA's refusal trotted out the same reasons that NICE had given in their reply to the Letter of Claim. The fact that they accepted without scrutiny NICE's unscientific assertions was proof to me that they were biased. As I wrote to Mathieu that same day, 'I find it strange that the Legal Aid Agency should so readily base their decision on NICE's reply without investigating whether the facts are as stated. Is that normal procedure?'

On 16 April Mathieu arranged a three-way telephone call to Eddie and me. It was a 'dear John' call. No legal aid, so no judicial review. There was no mention of the 'other options' that Mathieu had mentioned, many months before. No word about the unscientific claims that NICE had made, and the LAA had repeated.

It was at that point, confronted by the failure of the

NHS complaints system, the untruths of the Ombudsman and NICE, the Legal Aid Agency's failure to check its facts, and the prospect of legal action withdrawn, that I felt the game was over. The Minotaur was winking at me, with first one white eye, and then the other.

I wish I had kept three facts in view throughout this episode:

- that the only check on NICE, the only chink in its armour, is the possibility of judicial review
- that legal aid would never have been granted – my common sense should have told me this
- that the only chance of success would have been to find a legal firm that promised in writing to conduct the case free of charge, and failing that, to crowd-source the cost.

Of course one can never argue that because an outcome happened, it was intended. Certainly, however, the effect of Irwin Mitchell's apparent support for Eddie's case against the Ombudsman, their misleading reassurances about Eddie's standing, and his chances of getting legal aid – together with their delay in acting when the Guideline came out – prevented us going elsewhere until it was too late. I was the frog that sat in the water, not moving, until I was slowly boiled.

53 - THE MAIL ON SUNDAY

This second NICE debacle made me desperate at least to salvage some media coverage from it, as I had after SIGN's refusal. Lynne reminded me about an article I had written telling the stories of brave Christine Wrightson, who fought so hard for the SST to be exposed, and her friend Jill Mizen, which the *Mail on Sunday* had bought but never published. She said my best hope was to approach editor Barney Calman again and try, using this new hook, to get him to print the article. Lynne drafted me a wonderful email which began:

'Dear Barney

I hope you are well.
You've had my article about Jill Mizen for just over a year, and you've promised me you'll publish it. Now we have the nose it needs...'

Barney said yes, he would run it the next weekend.

Well, this was the best thing that had happened for a long time, and yet, somehow, very alarming indeed. This was Friday 9 May.

The following Monday lunchtime he phoned and talked me through the structure of the article, and what he wanted me to add. He also wanted me to get a quote from an expert criticising NICE's decision. I had faith that

Professor Thompson in Dublin would oblige, since he'd already called NICE 'deliberately delinquent' in the email I have quoted, but he was always busy and slow to respond. I spent Monday afternoon sending him desperate emails and phoning his friendly secretary Marie – who told me, to my dismay, that he was just about to go abroad. I didn't get down to rewriting the article until the evening, and ended up spending the whole night on it, sustained by a rush of something powerful – cortisol probably.

At eleven o'clock the next morning I emailed a Lynne-subbed version to Barney. About an hour later an email came through from Professor Thompson, calling NICE's decision 'nonsensical' just as I'd hoped. Whew! I forwarded that to Barney too, and thought that now I could relax, and just focus on getting through my childminding hours without falling asleep. But late that afternoon, when I had just dropped Katherine off at her drama group, I got a phone call from Barney – a somewhat uneasy, throat-clearing call, saying he wanted to 'rejig the article slightly' and would I look at my emails? He'd sent me a suggested framework.

His new version showed that he'd misunderstood. He'd thought that my point was that the NICE guideline was advocating a faulty test instead of a good, more costly one and that patients got checked routinely with the faulty test that didn't show up PTHP, and then got diagnosed with CFS/ME. This was understandable, because the previous version had all been about the short synacthen test. But what could I do now, how could I sort this out? I didn't see how I could use the new 'rejig' he'd sent me. Was everything going to collapse? Lynne said, 'Phone him.' I emailed him saying the problem wasn't that NICE were advocating the wrong test, but that they weren't advocating *any* test, synacthen or otherwise, and it didn't breathe a word about the risk of hypopituitarism. Could I phone him about it?

I spent the evening in high agitation. I could see, really, that Barney's rejig wasn't as impossible to stick to as I'd thought, as long as I kept to his structure, inserting different facts into the slots I worked away. Well into the next morning, and even when I had finished I was in a state of heart-thudding tension, incapable of relaxing.

On Wednesday, after a second almost sleepless night, I sent off the revised copy. Barney was happy, so all was well, and the article appeared (see appendix 2).

It attracted a lot of attention in ME, head injury, and endocrine circles, which was just what I wanted. Most of the ME, brain injury, and pituitary charities posted it on their websites. I used Bitly to create an abbreviated link so that I could tweet it to everyone I could think of. The benefit of such a link is being able to track how many people have clicked on it, and in what countries. Swiftly the clicks mounted to 1,500, reaching readers in the US, Canada, Australia, South Africa, Norway, and, more unexpectedly, countries where English is spoken less, like France and Peru. I still look to see how it is doing, rather in the manner of a gardener checking on seedlings, and a few clicks accumulate each week. At the time of writing the number had reached 2,070.

I wish I could find out if 200 people ever did get diagnosed as a result of my article, as Barney predicted. Somehow I don't believe that their journey will have been easy. By a roundabout route I got a glimpse into what two patients went through. I have to explain that when I wrote the original article, which focused on the evils of the short synacthen test, Barney told me that it wasn't enough to cite the review that showed how unreliable it was, and asked me to find an expert endocrinologist to endorse its findings. I chose Dr John Newell Price, a consultant endocrinologist who had recently, as chair of the Pituitary Foundation's Medical Committee, allowed the following statement to be posted on their website:

> 'Please note: for patients with symptoms that may suggest cortisol deficiency that a "pass" on a SST, may not always mean that cortisol deficiency is excluded, and that with persisting symptoms referral to an endocrinologist is recommended where testing may be carried out with alternatives such as the glucagon test or insulin stress test.'

I emailed him on 20 March 2013 asking if I could quote him, but got no reply, and although I made some attempts to phone him I never got through. In the end I decided that, as his statement was already in the public domain, I didn't really need his permission and went ahead anyway.

Although he had made this crucial statement I had never felt that he had a real desire to diagnose patients with hypopituitarism, because he never responded to any of my invitations to sign letters to the various concerned bodies. It was probably a mistake to suggest indirectly to ME patients reading the article that he might help them.

I think this because in September Barney forwarded me a letter from someone who had consulted him. It was from a woman who had been ill for many years with a non-specific chronic condition for which no doctor had ever supplied a definite, treatable, diagnosis. Her GP eventually diagnosed CFS but she felt this was as a last resort. 'My list of symptoms is vast, and my quality of life is at rock bottom right now.'

My article had excited her because she recognised her own symptoms and experiences in those of Christine and Jill, and she was even more pleased to see Professor Newell-Price quoted because he was based in her home town of Sheffield. Her GP (who 'raised her eyes because I think she is under the impression that I am just depressed, despite all my physical symptoms') grudgingly gave a referral and after some effort the writer got an appointment, sending a detailed medical history, test results, and symptom list to the Professor beforehand.

However, 'as soon as we got into the consulting room Prof Newell-Price referred to the *Mail on Sunday* article. He said he had nothing to do with the article, that his statements had been fabricated or misquoted, that he did not advocate the diagnostic and testing methods mentioned and that he didn't agree with any of the contents of the article.' So this unfortunate patient was simply referred to the Infectious Diseases and CFS Clinics, and offered anti-depressants, none of which gave her any help whatsoever.

Her next two paragraphs were very bitter:

'Bearing in mind how ill and fatigued I am this was the last thing I needed to hear. It had taken so much energy just to attend the appointment only to be told I had wasted my time [...] Since coming home [...] I have given up. I have had suicidal thoughts many times over this past year but this has sent me to the edge [...] I had such hopes that I was going to see someone who listened to the patient and could help. I really don't think anyone in good health can understand how demoralising it is to be shown a possible lifeline only to have it snatched away. Now what can I do?

I do not blame Prof Newell-Price, I lay the blame firmly and squarely at the door of The Mail on Sunday for printing the erroneous sections of this article. Once again I am back to square one in my search for answers, my hopes dashed due to lazy journalism by the author of this article [...] I think the least you could offer is to find the medical person who can help or at least will listen and test me.'

Lazy journalism! Oh dear! I was comforted by Barney's accompanying email. Barney told me he had telephoned Professor Newell-Price, 'who told us a number of patients had been referred to him for the same reason and seemed exasperated.' But he did at least acknowledge that he *had* said what I'd said he'd said, though he was uncomfortable with the context, as he didn't agree with the premise of the article. 'However,' Barney continued, 'he doesn't wish to take the matter further.' I wrote back explaining about the Pituitary Foundation website and how I'd tried to get in touch with the Professor but failed, and then decided to go ahead anyway. Barney said, 'No, you did the right thing. Don't worry, Joanna!'

I wrote to the lady who had complained, with the best advice I could give her. She told me she had been repeatedly hit on the head with a heavy glass object until she passed out, which made her think her illness could be pituitary damage.

By coincidence, shortly after that I received an account from a second patient of Professor Newell-Price, telling me, 'He said my scans are irrelevant, my previous diagnosis is irrelevant [cyclical Cushing's] and my symptoms could be anything. He said I could be depressed.' All this patient got offered was a morning cortisol reading (which is of course rarely enough to establish cortisol deficiency without further testing) and a recommendation not to waste time travelling to Sheffield.

I do not know how patients in other parts of the UK fared, but I am afraid the ones in Sheffield may not have got very far.

54 - THE PICTURE BROADENS

Eddie and Jill had led me into a new landscape, more desolate and vast than I had ever imagined, a Dante-esque circle of hell, where every day desperate people cry out on forums for help in understanding their test results, and plead for the names of doctors who will treat them knowledgeably and with respect instead of dismissing them contemptuously, where they complain about their years of suffering, share their despair at daughters or husbands who cold-shoulder them, confess to thoughts of ending it all – and where other equally sick people offer sympathy and do their best to help.

The themes of isolation, inappropriate testing, unsympathetic doctors, refusal by family and colleagues to believe anything organic is wrong – all these were familiar to me from hypopituitarism sufferers who had emailed me. Some of those people in life-rafts lost on the dark sea appear on forums around thyroid conditions. Somehow the fact that they weren't under a 'head injury' banner, meant that at first I didn't see them. Thyroid problems don't necessarily stem from the pituitary but may lie in the thyroid gland itself. But the more posts I read about the detail of testing for thyroid deficiency, the clearer it grew that many of these people *could* have a pituitary that wasn't working properly, and could well be suffering other pituitary deficiencies that they didn't know about.

The fact that so many of Thyroid UK's members had been given those catch-all diagnoses that can't be verified by laboratory testing, such as ME, chronic fatigue syndrome, and fibromyalgia – just like Eddie and nearly all the others who'd written to me – eventually took on its full significance, and I woke up to what was under my nose: the answer to the mystery about how so many hundreds of thousands of sick people could apparently remain invisible. The answer to my long-standing question, 'Where are all these people?' was that they were being diagnosed with fatigue syndromes.

The number of people currently being told they had one of these three 'vague' illnesses – illnesses that are a 'diagnosis of exclusion', something that doctors tell people they have when other tests have proved negative, illnesses that are considered to have a psychosomatic element, and for which there is no effective treatment – the combined number of these patients stands at around three million in the UK today. There is plenty of room in there for Mr Belli's estimated million PTHP sufferers to hide.

If I wanted to reach them, the most effective route was clearly going to be via the charities and support groups for so-called ME patients.

While I thought about this I did some googling about ME and also learnt a lot from Jill. I have to confess here that most of my life I had believed ME was an imaginary illness, yuppie 'flu. In the eighties and nineties I had unthinkingly absorbed the view, assiduously promoted in the media, that people with ME were spoilt and rich with nothing wrong with them really. I do remember being puzzled, however, at the news that Clare Francis the yachtswoman had it. To me, though she was clearly not poor, she did not fit the introspectively idle profile.

What Jill told me radically changed my ideas about this disease. She made me aware, for example, that a whole cache of documents about ME were locked away in the UK Government National Archives at Kew. The original release date for these was 2023, but has since been extended to 2073. When I told John this he couldn't believe it. He protested that files were only kept secret when they threatened national security – for example correspondence about foreign policy. How could documents about an illness possibly pose a security risk? I could not answer him. I had no idea either. But when, on Jill's advice, I looked at the ME Association website, I found a link to a Parliamentary question posed by the Countess of Mar in the House of Lords dated 21 January 2011 as to why these files were being closed to public access for seventy-eight years rather than the usual thirty, together with the reply by the then Minister of State for Justice, Lord Tom McNally, that 'Due to the personal nature of the content, the file remains closed until 2073 under Section 40(2) of the Freedom of Information Act.'

These documents were written during the period 1988-1997 and are about the allocation of grants by the Medical Research Council (MRC) for research into ME/CFS. But that organisation is a big bear trying to hide behind a small sofa. Thanks to the leaky nature of the internet, photographed copies of one such correspondence (stamped 'Redacted under FOI exemption(s) 40(2). Closed until 2073') can be viewed on the whale.to website. [http://whale.to/v/secret1.html]

The correspondence took place in 1992 between a Ms Doris Jones and a Dr Peter Dukes of the GMC, and relates to Ms Jones's application for funding to investigate physiological causes of ME, focusing in particular on the effect of vaccinations, antibiotics, and allergies. Her application, though supported by published research as well as a detailed, multifactorial, epidemiological research project she had recently completed herself, was turned down (An article by Christina England dated 6 October 2012, which appears above the facsimiles, provides evidence that, by contrast, the GMC chose to give generous funding to research carried out by the Institute of Psychiatry.) This example of a single application proves little on its own, but the GMC's bias towards research into psychiatric causes is supported by a talk given in 2006 by Dr Jonathan Kerr of St George's University in London at an ME conference. He said that the panel allocating ME grants was made up predominantly of psychiatrists, which immediately 'biases the decision-making process.' He said, 'It is a fact that currently the MRC does not fund any biological approaches.'

What this meant was that when NICE prepared its ME guideline there was a wealth of research at their disposal, all finding the CFS/ME was a psychological condition – a 'somatoform' disorder – and not an organic disease. In this way they were able to preserve a semblance of academic rigour when they advocated counselling and exercise and discouraged 'over-vigilance regarding symptoms and related checking and reassurance-seeking behaviour'. This instruction is what lay behind the letter to Eddie's GP which expressed concern 'that he may go on to undergo further investigation and medicalisation of his symptoms' and recommended counselling – a letter that could have ended his quest for a cure.

55 - MORE ABOUT ME/CFS

The more I read, the more I suspected there was a machine that the government holds at the ready for emergencies, for trundling out whenever people are falling ill in droves from a new sickness which has perhaps been caused by something poisonous in the environment, or by medical intervention such as vaccines – an illness which may mean paying compensation. The purpose of the machine is to persuade the public (and if possible the patients too) that the illness doesn't exist, and is all in the mind.

I brooded on the story of the Camelford water scandal as it was described in newspaper articles at the time. Most people remember how in July 1988 the water supplies of this small Cornish town were seriously contaminated with aluminium sulphate. There was a delay of 16 days before the water company, South West Water Authority, who were about to be privatised, confessed. People complained that the water was black, that they had stomach cramps and ulcers, but the water company told them that the water was safe and that all they needed to do was to boil it (In fact boiling is exactly the wrong thing to do as it increases the aluminium concentration). The public didn't stop complaining of health problems, and seven years later an article came out in the *Journal of Psychosomatic Research* by Professor Simon Wessely stating that the Camelford inhabitants were infecting each other with group hysteria and were influenced by the hope of compensation (I remem-

287

bered Professor Wessely's name from Christine Wrightson's Deep Throat-type phone calls that used to transfix me as I stood in shopping malls.) His conclusion was reported in the BMJ and widely publicised. It was not until 25 years later in September 2013, when a number of those affected had died and been shown to have abnormal levels of aluminium in their brains, that the British government 'apologised unreservedly' for its handling of the affair. As for compensation, some money was eventually paid out in 1997 (the claim was brought by Irwin Mitchell who often handle group actions from the public), but residents claimed that they had been railroaded into accepting inadequate sums by the threat that they would lose their legal aid if they refused.

Gulf War Syndrome was a similar story. Veterans fell sick in large numbers. Professor Wessely wrote an article in *The Lancet* in 1999 saying the malaise was caused by stress of combat, together with *anxiety* about vaccines and chemical weapons. The BMJ published an article in 2001 by Chalder (co-authored by Professor Wessely) finding that you were more likely to believe you had Gulf War Syndrome if you knew somebody else who believed they did. Twenty years after Operation Desert Storm the British government, in contrast to the US who have now paid compensation to their veterans, still refuses to admit that Gulf War Syndrome exists, and although some veterans now have war pensions, many are still waiting.

The mysterious sickness of ME/CFS first reached public awareness in the 1980s. In 1988 the familiar figure of Professor Wessely is recorded as advocating in his role as a senior registrar in psychiatry that a child with ME be separated from his/her parents: 'I feel that Ean needs a long period of rehabilitation (which) will involve separation from his parents, providing an escape from his "ill" world.' For a more detailed account of Ean Proctor's case, see the article by Eileen Marshall and Margaret Williams dated 25 July 2005 which quotes from the *Report of the Select Committee of Tynwald on the Petition for Redress of Grievance of Robin and Barbara Proctor* (dated 19 April 1991) and gives the full correspondence with dates. This can be found on the Hummingbirds website.

From the 1990s onwards, Wessely became increasingly vocal in his view that CFS/ME was a mental (somatoform) disorder, and that 'holding a belief that the illness is due to physical causes' leads to a worse outcome (*Quarterly Journal of Medicine*, March 1997). To this day, even in the face of the World Health Organisation's classification of the illness as a neurological condition, he persists in this opinion. He was knighted in 2013 for services to military healthcare and psychological medicine. And patients diagnosed with CFS/ME/FM are still being treated with exercise and counselling, and still not being properly investigated.

I found all this hard to absorb, and disturbing. It seemed clear that there had been enormous determination to present ME as a psychological illness. The Camelford and Gulf War Syndrome similarities made me wonder if a fear of litigation was involved, but ME is an international phenomenon, so the cause would have to be something used worldwide. Vaccinations? Pesticides? Fertilisers? Or was it not about compensation at all, but simply that too many people, if investigated properly, might turn out to need expensive hormone treatment? I could not understand how I had been ignorant of all this, how nobody else seemed to know either.

And I learned two more things, one of which made me

angry, the other heartbroken and furious. The one that made me angry was the PACE trial. This was a clinical trial carried out for a year (the report came out in March 2011) with around 600 patients, costing the tax-payer £5 million. It was designed to assess the effectiveness of therapies for treating CFS/ME, with the emphasis on cognitive behavioural therapy and graded exercise training. The Countess of Mar (a member of the House of Lords who was wrongly diagnosed with ME after exposure to organophosphates) has ably exposed the jiggery-pokery that went on to ensure that the study came to the 'right' conclusion. She revealed how certain data was withheld, how the goalposts were moved in the course of the trial so that if a patient was sicker at the end than at the beginning he/she could still be counted as having improved, how objective measures such as coming off benefits or getting back to work were studiously avoided and how, even with all this tinkering, the trial only managed to show that 15 per cent improved after cognitive behavioural therapy and graded exercise training – in other words, it made no difference to 85 per cent of patients.

As the Countess put it: 'The only information, published in "A Cost-Effectiveness Analysis of the PACE Trial", shows that there was no significant improvement [...] in the average number of days lost from work or the number of participants who lost days at work. In fact, claims for [...] benefits, and from private pensions and income protection schemes, increased across all intervention groups during the trial.'

What a waste of money. I wondered how many people might have been helped if the £5 million had been spent on investigating their pituitary function instead.

With this thought I come to the discovery that made

me furious and broke my heart. I learned about Dr Chandy.

One of my correspondents sent me a web link to a talk Dr Chandy had given at a conference held by the Pernicious Anaemia Society in 2013 (transcribed in appendix 3). Dr Joseph Chandy is a 75-year-old GP in Horden, County Durham, and he has achieved fame for his research using vitamin B12 to treat fatigue syndrome, even receiving the Glory of India award. Despite his distinguished reputation, the impression I got as I watched his presentation on my computer screen, was that he had the unassuming simplicity that you sometimes find in very good people, and that his audience loved him and he loved them. 'Am I all right for time?' he asks at one point. 'You'll have to speed up. [audience laughter] This is the time I always over-run, I get excited to see you all I think … [more laughter] Forgive me Martin, I get carried away.' After he finishes, a voice off-camera shouts, 'This is the first time in four visits he's actually finished early! The very first conference he went on for three and a half hours!'

His talk was carefully constructed, with a surprise at the end (the transcript can be found in the endnotes), and I am spoiling the surprise by revealing that one of his 'fatigue' patients was his own daughter Leanne. She was 28, practising as a lawyer, when they began to suspect something was not right, and by the time she was 33 she was having difficulty remembering things, and getting angry and upset. Dr Chandy came to suspect hypoadrenalism (a deficiency of ACTH, one of the pituitary hormones). When he referred her to the Royal Victoria Infirmary in Newcastle they gave her the short synacthen test and found she had low basal, pre-test cortisol levels, but decided that her illness was 'all in her mind'. She got worse, collapsing one day, and unable to get up or look after her two small children. Later she couldn't talk or breathe properly. Hartlepool Hospital and James Cook Hospital both said she needed to see a psychiatrist. 'Day and night I studied' says Dr Chandy, and after this rejection by three hospitals he took matters into his own hands: 'I must act, though we GPs are not allowed to diagnose and treat.' He started her on hydrocortisone. 'Probably if I didn't, she would have died.'

His success with her, and his experience of the short synacthen test being wrongly used to rule out hypopituitarism, made him alert to other patients and in all he saved 25 patients with chronic fatigue by giving them hydrocortisone as part of their treatment. In his talk he showed slides of them, ill and then recovered ('When you see this smile – doesn't it make you all well?').

Twenty-five patients! The BBC says there are 32,000 GPs in the UK. If, for the sake of argument, you imagine that all the GPs in this country imitated Dr Chandy, that would mean that 800,000 patients would get their lives back. Getting on for the missing million I'd been searching for. How could the GMC not give him a medal and swiftly roll out this practice to all the other GPs in the land?

Of course they didn't. They harassed him and restricted him on three separate occasions, starting in 2001, and have now banned him from prescribing B12 and hydrocortisone to fatigue syndrome patients, and barred him from doing private practice outside the NHS. His patients are left high and dry.

Nothing could show more clearly the General Medical Council's determination, and perhaps that of other outfits even higher up the chain, to ensure that deviation from clinical guidelines will not be tolerated, with the consequence that patients with pituitary conditions remain undiagnosed, condemned to endure the rest of their wretched half-lives in their bedrooms, alone and without hope. How much compensation would someone like Christine Wrightson be entitled to for the clinical negligence which made her so ill by delaying her diagnosis for three years and probably hastening her death? £100,000? What about people who have been kept unnecessarily ill for three decades, who have lost their relationships and their jobs? The compensation can of worms could be gargantuan.

56 - AMY

The discoveries I have just described propelled me to an ME conference in 2013. Although it did not seem the case at the time, my day there set in motion a long train of events.

It was held in London, in Westminster, in May. On the way there, while I was sitting at our local station tensely rehearsing what I was determined to say at question time, I'd seen a neighbour, James, who I'd rarely spoken to but had sympathy for because he and his wife had a severely handicapped son. He looked exactly like a young Daniel Day-Lewis, and it was somehow surprising to discover that he lived a normal suburban life, going off to work in a suit each morning.

I had told him about Chris and the ME conference, and he talked to me about his son, and as we got on the train he gave a smile tinged with sadness and said, 'We have to fight for our sons.'

Just as I had with Christine Lord, I felt that empowering boost that one grieving parent can give to another, and arriving in London I went more fortified into the conference than I might otherwise have done.

I managed to stand up and loudly voice how people who'd written to me had almost all been misdiagnosed with ME before getting a correct diagnosis of PTHP, how a million PTHP sufferers could easily be concealed in the three million so-called fatigue patients – and asked why people weren't checked for this? I got the reply that they *were* checked (plainly not rigorously enough), but I didn't mind, I'd launched my message and could only hope I had been heard.

Two people came and spoke to me in the coffee break. One a German GP who had diagnosed himself with a pituitary condition after being told he had ME and meeting with very little support from other doctors. The other was a lady who told me, intriguingly, that one of the organisers of the conference had commented, about me, 'We don't usually allow that kind of question.'

I thought that this was the end of it – that I hadn't achieved much for the £80 or so the day had cost me. But a week later I got an email from a 31-year-old woman called Amy Louise Hanson who had read an account online of what I'd said and wanted me to tell her which endocrinologist might test her properly for PTHP.

Amy had been dropped on her head first while a baby, again aged 12 during a dance routine after which she'd suffered depression, and then had been involved in a bad traffic accident aged 19. At university her concentration began to fail, she'd need naps, she put on weight, her depression returned, and she had to repeat a year. It was after this that the traffic accident happened, leaving her with broken ribs and whiplash. She knew something was seriously wrong when she fell asleep on a Friday evening and didn't wake up until Sunday. The following year she had to leave university with nowhere to live and nothing to show for her years of study except a £16,000 debt. A thyroid test in 2005 gave a normal level result and in 2006 she was diagnosed with CFS/ME.

I suggested she see Dr Kar, who had worked such a miracle with James Smith, spotting what was wrong with him within minutes. Amy got an appointment with him for the end of October. Strangely, though, all Dr Kar seemed inclined to offer her was a short synacthen test.

Amy wrote soon afterwards saying it had come back normal and he had instructed her GP to discharge her. She wrote in December asking him for an insulin stress test, but he replied that she was too ill for that and did not suggest any alternatives.

I was horribly mortified. I'd let Amy down. How could Dr Kar have changed his view so much from only a year before, when he had written so enthusiastically that 'hypopituitarism is indeed very close to my heart'? He must have suspected pituitary dysfunction from Amy's head injury history, yet he was avoiding giving her the test that would reveal it.

Amy gave me permission to email Dr Kar directly and I wrote to him in January 2014 on the same day as Amy wrote a long letter, with some input from me, asking for a glucagon stimulation test. I reminded him of how he'd recognised James's symptoms so quickly, and said that with Amy's own history of head injury I had wondered if he might do the same.

To my relief he answered the next day, 'No probs, I am working on it.' He answered Amy's long letter with a promise that he would 'discuss with our nurse and then get back to you asap'.

However, the next thing I heard was a despondent email from Amy dated a month later, forwarding Dr Kar's answer to her request for a glucagon stimulation test. He said the department had discussed it, but the consensus was not to give the test. 'However, hold fire – and give me a nudge end next week.'

At this point I felt I had to act. I wrote on 5 February summarising Amy's symptoms, pointing out the limitations of the short synacthen test, and reminding him that some tests for cortisol involved hardly any risk. 'Any testing risks have to be weighed against the fact that her current life is not worth living. It is shocking that such a young girl should be robbed of all chance of having a career, marrying, having children, feeling happy and fulfilled – if the path to getting her life back carries some risks, she might decide to take them.' I asked him to tell me frankly if it was a funding issue, because then Amy might do something privately.

I ended by giving him links to Eddie's, Jill's, and Christine's stories.

Dr Kar replied three days later, apparently forgetting that Amy had asked for the relatively safe glucagon test, and writing as if everything had been about the more dangerous insulin stress test (IST):

> 'In short, think I did offer Amy the glucagon test but she wants the IST. Looking at her health I am not sure she can go through it which she doesn't think is the case. As clinician I do have my concerns about going through with this, as do the nurses who have seen her ... thus the discussion.
>
> As regards the finances, on the contrary, doing the test gains us money via NHS structures ... so the easiest way is to do the test if purely for financial reasons.
>
> However, the clinical issue is a concern as if something does go wrong, which it can do in an Insulin Stress Test, the responsibility for that will sit with me, not anyone else.'

I did not try to sort out who had said what, but wrote to Dr Kar thanking him and sympathising with his position. I said I hoped Amy would agree to the glucagon test.

So Amy wrote to Dr Kar in February saying she would be happy to have the glucagon test and – wonderfully –

she was given it at last, in March.

There was the usual long wait, but then in April an email headed 'Surprised results' from Amy appeared in my inbox. She attached a letter from Dr Kar noting that her growth hormone readings were 'quite flat' and suggesting referral to the endocrine team at Winchester.

In due course her exact results were released and it turned out that Amy had only one twentieth the growth hormone that she should.

Painfully the wheels ground round. Amy was duly referred to a Winchester endocrinologist, but given an appointment months away, at the end of August. She made a private appointment with one of his team and saw him in June. To our surprise, he considered there was no risk in giving Amy the insulin stress test, and said he could do it on the NHS and she underwent it without mishap in August.

On 16 September she heard that this test too had shown she was growth hormone deficient. After an MRI scan and a further test, her endocrinologist said in September that he would give her a trial course of GH replacement. This began at the end of November.

Disregarding, for the moment, Amy's long years of being diagnosed with depression, it took 18 months from her first request to be checked out for PTHP to her being in line for some treatment. It's a long time.

Amy's story is ongoing. She had a bad reaction to the injections, as sometimes happens, and had to begin again with a lower dose. The miracle cure like James's has not happened yet, but we all live in hope.

57 - SOMETHING ELSE GOOD

Another breakthrough happened while Amy was waiting for her glucagon test. Dr Mark Porter, whom I'd been writing to since 2010, agreed to air PTHP on his BBC Radio 4 programme *Inside Health*. What persuaded him in the end were two academic papers, one stating 30 in every 100,000 succumbed to PTHP every year, and the other that 50 did. This of course multiplies to between 18,000 and 30,000 a year, and if you multiply by 40 for the past decades of non-diagnosis, then you get a rough and ready total of up to 1.2 million – though the real figure will be less, because of the suicides.

Dr Porter said that if I could get a consultant to endorse that estimate, he'd run the piece. Mr Belli, like a star, obliged.

The interview happened in March, and then there was a long, agonising wait. I was convinced again that something would happen at the last minute to make them pull it – it just seemed too good to be true – but in the end, on 9 April (John's birthday) it was aired.

It was perfect. Mr Belli said everything I could have wished. Both Mark and he described the pituitary and how easily it could be damaged. They had found a little boy called Luke Flavell whose recovery from a head injury had been suddenly stalled by pituitary failure, and then quickly put back on course again thanks to prompt diagnosis and treatment. (Mark: 'You've had quite a battle haven't you Luke?' Luke 'It's one of them things.')

Then the symptoms were discussed (they missed out

obesity for some reason), and I was pleased that Mark teased out the point that it wasn't 'all or nothing' – the gland might only fail partially – and that the onset might be delayed. And they included the crucial point that the injury need not be severe like Luke's, it could be something like a sports concussion where the patient hadn't even attended A&E.

But what pleased me most about the programme was the time they spent discussing the numbers of people affected. 'Some studies suggest a million people, some studies suggest probably half a million but still we're talking about very, very large numbers of people that are not recognised or treated.'

Finally Mr Belli said how effective treatment could be.

I was so happy that day. What lovely men Dr Porter and Mr Belli were. I could have kissed them both. It was not just that people listened to the broadcast that day, but that I had yet another credential for when I approached people. *Inside Health* was a respected, well-researched programme, and if I could quote that, plus the Early Day Motion, people would have to take the issue seriously.

How can one measure the impact of these things? I greedily looked at the audience figures for Radio 4, which run at about 11 million listeners a week – but did those 11 million listeners switch on to *Inside Health*? Could you reckon that perhaps a million would? That would be a sixtieth of the UK population, a sixtieth of the people I was trying to reach, bypassing NICE and all those other more or less obstructive health organisations.

I emailed the programme link to everyone I could think of. At any rate, I felt as if I had done my absolute best. And, as an unexpected bonus, Mark wrote an article about PTHP in *The Times*, on 10 September that year. *The Times* circulation during that period was 386,883, not as exciting as the Radio 4 listening figures, but still, they might be educated readers who I hoped had some clout. The *Mail*'s circulation is one and three quarter million. Little by little, I felt the cup was filling.

A friend said, 'Chris would have been proud of you,' but I always found that kind of comment upsetting, even though so kindly meant. Chris wasn't there. He couldn't be proud of me. All I could feel was that I had done my best to fulfil my mantra of 'Let everything that can be good, be good.'

When, as usual, I had looked up the diagnosis figures for hypopituitarism for the year 2013, I'd had a surprise. An enigmatic surprise. The website gave the primary diagnosis figure as 2,378 – not brilliant, about 150 up on 2012. But it also gave the secondary diagnosis figures for all conditions, which was something that had never happened before, and the figure for hypopituitarism was 11,128.

This looked good, but I didn't understand what it meant. Did secondary diagnosis mean a condition that was already there on the patient's notes when he or she went to hospital? If it did, that would be a historical diagnosis not a new one, so the total of new cases diagnosed would still be only around 2,000. However (and this is what I hoped) secondary diagnosis might mean 'other things found to be wrong with the patient while he has gone in for a different condition' – as, for instance, if a person went in to have a heart condition investigated, and then was found to have hypopituitarism as an extra complaint.

I wrote to Enquiries for clarification, but the answer didn't help. The conditions may be pre-existing or newly diagnosed, they said, and it was not possible to distinguish between the two in the data they held.

KENNETH STARR'S STORY

I was born in 1943 and grew up in Northern Ireland. In my youth I enjoyed playing hockey and tennis. I played these too at teacher training college in Manchester and later at senior level in Africa and in England. Even at that stage, I had some stamina and fatigue problems, and depression. Then I worked abroad teaching Agricultural Science and other subjects in Zambia in the late 1960s and early 70s and during that time I was exposed to an organophosphate (a pesticide called malathion) at work. It was then that my depression deepened and my muscles, gut and brain were affected. By 1971, just before my brother John (RIP) died tragically in a car accident, I was on anti-depressants. However, they made me much worse, so I stopped taking them.

In 1974 I suffered an unprovoked assault on my return from my second teaching contract in Zambia. I went out drinking with a friend and was going towards the hotel bar when I was struck a terrific single blow to the left-hand side of my jaw. I fell backwards and my head rebounded off the marble tiles. I came to, for a split second … felt a great rip inside my head … and then I was unconscious. I learned later that I had been shaking all over like a boxer when KO'd. Later that evening I was beaten up again and left unconscious outside my parents' home. I was suffering from what is now called Secondary Impact Syndrome (SIS) which can be fatal. Rugby and other sports bodies have recently become aware of this.

I didn't want to cause my parents further distress after my brother John's death, and I was too stubborn to go to the police or the hospital in spite of my seriously bruised spine, broken teeth, temporary double vision and the blood in my urine and faeces. I had to lie in a foetal position in the dark, as the light hurt my brain. The following year I had to terminate teaching contracts in Zambia where I had been for the previous five years, and Papua New Guinea. The contract in Papua New Guinea meant I had to have a battery of vaccinations at my local Army barracks before I flew out there, but I was too ill even to start teaching. I had to return.

After that my depression got much worse. I had shock treatment for seven or eight years and I was given eight bouts of electro-convulsive therapy (ECT). This psychiatric treatment regime caused me to suffer a severe breakdown in 1982 and I became suicidal after that. I had been on Ativan (which contains the active ingredient lorazepam – a benzodiazepine similar to valium, though I have been told it is at least ten times stronger) and I became seriously addicted to it for five years. Nobody in the NHS could get me off it. In fact I took part in a case study on Ativan addiction.

I took myself to a mental hospital for help. It was a terrible time. I ended up in 1982 locked up and fighting for my life. During my period in the mental hospital I became agitated, was restless and had hallucinations. I suffered from dreadful thirst and I was foaming at the mouth. I had at least one serious convulsion caused either by withdrawing from Ativan or by an injection I was given, which brought me close to death. I nearly bit my tongue off and my brain felt like a car engine with no oil, grinding on itself. My hearing and sense of smell were heightened but I seemed to have no taste left. An artery in my mouth burst and the thick, lumpy red blood nearly filled a jug that was handed to me. The damage to my mouth and tongue were permanent! Even during the recovery stage I was so weak, and unaware most of the time, that I had to be bathed. When I got home I prayed to die. I could take no more. All my energy had gone, and so had the elasticity in my body and skin.

After one of the ECT treatments my legs were like lead and I felt semi-paralysed. My condition was made worse by the fact that the consultant psychiatrist delegated my care to a trainee member of her team who had inclinations towards Christian Science, haranguing me about Jesus and forcing me to carry out demeaning and exhausting manual tasks.

The ECT, or perhaps the accompanying anaesthetic, worsened my condition permanently. Seemingly, ECT should not be given to B12-deficient patients or to those affected by organophosphates and the medical profession needs to be aware of this [see references to research in appendix 1].

My medical records covering this time have been destroyed, so I cannot check whether the large injections I was given increased the addiction problem and helped to cause this terrifying crisis and everlasting suffering. Afterwards, I was not able to play tennis or hockey any more and life would never be the same again, though eventually I found other interests.

I have suffered from steadily increasing depression and extreme fatigue for forty years plus and my weight gain has been abnormal. These are classic symptoms of growth hormone deficiency, yet it was only in 2014 that I was finally diagnosed with this, and also with low testosterone. It is likely that my hypopituitarism (PTHP) has been caused by the double effect of organophosphate exposure and head injury. I'm sure my brain has been injured in many other ways, but I think I would have had a better chance of a normal life if my pituitary damage had been spotted immediately.

Note

In the hope that it may help other people, I have described my other treatments and diagnoses here.

In 1983-4, Dr Kenneth McAll (now sadly deceased) treated me with vitamins B1, B3 and B6, which helped me tremendously. Dr Friedrich Staebler (London) also gave me hope and helped me with alternative treatments and I was well enough to complete an MSc in Crop Production in 1984-5.

Over the years I kept having tests (mainly private) to try to discover the reason for my depression, fatigue and ME/CFS type illness. I have PENE and PEM type symptoms.

I tested positive for Virus Protein 1, and tests for the Epstein Barr Virus showed I was likely to have been infected in the past.

I was found to be very low in vitamin B12 (93 iu) in 2005, as was my mother (my earlier treatment in the 1980s had not been followed up). In fact I was only given B12 injections regularly after I was diagnosed with pernicious anaemia and autoimmune gastritis in 2008.

I probably had hypothyroidism most of my life and although my TSH was high at about 5.5 (in USA people are treated at 3.0 and above), I received no NHS treatment. I had to have that seen to privately.

In 2006 I was diagnosed with hyperparathyroidism and informed that I had probably had this condition for more than twelve years (earlier diagnosis would have helped me!) and had the large tumour removed.

In 2007 I again was found to have candida which could be responsible for many of my bowel problems. I had also at various times tested positive for the parasites *Rickettsias conorii* and *mooseri*, *Blastocystis hominis* and *Dientamoeba fragilis*.

A Mitochondrial Profile Function Test showed I have a major problem with fatigue; my score was 0.85, which equates to about 45/100 on Dr Myhill's Disability Scale, and I have become much worse since then.

In 2007 I was diagnosed with 'partial peripheral thyroid hormone resistance' and advised to take T3 medication.

I also have severe osteoporosis which has increased the lower back pain which was caused by the assault and the ECT. I was told that the removal of my parathyroid tumour in 2006 should help my bone density to increase again, but there has still been no improvement in 2014. I imagine that the 12-year delay in finding and removing the tumour meant the operation came too late to help the osteoporosis. Also I now know that growth hormone and testosterone are necessary for better bone density and I have probably been deficient in these for years.

58 - EVERY EARTH STOPPED

The PTHP sufferer, faced with the intransigence of the various health organisations, is like a badger trapped underground. It seemed to me as I tried to get action taken that gamekeepers were on guard at every exit. Whichever burrow I tunnelled down, whether it was arguing for the inclusion of PTHP in the national suicide prevention strategy, or attempting to initiate a Cochrane review, or persuading the BMJ to publish an article about PTHP, it was as if light and air were blocked and dry earth choked my mouth.

Suicide Prevention

I have always been resistant to counselling. I don't want to be taught techniques to cope with my grief, to feel less bad. Grief for me is as effective as a cattle-prod in making me act, because I can't bear to sit still and let the thoughts come. Letting my rocket fuel dribble harmlessly into the sand means everything is lost.

This is why I bristled (unfairly) when, in November 2008 – very early on in my campaign, and in an attempt to influence suicide prevention strategy – I rang Paddy Bazeley, founder of Maytree. The charity runs a centre where suicidal people go to shelter until the crisis has passed, and I can hardly think of a more worthwhile project. I felt Paddy's warmth and charm over the phone, but … I could tell, she was instinctively slipping into counselling mode, asking how I was feeling (grrr) when all I wanted was for her to check if any of her clients had had a head injury and/or were suffering from sexual failure, and to implore them to get their hormones checked. She sensitively didn't push, was kindness itself, and offered to deliver my message to Professor Keith Hawton, the Director at the Centre for Suicide Research in Oxford, which feeds directly into the national suicide prevention strategy. In due course she forwarded me a study from him, the contents of which shocked me.

The paper – 'Suicidality after Traumatic Brain Injury' by Grahame Simpson and Robyn Tate – had been published six years previously and was a study of around two hundred head injury patients. It showed that more than a third had 'clinically significant' levels of hopelessness, about a quarter had suicidal thoughts, and 17 per cent ac-tually tried to kill themselves within five years of their in-jury. Googling further I found a vast Danish population study which established beyond doubt that brain injury survivors committed suicide three or four times more often than the norm. This study by Teasdale and Engberg had come out in 2001 in the *Journal of Neurology, Neuro-surgery and Psychiatry* and covered 145,440 patients admitted to hospital with head injury in Denmark. It found that the respective incidences of suicide after concussion, skull fracture, and bleeding on the brain were three times, 2.7 times, and 4.1 times the norm, respectively.

If I had known this, I would have treated Chris's account of his suicide attempt with utmost seriousness, instead of concocting a theory about him trying to distract us from his debt. I would have been on the watch all the time, talked to him more about it, I might even have discovered about his impotence. I might have saved him.

But he had had his accident too soon. The World Wide

Web didn't exist in 1984. If only I had thought more about the nurse who had warned me, 'His pituitary gland may be damaged' – I never forgot it – and done some retrospective browsing. But it's no good crying over spilt milk – or spilt life. It makes no difference now.

In passing on this study to me, Professor Hawton had given me something important to add to my collection of hard facts to quote. I knew that the increased risk of suicide wasn't necessarily caused by hypopituitarism – a head injury has any number of ways of screwing you up – but the more PTHP sufferers I met who had nursed suicide plans, or made attempts, the more I couldn't help suspecting that part of it was. .

I read the National Suicide Prevention Strategy, which listed groups of people who were at high risk, from beginning to end and found that, inexplicably, head injury patients weren't mentioned once. How could this be, when Professor Hawton, one of the experts behind it, clearly knew about them?

When I wrote to Professor Louis Appleby (National Clinical Director for Health and Criminal Justice) querying this, I found myself in that territory of illogicality which became so familiar as time went on. He quoted four criteria necessary for including head injury patients as a high risk group: the group had to be shown to have a statistically increased risk of suicide; the actual numbers of suicides in the group had to be known; evidence had to exist on which to base preventive measures; finally, there had to be ways of monitoring the impact of preventive measures.

What was extraordinary was that he was quoting these criteria as if they excluded head injury survivors, whereas they didn't – in my opinion all the criteria were met. The Danish study showed a 'statistically increased risk of suicide', it quoted the 'actual numbers', and there was evidence that if you educated GPs about the risk to a particular group, you could cut that risk by between 22 and 73 per cent. And as for monitoring, you could easily begin distributing leaflets about PTHP in a pilot area, say Wales, and see if the suicide rate dropped there more than in other places. Every year the Samaritans publish a Suicide Statistics Report, breaking down the numbers into geographical areas such as Wales, Scotland, and Northern Ireland, so any fall in the rate would be obvious.

But arguments like these had no effect.

I did have some brief success with the Kensington and Chelsea local suicide strategy authors, who took the research I sent them seriously and told me they would include head injury patients as a high risk group. When I looked this up recently to see if it was still there, I could find nothing.

I didn't at that stage understand how powerful a weapon a suicide strategy could be. Implemented, it could have meant that every GP's surgery had leaflets in its waiting room about the high risk to head injury survivors, a brilliant way to warn the public, not to mention the GPs themselves. I don't know why I didn't see this, but I didn't, and I forgot about suicide strategy until 13 September 2014.

That was when I clicked on an email which I won't forget. It said, 'I hope you don't mind me emailing but I believe my son may be another victim of undiagnosed PTHP.' Later this mother told me:

'We lost our lovely 26 year old son [...] he was a normal, delightful lad. Good fun, loving, kind, a hard worker [...] he had been to our GP because he was weeing such a lot [...] he had a breast tissue growth

314

that was unexplainable [...] He'd a head injury seven years ago [...] We adored him and loved him to bits. I miss him with every breath I take. Can I possibly speak to you?'

I can't describe how upset I was. I felt as if Chris had died all over again. And I can't describe how angry I felt either. I'd been working away for five years trying to change things, and still this could happen. Excessive weeing and man-boobs (polyuria and gynecomasty) were well documented symptoms of hypopituitarism, and everything I'd read suggested that these symptoms could have been caused by the head injury.

This mother, whom I shall call Mary, stayed in close touch for a while, suggesting people to approach. My only way of expressing what I felt was to follow up her leads gratefully and report on what happened. Through her I contacted the SOBS groups (Survivors of Bereavement by Suicide) and reached John Asher, a volunteer suicide prevention lead and trustee of the Cumbria Mental Health Group. He was wonderful and he knew something about pituitary disease. He was intuitively convinced I was right, more especially when he did a spot check of a bereavement group and found that two out of the eight attendees were mothers whose sons had suffered brain damage. John must have spent hours rooting out the contact details of influential people. Professor Appleby was on his list, and so was Professor Hawton, so I didn't expect much from them, but duly wrote all the same. Professor Appleby's response to my long email was:

'As things stand, we read the evidence as saying that brain injury can lead to suicide, the link being mediated by mental disorder and psychosocial factors – both of these are highlighted in the national strategy.

Once again, my sympathy for the loss of your son – it is a terrible experience.'

I did not welcome Professor Appleby's sympathy, unaccompanied as it was by any undertaking to change the silence which may have contributed to our son's death, but I could only respond graciously and point out that the evidence suggested that the link was direct, not 'mediated' by anything, otherwise why would the degree of risk be so clearly reflected in the type of injury? I reminded him that the Danish survey showed that the risk was exactly three times the norm if you have had a concussion, a bit less if you've had a skull fracture, and four times if you've had bruising or bleeding on the brain. Professor Appleby did not reply.

To Professor Hawton I had already written comparatively recently (30 May 2011) asking why head injury survivors were omitted as a high risk group. He had said not enough research had been done. I, having become wilier over the years, had not said, pantomime style, 'Oh yes it has!' but rather:

'What I'd like to do now, if you would bear with me, is to consider, one by one, the criteria for a high risk group as defined on page 12 of the National Suicide Strategy, and ask you what remains to be done for them to be fulfilled, in respect of head injury survivors.'

And then I gave the four criteria, much as I have done above, with the research that supported the evidence of risk, the actual numbers, the evidence for the effectiveness of intervention by warning medical professionals, and the ways that intervention could be monitored in the case of head injury. I said I'd be so grateful if he'd tell me what obstacles there were to naming head injury survivors as a high risk group.

When no answer came I chased him. Eventually I got his PA who said she'd just come back after being on holiday since 30 May, so he hadn't been able to email anyone in her absence. 'Poor helpless man!' I thought. 'Normally we go on holiday together,' she said, adding carefully, 'well, not *together*, but at the same time.' Professor Hawton never answered my email. And there I left it.

John Asher suggested several other influential people including Hamish Elvidge who runs the Mathew Elvidge Trust set up in memory of his son, and Helen Steele, Senior Policy Manager for Suicide Prevention at the Department of Health.

Hamish, who as John said 'wore the T-shirt' of suicide bereavement, talked to me on the phone and was helpful. He discussed the issue with Helen Steele, who, all credit to her, did not go in for 'Appleby logic' but corresponded with me rationally, answering my points and my counter-arguments. I asked her why it was 'hard to estimate' the risk to head injury survivors, as she claimed. I could not see why it was any harder to estimate that risk than it was to measure suicides among those with, say, a history of self-harm (the third high-risk group listed). 'I imagine both investigations would be quite similar, requiring reference to the person's medical notes.' Her reply, put simply, was that looking at patient's notes cost money, and the way they dealt with the self-harm group was to take the attendances recorded at six Emergency Departments in three cities after an episode of self-harm,

317

and then match the records for those patients with records of their death. However, the business case for doing this was that 50 per cent of suicide deaths occurred in this group. She said that my figures suggested that head injuries would only account for around 1-2 per cent of suicide deaths.

If I had been more on the ball, I would have asked what 1-2 per cent meant in real numbers (In fact, when I looked it up later, it meant around 132 people, because in 2012 there were 6,600 suicides). I could then have said that, according to a report published by the Department of Health in 2011, each suicide of someone of working age costs £1.67m (at 2009 prices), taken over a lifetime's taxes on earnings and including societal costs such as the increased risk of mental illness and consequent unemployment in other members of the family, and that therefore we were talking about nearly £200 million, a loss surely worth spending a little money to avoid.

However, I accepted her reasoning, and was in fact relieved to have a reply that made sense, so I thanked her. I said I could see it wasn't economical to spend a disproportionate amount on preventing only 1-2 per cent of suicides and instead I focused on discovering whether it really was such a small percentage.

I pointed out I'd based my figure on in-patient head injury cases, whereas everyone knew it was well documented that sports concussions – which are often not even reported – could cause depression too and might be the cause of the 'notorious suicidality' of footballers. Given the alarming possibility (or probability, given the figures I could show her) that the percentage was far higher, shouldn't there be some investigation? I suggested a pilot study, in which two or three individual coroners could do a box-ticking exercise asking families whether the person had ever had a head injury, including an apparently minor concussion.

She did not reply. When I reminded her a fortnight later she wrote, 'Just a quick note to let you know that I know you are still waiting […] but it is a very busy time for me […] I will come back to you again.'

This had been in November 2013. I nudged her six weeks later, but she did not answer. I tried a couple of times after that, still with no success.

I could see no reasonable excuse she could give for refusing to take such an inexpensive step to investigate such a crucial question. I think she was too honest to concoct one.

Anyway, that concluded my digging along that burrow – at least for the time being.

The British Medical Journal

The BMJ were helpful at the beginning. I wrote to them in 2008, soon after Chris's death, and the editor Fiona Godlee suggested making his story a 'Lesson of the Week'. This would have been excellent, but Chris's GP practice (The Fisher Medical Centre in Skipton) would not cooperate. The GP said he was 'regrettably' prevented from writing an article by the common law duty of confidence towards patients both living and deceased. However, this wasn't really true. The BMJ often published articles about deceased patients and told me their policy was to ask the relatives' consent. They suggested instead that I should ask a specialist involved in Chris's care, but of course the problem was that he'd never seen a specialist – or certainly, not the right specialist. So that initiative failed.

The next year I had a stab at writing a 'Patient's

Journey' article, which is the slot where laypeople can describe their experience, but when that failed I wrote off the BMJ.

My mailshot to consultants, which I carried out in 2009-2010, had elicited a kind letter from Dr Beckett, an A&E consultant at West Middlesex University Hospital. 'Clearly this is something that all doctors need to know about and I think it's very admirable that you are working to raise awareness.' One of his suggestions was to phone the BMJ editor and get their advice on writing a 'layman's view' type article. He also suggested the journal of the Royal College of GPs. but that led to nothing (This journal, I note, contains only six items on hypopituitarism, all dating from before 1994).

I told him about my earlier failures with the BMJ but he gently insisted that ringing them up was the best way. I was still crippled back in 2010 by a dreadful shyness on the phone; if it had to be done, I used to write myself a script and deliver it in a somewhat robot-like manner, like someone reading French aloud from a phrase book – and like a phrase book user, I was often panicked by the reply. I don't think I rang either the BMJ or the Royal College of GPs. My time was eaten up then by being a granny. Katherine was only three months old, Jenny had only recently recovered from her Caesarean, and I was childminding every day.

In September 2012 I approached Dr Beckett again, asking him to sign the letter to the Scottish equivalent of NICE, the SIGN (see chapter 46), and then the letter to the BMJ. He agreed to both, but returned to urging what he had originally suggested. He asked what the letter to the BMJ was for – to change SIGN's mind or to raise awareness? If the first, it wouldn't work, and if the second, then a much better way would be to write an article. He suggested finding an expert and approaching the BMJ jointly. This was such good advice, and I was so lucky to be getting suggestions from an expert who knew how everything worked from the inside, who was giving up his highly paid time to help me. He must have groaned sometimes – I didn't try hard enough to find an expert, and the 'Patient Journeys' editor (Peter Lapsley) rejected me, though he said they would discuss at a forthcoming meeting if there was another slot that would be suitable.

Mike Beckett then suggested getting a sympathetic endocrinologist to write to Peter Lapsley before the meeting saying there was a lot of ignorance among doctors about this. 'Easier to influence the decision before it's made.' However I didn't manage this either.

On 5 December, Peter wrote to tell me that the PTHP topic had none of the characteristics of a 'Patient Journey' article, and did not fit with any of the types of article they published. I found this puzzling, given that the proposed PTHP article could be summed up as, 'People have an illness called X, and they need diagnosis and treatment. Here is how to diagnose them. Here is how to treat them.' The Journal had been publishing articles based on this template since it was first published in 1840.

Cochrane Review

The third burrow I went down – this was in 2010 – was suggested to me by my psychologist neighbour: why didn't I write a Cochrane review? He explained that a Cochrane review was a summary and interpretation of all the research available on a particular topic, which is consulted by such bodies as NICE when writing guidelines. He said anyone could write one – the Cochrane Foundation would supply the methodology and give support – or I could persuade a medical student to do it.

I duly approached Emma Sydenham, the Managing Editor of the Cochrane Injuries Group. Our correspondence lasted no more than a fortnight, but was intense.

On 5 May she wrote a most encouraging reply, saying she would be happy to help me and to meet sometime to discuss things. She thought the first step would be for someone to write a systematic literature review of the available evidence, which would clarify areas needing research. She said her supervisor, Dr Pablo Perel, would very much like to help me. She told me to feel free to ring her and gave me her number.

I was hugely delighted. Here was someone who saw how important PTHP was and seemed prepared to do something. I sent her a list of the research. Her next email came an hour later. She'd read the important Schneider review and now asked me for a link to the NICE guideline. Had NICE explained why they'd ignored the recommendation to screen head injury patients? Still that same day, she asked if I had requested a separate guideline as Andrew Dillon had suggested, and proposed that we met on the Thursday of the following week. The day before our meeting, she told me to call her on her extension and she would collect me.

On the Thursday I was poised to set off when the phone rang. It was Emma, obviously distressed, cancelling our meeting. 'We've decided that there would be no point in your coming in, we couldn't add much to the review you sent us…' I was stunned. I couldn't help suspecting that a superior had put a stop to the meeting. Yet saying so would make me sound paranoid. I said, 'Has something happened?' but she said nothing had. I sensed she was near to tears, as I was too. I repeated, 'But what has happened since you suggested the meeting? Can't I come in anyway to talk to you?' 'No,' she said.

I don't know why this particular setback should have upset me almost more than all my battles with NICE and Headway, but when she rang off I walked round the house beside myself, unable to do anything but cry the tiny useless tears that are all I can manage and which give no relief to the heart. I emailed my old friend Frances forlornly and she phoned instantly, even though she was at work, and comforted me, which I will always remember.

Later I wrote to Emma reverting to my first request, to do the review myself under Cochrane's guidance, and she enthusiastically offered her help. But I discovered that I'd have to travel to workshops that lasted several days, and give up around a year to the work, and even after that, would have to arrange for the review to be updated regularly forever. At the time Katherine was just six months old. I knew that if I took on this big task I'd be letting Jenny down when she needed me and I'd be breaking my vow never to put my dead child above my living ones. Sadly I dropped the idea, at least for the time being.

There were many other dead-end burrows that I explored, but it is disheartening to describe them all. The Royal College of GPs did not even acknowledge the letter I sent to them, signed by 30 consultants, despite several reminders on my part. The Royal College of Emergency Medicine steadily refused to consider PTHP as being within their remit, even though the Journal of Emergency Medicine had obviously thought it was when they published my letter. The Royal College of Paediatrics and

Child Health did nothing. And so on.

I sometimes escaped the claustrophobia by imagining myself walking in Skipton, Chris's home for the last five years of his life. Skipton is called the Gateway to the Dales, and I had often walked that wild limestone country with him, where you can see for miles over rough grassland and heath to a horizon of bare hills. It is quiet there. You would not guess that gurgling deep under your feet there is a network of dark waterways, invisible torrents, waterfalls, lakes. You might wonder how these could ever be charted, but people have worked out which rivers conjoin, and which are separate, by adding dye to those streams that suddenly dive into the earth and seeing where they re-emerge. If two streams burst scarlet into the open air, however many miles apart they may be, you know they are linked higher up.

The secret pathways of power reveal themselves in the same way. The Army have reacted to the information about PTHP with natural humanity. Their stream-mouth runs crystal clear, and that is a comfort to me. NICE and the Royal Colleges have not reacted naturally – what could be more unnatural than to suppress information that might stop people killing themselves? I would guess their responses are linked. Maybe that's not surprising – they're not miles apart, after all – but what does the apparent unanimity of other, far more disparate organisations like the Suicide Strategy Group and the Manchester Academic Health Science Centre tell us? How far upstream must we look?

CONCLUSION

When the elation at getting the *Mail on Sunday* article published had worn off, a reaction set in. I felt very tired, as if I'd shot my bolt. The only thing I could think of left to do was to write my story. The judicial review debacle had taught me that I needed to reach people at large, I needed a voice. If NICE said hypopituitarism couldn't happen straight after head injury, and I said it could, who would people believe? Who would even hear me? It is only by reaching out a hand and pulling the reader with me (rather as my second little granddaughter, Jessica, drags grown-ups into the playroom), so that he or she lives through what I've experienced, that I have any hope of convincing people.

There are those who see conspiracy everywhere, and those who staunchly believe that nobody has ever conspired since the Dawn of Time. Of the two, I find those who trust other people much more likeable, yet both groups are equally at fault if they ignore the facts.

Nobody can have read this book without realising that I believe that there *is* a conspiracy, stemming from a level higher than the NHS management, higher than the BBC, higher than the National Suicide Prevention Strategy, higher than the Cochrane Foundation, to keep a stranglehold on information about pituitary disease. It is a conspiracy to keep doctors unaware, to make them use a 'diagnostic' test that will fail to diagnose, and to encourage the public to believe that sufferers have CFS/ME and that it is 'all in their heads', when a substantial proportion are biologically ill.

It is a conspiracy to deny more than a million Britons a proper life.

The facts are these:

- Hypopituitarism is life-wrecking
- Head injury gives you a one in three chance of getting it
- If you're in the Army and have a head injury you are screened for it
- If you're a civilian NHS patient you aren't warned of the risk, nor is your doctor
- Footballers and others who sustain repetitive concussions are at risk
- The short synacthen test is officially endorsed by the Society for Endocrinologists as the right test for diagnosing hypoadrenalism and is widely used. But it isn't reliable
- The number of people in the UK who have suffered dreadfully as a direct consequence of the preceding facts stands at around a million.

Think about a million for a moment. A good visual image is that host of ceramic poppies that were installed round the Tower of London by Paul Cummins and Tom Piper in November 2014, to bring home to us how many soldiers died during the First World War. There were 888,246 – not quite a million, but approaching that. Can we stand by and let all these people, who could be our cousins, our aunts, our friends, suffer?

While I was slowly and painfully writing this book I encouraged myself by reading about Samuel Plimsoll, the man who successfully campaigned a century or so ago to stop ship-owners sending over-insured, over-loaded, ancient vessels out to sea where they would flounder in the first storm, drowning all on board. He wrote a book. He ended it with a direct address to the reader:

> 'I tell you, you who read these lines, if you are a man, you deserve to perish suddenly, lacking sympathy and succour in your hour of utmost need, and leaving your nearest and dearest only the cold charity of the world to depend upon – for this is how sailors die – if you don't help.
>
> If you are a wife, you deserve that your husband should be taken from you without warning, and that to the anguish of bereavement should be added the material miseries of hunger and destitution – for this is how sailors' wives suffer – if you do not help...'

I have only quoted some of this, to give an idea. The Victorian public were used to being ranted at from a pulpit – they sat with clasped hands in their pews accepting it every Sunday – and they responded in a warm and human way, which led to Plimsoll's eventual victory. I like the Victorians. I believe that if Plimsoll had written this book instead of me, he would have ended it like this:

> 'I tell you, if you are a man, you deserve to become impotent, constantly tired, unable to hold down a job or provide for your family, depressed and robbed of all self-esteem – for this is what can happen to PTHP sufferers – if you don't help.
>
> If you are a woman, you deserve to lose your looks, to become grossly obese and infertile, and to

be told by those around you that you are making yourself deliberately ill – for this is what can happen to PTHP sufferers – if you don't help.

If you are a parent, you deserve to see your teenage daughter lose her periods, gradually retreat from friendship and study and life and fun – for this is what can happen to PTHP sufferers – if you don't help. You deserve the anguish of seeing your much loved son commit suicide – for this is what PTHP sufferers can do – if you don't help.'

So if you want to help, what is the best way? I wish I could urge you with confidence to write to your MP, write to Sir Andrew Dillon, write to the Secretary of State for Health, but I have done all this, and I am not confident. The Countess of Mar (founder of Forward-ME), who often hits the nail on the head, has voiced her opinion that the scandal whereby patients are told they have CFS/ME/FM when they really have organic illness, will only be resolved 'from the bottom up'. For the PTHP scandal too, entwined as it is with the chronic fatigue complex, I believe the same holds true.

Resolving things from the bottom up means telling those immediately around you. If everybody in the UK shares a common knowledge that fatigue, depression, obesity, lack of libido, and infertility, separately or together, can be signs of hypopituitarism, and if they are warned about the tests that wrongly exclude this, then armed with that knowledge they have a sporting chance of getting treatment, or at least of making their voice heard in such numbers that they cannot easily be ignored. In other words, if you feel as angry as I do about the treatment of so many of your fellow-citizens, start sharing.

Tell your GP. GPs are having a terrible time but they still care about their patients and want to do their best. Leave a copy of this book in the waiting room. Tell the A&E department in your local hospital and leave a copy there too. Make sure that your local school warns parents about what can happen after a sports concussion. Best of all, make sure every person you know who is suffering depression or fatigue, or who has had a concussion or worse, or who is struggling with weight gain, or having difficulty in conceiving a child, who has a strange intolerance of heat or cold, has a working knowledge of the pituitary.

So, is there a conspiracy or not? There is an easy way to quieten my suspicions. It is to:

- Warn these people
- Diagnose these people
- Treat these people

Nobody would be more delighted than I to be proved wrong.

EPILOGUE

There have been several cases of little boys shot, caught in the cross-fire between gangs. I can't remember which one died crying for his mum, who couldn't get there in time, but I know it will be an anguish for her, until she herself dies, that she couldn't.

This is my pain too. It is the pain of not having been there to comfort Christopher when he needed me so much, and if I ever let myself think about that, I'm lost.

I used to like walking along the tops of walls when I was little, just like Jessica today. The trick is to look at the wall itself, not the drop on either side. 'Be grateful for what you have and don't think about what you've lost,' said a friend whose two-year-old grandson died suddenly in his sleep, and she's right.

So I think about Katherine and Jessica, their naughtiness, their sweetness, the way they love me, and I think about my two dear daughters and my darling John, and I get by.

The stump of the tree that Chris cut down is still there, darkened and shrunken now. It's in the corner of the garden, with the road on two sides, and Katherine likes to wriggle out of my arms and escape there when I'm trying to put her into the car. She stands on it poking her head out between the foliage of the other trees, looking over the wall. Once a woman passing by saw her and smiled. 'Oh, you startled me!' she said. 'You're like a lovely plant growing there.'

If we're lucky, new life sprouts above the old. Life

goes on, things change, people recover. But nothing can ever change now for Christopher, who died when he could have lived, isolated, misjudged, cut off from the love I would have given him, the energy with which I would have fought for him, if only I had known.

APPENDIX 1

A NOTE ON THE RESEARCH AND THE NUMBERS

Over the years after Chris's death I made a collection of all the literature I came across which found a high incidence of hypopituitarism after head injury. I have listed these below. The one at the top of the list, which was the one I quoted most often, was a large systematic review by Schneider et al, covering 19 studies and more than a thousand patients and finding that 27.5 per cent had hypopituitarism.

The Schneider review, which quoted an annual incidence of 30 PTHP cases for every 100,000 of the population, was one of the sources of my claim that there had to be around a million undiagnosed people in the UK. The other was a review by Fernandez-Rodriguez et al (the 'et al' included the well-known endocrinologists Professors Kelestimur and Casanueva) which gave an incidence of 50 per 100,000. The two figures equated respectively to 18,000 and 30,000 cases each year in the UK. I am not an epidemiologist, and my rough and ready way of arriving at an estimate of the total number of the undiagnosed was to multiply by forty, for the past four decades of neglect. I usually explained my reasoning to whichever consultant I was writing to, hoping that one of them might suggest a more accurate method, but nobody did. I do not in fact know if there is any methodology for arriving at a figure for undiagnosed prevalence. Mr Antonio Belli said on the BBC programme *Inside Out* that 'some studies suggest a million people, some studies suggest probably half a million'. Dr Mark Porter wrote more conservatively in his article in *The Times* referring to 'some estimates suggesting there are currently as many as a half a million people in the UK with some degree of PTHP'.

A review by Tanriverdi and five other big names in the PTHP field has come out recently [1], which has taken on board all the objections about different cut-off points and varying tests, and whittled the incidence figures down to an irreducible minimum – six per cent for multiple pituitary deficiency (i.e. when more than one hormone is affected) and around 18 per cent for a single deficiency. 'Applying a very conservative approach, with the arbitrary assumption that relevant neuroendocrine dysfunction is present in only 6% of TBI survivors (for reasons of simplicity, assuming that only those with multiple hormone deficiencies are relevantly affected by pituitary dysfunction), we would expect an incidence of seven cases per 100,000 persons per year in the population.' This means 4,200 PTHP cases a year in the UK for multiple deficiencies and about 12,000 for single. Multiplying by forty would give rough prevalence figures of 168,000 and 480,000 cases for the two categories. To give an idea of scale, the combined populations of Oxford and Cambridge come to 270,000.

Perhaps in the light of this I should abandon that comparison with the poppies round the Tower? Well, I don't think so, for several reasons. One reason is that head injury is not the only cause of hypopituitarism: it is one of many – exposure to organophosphates, for example, pituitary tumours, genetic predisposition, and so on, not forgetting the Gulf War vaccinations and possibly others.

Another, more important reason, is that the Tanriverdi

review has necessarily focused on moderate to severe head injury, because that is where the research exists. The new paper says little about concussion. Yet 140,000 people are hospitalised for concussion each year and a million visit A&E as outpatients. There is evidence that around 15 per cent of concussions cause distressing after-effects – concentration problems, headache, dizziness, depression, and irritability – and the risk of suicide after concussion is tripled. There is no particular reason to expect the hormonal risk to be negligible. Even if the incidence of hypopituitarism after concussion is tiny – say, two per cent – we get a figure of 22,000. Forty times that is 880,000 [2].

[1] Tanriverdi F et al, Pituitary Dysfunction after traumatic brain injury: a clinical and pathophysiological approach, 2014 *Endocrine Reviews*

[2] Hypopituitarism is known to occur after concussion. Schneider's review (listed below) gives a 16.8 per cent incidence after mild traumatic brain injury. Professor Charles Wilkinson has found 42 per cent in his recent study of hypopituitarism from mild traumatic brain injuries caused by blast (also listed below). There is a much quoted case of a 14-year-old who had four concussions playing soccer – only the 4th injury was 'medically diagnosed' as concussion, and there is no mention of hospital admission.

He stopped growing for two years and his strength declined, until finally he was diagnosed with hypopituitarism

(www.ncbi.nlm.nih.gov/pmc/articles/PMC1978466/).

How many more could there be like him?

The Research
Post-traumatic hypopituitarism

1. Schneider HJ et al, 'Hypothalamopituitary Dysfunction Following Traumatic Brain Injury and Aneurysmal Subarachnoid Haemorrhage: A Systematic Review', *Journal of the American Medical Association,* 2007

Based on the incidence of patients hospitalized for TBI and SAH reported in the literature and the frequencies of hypopituitarism in these patients, we have previously estimated the incidence of hypopituitarism caused by these disorders to be more than 30 patients per 100 000 population per year.

jama.jamanetwork.com/article.aspx?articleid=208915

2. Acerini CL, 'Head-injury-induced pituitary dysfunction. An old curiosity rediscovered', *Archives of Disease in Childhood,* 2008

A review: '…studies variously report the prevalence of pituitary hormone deficiencies to be between 23% and 69%. It is clear from these studies that one or any number of hypothalamic-pituitary hormone axes may be impaired in the chronic phase following head injury, with the growth hormone (GH; 10-33%), adrenal (5-23%) and gonadal axes (8-30%) apparently the most vulnerable to problems. Further clinical complexity is also evident from prospective, longitudinal observations, which suggest that for many head-injury survivors pituitary hormone dysfunction *may not develop until at least 6 to 12 months after TBI,* whereas, in others deficiencies can be transient and resolve spontaneously during the year after the trauma.'

adc.bmj.com/cgi/content/full/93/5/364

3. Agha A et al, 'Anterior Pituitary Dysfunction in Survivors of Traumatic Brain Injury', *Journal of Clinical Endocrinology & Metabolism*, 2004

102 consecutive survivors of mod/severe TBI at a median of 17 months (range 6-36) post event. 28.4% of these had at least one anterior pituitary hormone deficiency.

jcem.endojournals.org/cgi/content/abstract/89/10/4929

4. Agha A, Phillips J, Thompson C H, 'Hypopituitarism following traumatic brain injury (TBI)', *British Journal of Neurosurgery,* 2007

A review: 'Recently several studies have shown that hypopituitarism is a common complication of head trauma with a prevalence of at least 25% among patients who were studied months or years following injury.' Summarises available data i.e. 658 patients.

www.ncbi.nlm.nih.gov/pubmed/17453791

5. Aimaretti G et al, 'Residual Pituitary Function after Brain Injury-Induced Hypopituitarism: A Prospective 12-month Study', *Journal of Clinical Endocrinology & Metabolism,* 2005

Seventy TBI patients, 32 SAH patients tested at three months and 12 months post-event. At three months, 32.8% had hypopituitarism. At 12 months only 22.7% had it – however, although in some cases hypopituitarism had disappeared at 12 months, in others, though rarely, new deficits had appeared.

jcem.endojournals.org/cgi/reprint/90/11/6085.pdf

6. Benvenga, S et al, 'Hypopituitarism Secondary to Head Trauma', *Journal of Clinical Endocrinology & Metabolism*, Apr 2000; 85(4): 1353.

'We learned, in fact, that head trauma can be minor and had occurred several years earlier, so that the patient may lose recollection of it.'

jcem.endojournals.org/content/85/4/1353.long

7. Berg, C et al, 'Prevalence of Anterior Pituitary Dysfunction in Patients following Traumatic Brain Injury in a German Multi-centre Screening Program', *Experimental and Clinical Endocrinology & Diabetes,* 2010; 118: 139-144.

246 TBI patients screened across five German endocrine centres at around 12 months after injury. 'In summary, in this large series carried out on an unselected group of TBI survivors we have found hypopituitarism in every fifth patient with predominantly secondary hypogonadism and hypothyreosis. Regarding somatotrope insufficiency IGF-1 is decreased in 50% of GHD patients. Conclusion: These findings strongly suggest that patients who suffer head trauma should routinely undergo endocrine evaluation.'

www.ncbi.nlm.nih.gov/pubmed/19691014

8. Blair JC, 'Prevalence, natural history and consequences of posttraumatic hypopituitarism: A case for endocrine surveillance', Review, *British Journal of Neurosurgery,* Feb 2010; 24

www.ncbi.nlm.nih.gov/pubmed/20158347?tool=bestpracti ce.bmj.com

9. Dubourg J, Messerer M, 'Sports-related Chronic Repetitive Head Trauma as a Cause of Pituitary Dysfunction', *Neurosurgical Focus,* 2011; 31(5):e2.

www.medscape.com/viewarticle/753229_1

10. Fernandez-Rodriguez E et al, 'Hypopituitarism following traumatic brain injury: determining factors for diagnosis', *Frontiers in Endocrinology,* 25 Aug 2011 (doi: 10.3389/fendo.2011.00025)

The incidence of hypopituitarism following TBI is around 50 patients per 100,000 individuals per year, which results in a high number of patients affected.
www.frontiersin.org/Pituitary_Endocrinology/10.3389/
fendo.2011   .00025/full

11. Gasco V et al, 'Hypopituitarism following brain injury: when does it occur and how best to test?' *Pituitary,* 2010

'In patients with TBI or SAH, a high risk exists for hypopituitarism, but symptoms are usually masked by the sequelae of BI. In these individuals, endocrine assessment should be done routinely, particularly in severe or moderate cases or if the brain injury has led to prolonged admission.'

www.springerlink.com/content/92527qj442046317/

12. Ghigo E et al, 'Consensus guidelines on screening for hypopituitarism following traumatic brain injury', *Brain Injury,* 2005; 19(9): 711-724.

'Signs and symptoms associated with hypopituitarism often mimic the sequelae of TBI, although the severity of the symptoms is not necessarily related to the severity of the injury [...] systematic screening of pituitary function is recommended for all patients with moderate-to-severe TBI at risk of developing pituitary deficits'

http://www.ncbi.nlm.nih.gov/pubmed/16195185

13. Guerrero AF, Alfonso A, 'Traumatic brain injury-related hypopituitarism: a review and recommendations

for screening combat veterans', *Military Medicine,* Aug 2010; 175(8): 574-80.

Says 15% of mild TBIs have long-term consequences, and of these, 15-30% develop neuroendocrine dysfunction (NED).

www.ncbi.nlm.nih.gov/pubmed/20731261

14. Hohl A et al, 'Hypogonadism after traumatic brain injury', *Arquivos Brasileiros de Endocrinologia et Metabologia,* 2009

www.scielo.br/scielo.php?pid=S0004-27302009000800003&script=sci_arttext

15. Kelly DF, 'Hypopituitarism following traumatic brain injury and aneurismal subarachnoid hemorrhage: a preliminary report', *Journal of Neurosurgery*, 2000; 93:743-752. www.ncbi.nlm.nih.gov/pubmed/11059653

16. Klose M et al, 'Acute and long-term pituitary insufficiency in traumatic brain injury: a prospective single-centre study', *Clinical Endocrinology (Oxford),* 2007

46 consecutive TBI patients assessed within 12 days, then at three, six, and 12 months post-injury. In early stage 76% had hormone alterations, at 12 months 11%.

www.ncbi.nlm.nih.gov/pubmed/17880406

17. Klose M et al, 'Prevalence of predictive factors of post-traumatic hypopituitarism', *Clinical Endocrinology (Oxford),* 2008A study of 104 survivors of mild, moderate and severe traumatic brain injury. 16% had pituitary dysfunction.

www.ncbi.nlm.nih.gov/pubmed/17524035

18. Krahulik D et al, 'Dysfunction of hypothalamic-hypophysial axis after traumatic brain injury in adults', *Journal of Neurosurgery,* 2010; 113: 581-584.

A study of 89 patients Glasgow Coma Scale 3-14. 21% had primary hormonal dysfunction. Some patients recovered from defects, others developed new defects during year after TBI.

www.ncbi.nlm.nih.gov/pubmed/19929195

19. Leal-Cerro A et al, 'Neuroendocrine dysfunction and brain damage. A consensus statement', *Endocrin Nutr.,* Jun-Jul 2009; 56(6): 293-302.

'This consensus is based on the recommendation supported by expert opinion that patients with a TBI and/or brain haemorrhage should undergo endocrine evaluation in order to assess pituitary function and if deficiency is detected, should receive hormone replacement therapy.'

www.ncbi.nlm.nih.gov/pubmed/19695511

20. Norwood K et al, 'Traumatic Brain Injury in Children and Adolescents: Surveillance for Pituitary Dysfunction', *Clinical Pediatrics,* 2010; 49(11): 1044-1049.

A study of 31 children and adolescents of whom five (16%) had GHD.

21. Pickel J et al, 'Hypopituitarism and brain injury: recent advances in screening and management', *F1000 Medicine Report,* 2009; 1: 63.

www.ncbi.nlm.nih.gov/pmc/articles/PMC2948313/

22. Popovic V, Aimaretti G et al, 'Hypopituitarism following traumatic brain injury', *Growth Hormone and IGF Research,* 2005

A review: claims hypopituitarism and in particular growth hormone deficiency is common among TBI survivors tested 'several months or years following head trauma [...] the subjects at risk are those who have suffered moderate-to-severe head trauma although mild intensity trauma may precede hypopituitarism also. Particular attention should be paid to this problem in children and adolescents. Onset of pituitary deficits can evolve over years following injury. For the assessment of the GH-IGF axis in TBI patients, plasma IGF-I concentrations, plus dynamic GH testing is indicated. Some degree of hypopituitarism is found in 35-40% of TBI patients.

www.ncbi.nlm.nih.gov/pubmed/15935980

23. Schneider H J et al, 'Prevalence of anterior pituitary insufficiency three and 12 months after traumatic brain injury', *European Journal of Endocrinology / European Federation of Endocrine Societies*, 2006

78 patients tested at three and 12 months after TBI. At three months, 56% had hypopituitarism, after 12 months 36% were affected but in some cases new impairments occurred. *Conclusions*: Hypopituitarism occurs often in the post-acute phase after TBI and may normalize later, but may also develop after the post-acute phase of TBI.

www.eje-online.org/cgi/content/abstract/154/2/259

24. Tanriverdi F et al, 'High risk of Hypopituitarism after Traumatic Brain Injury: A Prospective Investigation of Anterior Pituitary Function in the Acute Phase and 12 Months after Trauma', *Journal of Clinical Endocrinology & Metabolism*, 2005

52 TBI patients. Pituitary function evaluated within 24 hours of admission and after one year. Conclusions: GHD

is the most common pituitary deficit 12 months after TBI, and 50.9% of the patients had at least one anterior pituitary hormone deficiency. Pituitary function may improve or worsen in a considerable number of patients over 12 months.

jcem.endojournals.org/cgi/content/full/91/6/2105

25. Tanriverdi F et al, 'Hypopituitarism due to sports related head trauma and the effects of growth hormone replacement in retired amateur boxers', *Pituitary*, Jun 2010; 13(2): 111-4. (doi: 10.1007/s11102-009-0204-0)

www.ncbi.nlm.nih.gov/pubmed/19847653

26. Urban RJ et al, 'Anterior hypopituitarism following traumatic brain injury', *Brain Injury*, May 2005; 19(5): 349-358.

'This article has a two-fold objective: to review the evidence indicating the existence of a substantial sub-population of patients with TBI-induced endocrine disorders and to underscore the importance of screening patients with TBI most at risk for hypopituitarism. These data suggest that treatment of hypopituitarism in this group of patients may have major beneficial effects in terms of morbidity and quality of life.'

www.ncbi.nlm.nih.gov/pubmed/16094782

27. Wilkinson CW et al, 'High Prevalence of Chronic Pituitary and Target-Organ Hormone Abnormalities after Blast-Related Mild Traumatic Brain Injury', *Frontiers in Neurology*, 2012; 3: 11.

11 out of 26 participants with blast concussions (42%) were found to have abnormal hormone levels.

www.ncbi.nlm.nih.gov/pmc/articles/PMC3273706/

28. Zaben, M et al, 'Perspectives in Rehabilitation: Post-traumatic head injury pituitary dysfunction', *Disability and Rehabilitation*, Mar 2013; 35(6): 522-525. (doi:10.3109/09638288.2012.697252)
informahealthcare.com/doi/abs/10.3109/09638288.2012.6
97252

There are, to my knowledge, only four studies finding little or no incidence of PTHP after TBI.

Suicide

29. Teasdale TW, Engberg AW, 'Suicide after traumatic brain injury: a population study', *Journal of Neurology, Neurosurgery & Psychiatry,* 2001
jnnp.bmj.com/content/71/4/436.full

30. Simpson G, Tate R, 'Suicidality in people surviving a traumatic brain injury: prevalence, risk factors and implications for clinical management', *Brain Injury,* Dec 2007; 21(13-14): 1335-51.
www.ncbi.nlm.nih.gov/pubmed/18066936

Testing for adrenal insufficiency

31. Dorin RI, 'Diagnosis of Adrenal Insufficiency', *Annals of Internal Medicine,* 2003
For this review the MEDLINE database was searched from 1966 to 2002 for all English-language papers related to the diagnosis of adrenal insufficiency, and it was found that for diagnosing secondary adrenal insufficiency, the sensitivity of the short synacthen test was 57-61% i.e. it missed two people in every five. This review is ten years old, but to my knowledge its findings have never been overturned.
annals.org/article.aspx?articleid=716603

32. Thorogood N, Baldeweg S E, 'Pituitary Disorders: an overview for the general physician', Symposium on the Head and Neck, *British Journal of Hospital Medicine*, Apr 2008; 69(4)

'A morning cortisol value below 100 nmol/L indicates adrenal insufficiency. Cortisol values of 500 nmol/L or greater are consistent with an intact hypothalamic-pituitary-adrenal axis. The values in between *do not exclude secondary adrenal insufficiency and dynamic testing is therefore warranted.*'

33. Countess of Mar on the PACE trial: full speech can be found in Lords Hansard at 8.16pm

https://hansard.parliament.uk/Lords/2013-02-06/debates/130206114000195/PACETrialChronicFat igueSyndromeMyalgicEncephalomyelitis#contributio n-130206114000058

Notes on Kenneth Starr's Story

34. Schilling R, 'Is nitrous oxide a dangerous anesthetic for vitamin B12-deficient subjects?' *Journal of the American Medical Association,* 28 Mar 1986; 255: 1605-6.

jama.jamanetwork.com/article.aspx?articleid=403433

35. Hadzic A, Glab K, Sanborn K, and Thyrs D, 'Severe neurologic deficit after nitrous oxide anesthesia', *Anesthesiology,* 1995; 83:863-6.
anesthesiology.pubs.asahq.org/article.aspx?articleid=1949 600

APPENDIX 2

DUNIYUL'S FUNERAL ADDRESS

I am truly honoured to have the opportunity to talk about Chris today.

My name is Duniyul Dossa and Chris was my oldest friend and part of my life for about 30 years.

Growing up, Chris was my hero. He taught me so much and I always looked up to him and as a kid knew that he would look after me. Today it's clear that we have all lost a great man, loving, caring, selfless and filled with a sharp imagination and wonderful creativity.

Chris would have been so surprised by today. Why? He would have asked, Why have these people come? Why have they taken time out of their busy lives for me? You see Chris found it so difficult to believe in himself, to recognise the things he did as important and to realise how many people's lives he touched deeply with love.

Almost every childhood memory that I have includes Chris.

I was always hugely jealous of his vibrant imagination. This brilliant imagination would always shape our time together. Age 3 or 4 we used to play a make-believe game invented by Chris. Helen, another friend of ours, and I were man and wife. Jenny was our baby. Ruth was yet to be born. Chris was … well Chris was our cat! Not just any cat but a cat that his owner, me, was allowed to ride on the back of. A cat that had a superpower which enabled it to build houses with sofa cushions and a cat that could only be steered by covering one eye as it was moving forward ... there was always a different story that we were acting out and it all came straight from Chris's young imagination. We were very young and very innocent and we called the game Christopher Pussy – we used to play it exhaustively without pause sometimes for hours at a time. Until his death last week I used to always greet him by saying 'Alright CP', which stood for Christopher Pussy. It was our little secret – nobody else knew what it stood for – I wish I could tell Chris just how much I loved calling him that and how special that secret was.

While Chris had a beautiful imagination he also had a special technical awareness. While I was just about managing to colour code the Lego bricks while building basic houses, Chris was creating hugely complex and technical Lego machines that would shame most engineers! Similarly, while I was using my bucket and spade to produce painfully delicate castles on the beach, Chris was building veritable forts with moats, dams and river systems. Our parents used to take us on long walks. Often, the kids, Chris, Jenny, Ruth, Adam and I used to be allowed to play on our own, diverting a stream or building some steps – Chris would direct and the rest of us would try not to mess it up. As Chris grew up these childhood games matured and became an important part of his life culminating in him spending considerable chunks of his personal time caring for the environment firstly becoming chairman of his university conservation society and then through BTCV a charity whose mission statement reads,

"To create a more sustainable future through inspiring people and improving places". Chris pursued this mission with BTCV on many occasions.

While on a Dales walk with Chris he told me that his love for the countryside was inspired and nurtured by his parents. I can understand that. Jo, with her soft and gentle love of the countryside and caring for nature and John, an engineer who developed Chris's technical abilities and guided him from structurally sound sand castles through to repairing his car after his too frequent bumps. This nurturing by Jo and John led Chris to combine nature and making things which I believe gave him great comfort and focus throughout his adulthood.

Family pride was such a large part of Chris. I remember in particular the way that he used to talk about his sisters – he was so proud that Jenny is so hugely successful in the property industry and that Ruth, 'little Ruth' as we used to joke remembering her as the youngest in our troop, is a smart and successful lawyer. He took huge pride and colossal joy in following your lives and he often spoke to me about you both with deep love. I remember him in his tails at Jenny's wedding, beard neatly trimmed and hair cut, simply beaming with pride and radiating love at the choice of your husband Nick. I remember too the way he described the mammoth walking holiday that his parents had just been on – proud of their stamina and determination.

In adulthood as Chris moved out of London and I started a family we spent less time together. Our true friendship was measured simply by our ability to pick up exactly where we had left off even if it had been months since our last meeting. Our closeness didn't dissipate over time, it simply changed to a curiosity about each other's separate lives. Chris was there with me and for me at all of the important moments in my life. My first day at school, first school disco, first school play, wedding, brother's wedding and every important moment in between. I called Chris the day my wife and I found out that we were to be parents so excited about telling him that I ignored the 'keep it quiet before 12 weeks' rule. After speaking to him for half an hour or so at around 7pm I put down the phone. Just before midnight there was a knocking on the door. Chris had driven all of the way from Skipton to London simply to shake my hand and say congratulations in person ... he had work the next day and drove all the way back home that night!

It has been revealing over the past week or so to compare stories and notes about Chris with other friends. There have been so many happy times. We all remember the drunken teenage nights, the weekends abroad as a group, the stag do's and the moans and groans as Chris took us on countryside walks which by the end we were converts to. We remember with laughter Chris being such a terrible traveller, throwing up at the slightest airplane bump yet enthusiastically planning out things to do once we arrived. We remember his immense creativity, the birthday cards he spent hours hand drawing for us, the signs he used to make for his sister's plays and we recall the decoration that used to go along with every school book and file as well as his invention of a pictogram system for his school timetable. We don't remember a saint but a normal, a *lovely* guy, a guy that nobody can remember ever doing anything even vaguely selfish. A guy whom we all loved dearly and who will be missed sorely. Somebody who we will keep looking over our shoulders expecting to see with us, laughing with us, being with us and looking after us.

Chris' death has suspended reality for so many of us. I've dreamt only of him since I was told last week of his passing.

When Christopher was at primary school he had a dreadful accident falling from a tree at Godstone farm and lying in a coma for a week. Jo and John kept a long and constant vigil by his bedside and I believe by their sheer willpower and prayers and Chris's amazing determination he clawed his way back to his family and friends. This shouldn't surprise us since Chris was not one to give in easily. Today my belief is that we can take some comfort from that. Chris would not have made the tragic decision to end his life lightly or without considering all the other options. This was not an impulsive decision but one which he most certainly wanted. It is painful to respect his decision but I believe that is what we must do for that is what I believe he would have wanted us to do. His life may have been short but we must remember him as he was. A selfless sometimes troubled friend and an extremely loved and loving son and brother.

Chris you will be missed more than you could ever have imagined.

EMAIL FROM HIS COUSIN OLI

I have loads of fond memories of Chris; he was like an incredible older brother who had already worked everything out.

I remember playing an old flight simulator with him that was loaded from a huge floppy disk. We wanted to see if we could go all the way around the world. He'd set up some sort of cheat that allowed you to fly super-fast and so we pointed east and watched the world rush by. It took a long time so we went off to do something else and popped back to check it occasionally. I remember being crazy excited when we came back in after several hours and saw that we'd hit land again. Turns out we were back in America and the world just looped indefinitely.

It breaks my heart that he imagined he wouldn't be missed and I guess I just wanted to share this photo with you and say that I do miss him and remember him often. He was an inspiration to me as a young child and I'm certain part of the reason I became an engineer.

THE MAIL ON SUNDAY ARTICLE

'How doctors are failing to spot the brain injury that could be behind 30,000 cases of "chronic fatigue"'
By Joanna Lane
Published 17 May 2014

Thousands of British patients suffering from chronic pain and fatigue could be misdiagnosed with psychological problems when they unknowingly have a type of brain damage.

Those people who complain of the symptoms are not given a series of blood tests that can pinpoint the problem, meaning the true cause is not spotted. Patients are then condemned to years of misery and ineffective therapies.

The major cause of the damage is head injury, which

can be relatively mild. However, viruses, tumours and even animal bites [should read 'snake bites'] can be a trigger.

The National Institute for Health and Care Excellence was considering including the condition – called post-traumatic hypopituitarism (PTHP) – in its most recent guidance to doctors on how to treat head injury.

It would have meant patients who turned up at A&E departments or GP surgeries with head injuries would be warned that the symptoms of PTHP – which also include depression, obesity, high blood pressure, loss of libido and even infertility – could take years to emerge.

However, when the new recommendations were published in the spring, there was no mention of the problem. The decision has been condemned as 'nonsensical' by an expert who treats PTHP.

Currently, patients who present with tiredness and chronic pain are often told they have chronic fatigue syndrome (CFS), or fibromyalgia, once other physical causes have been ruled out. They are offered psychotherapy, exercise and anti-depressants. However, these are currently found to be ineffective in up to 70 per cent of CFS cases.

Numerous studies have shown that between 20 and 30 per cent of the 135,000 patients who suffer a serious head injury also experience damage to the pituitary gland, which is situated below the brain, behind the nasal cavity.

The gland produces vital hormones that govern many bodily functions, including growth and repair, the sleep-wake cycle and how we react to stress. If the pea-sized organ is damaged, it may stop producing one or more of the essential hormones, triggering the wide-ranging symptoms of hypopituitarism.

Studies suggest there could be between 18,000 and

30,000 cases in the UK each year.

Treatment involves lifelong hormone replacement therapy, which is said to be highly effective but costs up to £6,000 a year.

Professor Christopher Thompson, one of Britain's foremost experts on PTHP, says, 'The overwhelming evidence from research studies carried out independently in a wide range of places, including the USA, Europe and Turkey, is that hypopituitarism occurs in up to 30 per cent of people who have survived moderate or severe traumatic brain injury. There is no debate.

'However, the failure to make the right diagnosis after such injury means patients miss out on essential treatment. That it's not included in the NICE guidelines [for treatment of head injury] is nonsensical.'

Serious head injury is defined as an injury causing unconsciousness for more than 15 minutes. However, some studies suggest even knocks that lead to a minor concussion, or repeated small impacts such as heading a football, may damage the pituitary gland.

PTHP sufferer Jill Mizen, 67, was misdiagnosed with CFS in 2006, having suffered from pain and blood pressure problems for almost 20 years. A former BT manager, she was advised to exercise more, but found her condition worsened.

During her illness, Jill was screened for deficiency in the hormone cortisol, a characteristic of hypopituitarism. However, the test – known as the short synacthen test (SST) – produced a normal result. 'That was when I was told I had CFS,' she says.

Yet SST misses two out of every five cases where the cause of cortisol deficiency is damage to the pituitary. In 2007, Jill came across a magazine article about Christine Wrightson, who was incorrectly diagnosed with CFS when in fact she was suffering from hypopituitarism.

'Eventually, after huge persistence, Christine was able to pay privately for a test which the NHS would accept. This proved she had been right all along – her pituitary was faulty. Her story opened my eyes,' says Jill.

Coincidentally, the two women were patients at the same hospital and struck up a friendship. Jill says, 'Doctors believe Christine's hypopituitarism was caused by inflammation – she suffered rheumatoid arthritis for 30 years. In 2005 she had a virus that wouldn't go, and the fatigue started then.'

Jill chose to be retested privately with the more reliable glucagon stimulation test, and was diagnosed as being deficient in cortisol and growth hormone. This proved she too had hypopituitarism.

Sadly, Christine died in July 2011 from complications related to her arthritis treatment, perhaps exacerbated by the fatigue she had suffered for so many years.

Dr John Newell Price, consultant endocrinologist at the Royal Hallamshire Hospital in Sheffield and chairman of the Pituitary Foundation Medical Committee, says: 'A "pass" on an SST may not always mean cortisol deficiency is excluded.' He recommends referral to an endocrinologist if symptoms persist, so that the glucagon test can be carried out.

Today, Jill wonders whether a concussion she suffered after jumping off a roundabout as a toddler could have caused the damage. Now she is having hormone therapy, her symptoms have improved.

Last Christmas she once again had the energy to cook a proper family dinner and put on make-up. 'It sounds silly,' she says, 'but I hadn't had the energy to do that for years.'

APPENDIX 3

DR CHANDY'S TALK

Note This transcript should be read while viewing Dr Chandy's talk on youtube.com/watch?v=qVYIAwHukF8

Addison's then and now

In those days it was thought it was caused through tuberculosis. Addison in fact in 1985, he is the man who diagnosed pernicious anaemia and he is the one who did post-mortem and he found the adrenal glands were shrunk. He was a doctor who will not sleep until he found the cause, very dedicated man and he is known as the father of endocrinology. And also of course his name, Addison – pernicious anaemia was also codified by him because as Martin said it is a threat of anaemia.

Two lives saved in my practice by looking for it. Not to say that they only have B12 [deficiency]. And this (showing slide) is the normal circadian rhythm. From about four o'clock in the morning we are getting prepared for our day to day tasks and you can see slowly the cortisol level rises. The normal morning cortisol level we expect is 550-750 and we may notice in the afternoon it starts to go down. Why? Because it's preparing us to go to bed, so the level drops to about 100. Now this is a patient (new slide) who was diagnosed before she came to my practice with everything under the sun, and she was collapsing, fainting, from age 14 and she was diagnosed with epilepsy, she was diagnosed with various conditions which I will come to, and then she joined our practice in 2009. She had B12 deficiency, I corrected the B12 deficiency, I looked for other things, vitamin D, corrected that, still she wasn't right, so I did the cortisol level, Dr Suter mentioned about it, and the importance of it, and you may notice the basal levels are low, the expected level is at the top (i.e. 500-600) – and so I duly referred her to RVI (Royal Victoria Infirmary Newcastle) and there they did this well-accepted synacthen test, that's a stimulation test, and they do large dose of adrenocorticotropic hormone that stimulates, that's supposed to stimulate the adrenal gland, and on both occasions the consultant wrote to me saying it was suboptimal but in spite of that they didn't follow her up. And these (new slide) are the synacthen tests they did, you will notice the first one only was up to 550 but the others are very low, and then in blue you will see, it was only two months ago, I found she was near to death and her level was 34, and I referred her to James Cook Hospital.

These are the three hospitals, previously relying on high dosage ACTH and they didn't take notice of the signs and symptoms. She was fainting, she had to sell her house and go live with her parents because she was a danger to herself. This is her. From age 14 onwards, dizziness, fainting, tired, weak, cold all the time, nauseous, weakness, muscle cramps, hair loss, IBS, stomach pain, depression, panic attack and she was diagnosed prior to that (of course she was B12 deficient as well) with all the other conditions, ME, CFS, fibromyalgia, all these conditions.

This is another patient of mine, this is a lawyer, 33 (28 when we first began to suspect something was not right), a very bright girl who studied at University College, London and she also knew something was not right because she had difficulty remembering things, she was getting angry, upset, the parents said, and you may notice in 2008 I suspected that she was hypoadrenal after having excluded other conditions, and then I referred her to RVI and her level was low, it was 70 and they said, it is all in her mind. The Marcel [?] biopsy even shows in this 28-years-old girl, damage to her left leg muscles, her reflexes were diminished, she, one day, the husband rang me at 10 o'clock. 'Dr Chandy she is on the floor, she can't get up' and she has two little girls at that time, three years old and one year, to look after. Then one day she couldn't breathe, she couldn't talk, and I was called out. I admitted to Hartlepool Hospital, local hospital, and they referred her back to James Cook. Hartlepool said, 'It is all in the mind, she is putting it on.'

At James Cook they did all the tests and they also said, 'I think she needs to see a psychiatrist.' So it went on like that, three hospitals rejecting her, and I decided, I must act, though we GPs are not allowed to diagnose and treat. I started her on hydrocortisone. Probably if I didn't she would have died, and you may notice in spite of having the hydrocortisone treatment her adrenal gland, or the pituitary gland was damaged, her level one morning was 34 … she hasn't yet got a diagnosis from our respectable professors of these teaching hospitals.

This is the synacthen test she had at RVI, and you may notice there is a near normal curve after 60 minutes, it is measured at 30 minutes and 60 minutes, and of course the basal, but even there the basal was low. So every other hospital and every professor said, she is OK. This is the hydrocortisone day curve which is usually done at hospital, but because her condition was so serious I did this myself. Because people will say, use steroids and you can get the opposite of hypoadrenalism, which is moonface, Cushing's syndrome, osteoporosis, gastric ulcer, but here we measure the hydrocortisone day curve and make sure the level never goes above 500 – that it matches the diurnal variation or the circadian rhythm. This is the patient. And you can see she had all the symptoms which you can class as fibromyalgia, which they did, chronic fatigue syndrome, or it is all in her mind. So there is, you can see they were only concentrating on the adrenal gland, but this autoimmune process can affect the pituitary as well as the hypothalamus and I believe even the supra hypothalamus. No test can really point out exactly where the trouble is. They were pinning it all on just the adrenal gland and they were missing … also they were using high dose stimulation, instead of physiological dose, so the physiological dose they should use is 1 microgram, instead they are using 250 microgram. Why [not] put in there, too, the low dose which is also done, instead of saying, 'It is all in the mind, she should see a psychiatrist'? And she could have been dead and gone by now.

So there is primary hypoadrenalism which Kennedy had. Fortunately, at that time glucocorticoids were just available and that saved his life, otherwise he would have died, and also B12 he was getting because at that time in 1945 B12 was identified by Dr Smith in London and someone else at the same time in USA. So you can have secondary or tertiary or suprahypothalamus hypoadrenalism, they are not looking for it, unfortunately, so there is just like pernicious anaemia the problem, this is a huge problem what is happening, many of these patients are put on depression tablets or they become psychotic, very powerful poisonous drugs, that is what is going on.

Which is very, very sad.

So I went on discovering in the last – since that girl is so ill – it has alerted me, my clinical mind is alert, and I make sure everything is tested, like the [inaudible] endocrine group of things and any essential elements that is missing, if you correct them, if quickly give an example, this is a very clever patient of mine, his mother, sister, they are all B12 deficient, so he came with all these neuropsychiatric symptoms, he read up like you all, and I found his B12 level was 126, so I started giving him injections and he improved, but something still was not right, he was having headache, he kept on coming to see my colleagues and myself and we couldn't find the cause of the headache, so, because he goes and sees the other doctors as well, there was no continuity, he got fed up, got angry, and he changed the doctors, he went to another big practice. Within two weeks he came back to see me, apologising, then I thought it is time I put my thinking hat, and I looked through all the tests the other doctors had done and I found his thyroid TSH level was 4.5, that is, marginally, he is hypothyroid. But of course, clinically, it is more than marginally. I started giving him 50 micrograms of thyroxine, and he came in one week, he came and said, 'Dr Chandy, I'm fine', and gave me a big hug, 'I'm sorry for leaving your practice, you have saved my life.' So you see everything, we doctors, must look for all these things.

So these are the other patients you can see there (shows before and after pic of mum) when she came to see me, and see the difference. Now she is B12 deficient, her mother is B12 deficient, and this boy was brought to see me, 'Will you take him to a mental ... to a psychiatrist, because he's really disruptive, he may have autism, will you refer?' I said, I asked her, what is the matter with you, you're B12 deficient, you're well now. Your mother is B12 deficient and your 16-year-old is B12 deficient, don't you think little Johnny has B12 deficiency? You could diagnose it, I said, you don't need me. So before referring to a psychiatrist let me check the B12 level. His B12 level was 194. I started giving him injections, because they were going to throw him out of the school. One month later the headmistress ran after the parents and said, 'Look this, a certificate saying that he is the best improved student in the class.' Just a few weeks ago she came and told me, 'He is going to get a scholarship for a brilliant boy.'

[...]

This is a girl again, came to me from another practice, her B12 level was 170 which dropped to 132. After correcting it she wasn't fully well, I checked her cortisol level it was 133, and I started her, I didn't bother to refer her to the specialist, I thought I am going to treat her, and you can see she is smiling. Previously she worked [?] for her dad and in the middle she had to go and lie down before she could get up.

This is a case of vasculitis which was diagnosed by the specialist as urticaria. She came to see my colleague, my colleague said, 'You'd better go and see Dr Chandy.' So she came to see me, she was on a [something] full of Piriton and all that, and one look at her, I said, 'I know what's the matter with you. You have two problems, one is your B12 deficiency and two, you are hypoadrenal.' And I was proved right. Her B12 level was 243, and you can see I gave her 5,000 microgram of B12 straight away and also I gave her 100 microgram of hydrocortisone intravenously and within days it cleared itself.

This is the lady who had been to ... (Am I all right for time? 'You'll have to speed up.' Audience laughter. 'This is the time I always overrun, I get excited to see you all, I think.' More audience laughter. 'So forgive me Martin, I get carried away.' You see when you see this smile (on slide) – doesn't it make you all well? For four years she was going to James Cook Hospital and they said, 'You have gastritis, take some antacid,' or 'You have some sugar [something, deficit?] go and have some chocolate.' She couldn't breathe so they put her on inhalers. One inhaler had cortisol, you know, steroid inhaler, so that gave her some relief, it went on and on, she is from Hartlepool, she is not from my district, she found Martin's website and somehow somebody mentioned about me and I was about to go to India and she rang me and she said, 'Dr Chandy I am desperate, I want to come and see you.' I said, 'You are not my patient … OK I will see you when I return.' So when I returned I rang her on a Sunday and asked her to come – so she had B12 deficiency at 273 and of course James Cook couldn't treat her. So she came and I checked these things and I started treating her and oh, she was so happy. In spite of that there was something missing, something was not right, and James Cook four years ago did do her cortisol level, and again it was using the high dose synacthen test, and they didn't diagnose so I did series of early morning cortisol level and I found she was hypoadrenal and I started to treat her, she improved, I referred her back to James Cook and now they admitted they were wrong.

And this is another girl, a young mother with a child, a sad case. It had just recently, I did series of cortisol tests, she was B12 deficient, her level is I think 130, I started treating her then I found she has cortisol deficiency of 160, slowly it came down from 200, came down to 160, then 140. I sent her to Hartlepool Hospital, they gave her high dose synacthen test and I got a letter yesterday, it really broke my heart, 'Oh she hasn't got hypoadrenalism, go away.' But I told her not to worry, I will follow you up and I will start treating, even if I will lose my registration,' (applause) 'I am going to risk my career for you' (more clapping).

Slide: Nearly 25 patients saved since 2007.

This is another lady who went to Hartlepool and James Cook, was misdiagnosed, now she is better – so these are the signs and symptoms, I have created my own protocol, based on my patient experience, not from textbooks, you learn more from life, you learn more from patients, that's a basic thing. Instead of that we doctors now concentrate on looking at the computer, and tick box, so that they can get the highest score of points.

So by this time, this doctor who came for 20 minutes to see me and to see what is going on: 'why is he doing so many cortisol – is he an outlier? And he is going of course again going to be reported'. Like last night I mentioned, twice my patients' B12 treatment was stopped by two separate Primary Care Trusts for a period of 15 months and one patient died of pneumonia during that time. Are they going to do the same, stop treating with hydrocortisone [because] I am not an expert? This may be the reason why he came, but he only came for 20 minutes and by the time he left it was three o'clock in the afternoon, so by that time he laughed because he asked me, 'Dr Chandy in 2002, you wrote to Tony Blair about the health service,' so the photograph (looks, can't find it), never mind, so I wrote to Tony Blair when he came into power about what is wrong with the NHS and I did 2,000 copies, sent to every MP, sent to chief executives and I know, danger, so I told him, I had a protection there, who was it? I said I wrote to Cherie Blair at the same time (audience laughter) and enclosed this booklet, and also I

put well congratulations card that is the time Cherie had
the baby, boy, I forgot his name, so I said, also I put a
third thing, which I'm not going to tell you. Well actually
I told him and he laughed the head off what I inserted, and
I said, 'That is my protection.' So many chief executives
try to see whether they can do something with me, but as
you can see I am still practising. So then he understood.
'Now I know what you meant by destiny, and that is why
you're here, I can see that, but please take care of that
girl.'

As I told you, I lost a baby girl in 1979. After seven
years, with a lot of prayer, we got a baby girl, and that
was that girl you saw, second patient, she's Leanne, she's
my daughter, and if it isn't for her becoming ill, I couldn't
have branched off into this. Since she became ill, and
these hospitals rejected her and said it is in mind, day and
night I studied, and now I am also diagnosing other
patients, and I am hoping we can publish this, and that I
can influence the establishment to change their policy. I
will stop there, I have overrun (applause). (Other person:
'This is the first time in four visits that he has actually
finished early, the very first conference he went on for
three and a half hours!')

Chandy, J, 'B12 Deficiency and Autoimmune
Polyendocrine Syndrome (APS), Part 2', Pernicious
Anaemia Conference 2013

ACKNOWLEDGMENTS

I would like to thank all the medical consultants and researchers who so generously gave me their time, advice and information. There are too many to list. Without them I could have done nothing, and certainly not written this book.

My next great debt is to those in the media, including all those who published my articles or wrote about our son themselves. My thanks to artist Joe McLaren. Those with websites who publicized PTHP, particularly Nick O'Hara Smith, Neurobonkers, Sharon Lister, Rebecca Aris, and those who enabled me to attend conferences, and give talks, such as Lorraine Cleaver, Margaret Palmer, Vicki Gilmore and Chloe Hayward.

Coming now to my various circles of friends my thanks go to those in the Saturday Walkers group who supported me in so many ways, ranging from IT advice (Andrew Murphy) to corresponding with NICE (Yvonne) to getting PTP a mention in Men's Health magazine (Miriam Greenwood), to advice on an academic paper (Neil Reeder), to reading the manuscript (Sylvia Godden, Margaret Chambers). Then I have to thank my husband's ex-VSO friends, particularly Anne Smedley and Graham Brodie, and my university friends Frances, Helen, Rosalie and Katharine for their time and support. Other friends who have given real help are Olga and John Clarke and their extended family, Sue and Imtiaz Dossa, and Sarah and Neil Jackson. My writers' group was a constant source of shrewd feedback on my manuscript. I particularly owe Debs Grayson and Eileen Muwonge for their close reading and comments.

Members of my mother-in-law's church St John the Baptist in Purley gave great support, signing my petitions. Sometimes software salespeople spent time helping me with queries out of kindness. I promised faithfully to one such person that I would acknowledge him, but now I can't find his name.

Thank you to my family for all their help, particularly Martin, Alex, Bernie, Andrew and David. My husband John was my great IT trouble-shooter, and the one who always listened when I said "Does this sound all right?"

I am grateful to Dr Andrew McNinch who explained to me what it is like to be a doctor, Sarah O'Halloran who told me what it is like to be a nurse, and to Julia Oakley who showed how it feels to be a patient denied access to her medical notes until too late.

Finally I have to mention the hard work Lynne Wallis did on my manuscript before I submitted it to publishers. It was an ungainly woolly sheep then, but she did a good clipping job, and after my editor Rebecca Lloyd had given it a second shearing, the sheep skipped free. I cannot thank Accent Press enough for publishing this book.

There will be people I have forgotten to thank, and I apologize. I hope they will remind me and give me a chance to make amends.

Hayley Okines was just like any other teenager: she loved clothes, shopping, and boy bands, and hated getting up in the morning. But she had progeria, which meant she aged eight times faster than normal, giving her the body of a 126-year-old. Her positive attitude and infectious smile charmed millions of people through her *Extraordinary People* TV documentaries.

At the age of seventeen, in April 2015, Hayley tragically lost her battle to be the longest survivor of progeria, succumbing to pneumonia in the arms of her mother. This book tells Hayley's story in her own words, continuing from the bestselling *Old Before My Time*. She reflects on the pains and perks of growing up with progeria – from the heartbreak of being told she will never walk again to the delight of passing her exams and starting college. Hayley considers mood swings, marriage, music, and what it's like to be 'famous' and is heartbreakingly positive about a future that wasn't to be.